HISTORY

Borgo Press Books by ROBERT BLACKEY

History: Core Elements for Teaching and Learning

HISTORY

CORE ELEMENTS FOR TEACHING AND LEARNING

ROBERT BLACKEY

THE BORGO PRESS

MMXI

H I S T O R Y

FIRST EDITION

Published by Wildside Press LLC

www.wildsidebooks.com

DEDICATION

For my loving and lovely wife,

CAROL PIXTON,

Who is the hardest-working and most dedicated and giving teacher I have ever known. I am a better teacher and historian for having worked with and been advised by her for more than twenty years.

CONTENTS

Introduction. 9

PART ONE: Lecturing and Classroom Techniques

1. New Wine in Old Bottles: Revitalizing the Traditional
   History Lecture 15

2. To Illuminate History: Making Teaching Picture-Perfect 51

3. Early Bird Specials: Some Thoughts on Use of Class
   Time Before Class Begins. 71

4. And Now for Something a Little Different: Constructive
   Breaks in the History Lecture. 85

PART TWO: Written Assignments and Writing

5. Writing in the Major: A Novel Approach That Works. . .97

6. University Students' Writing. 105

7. Words to the Whys: Crafting Critical Book Reviews . . 107

8. The Light Side: Being Serious About Teaching Writing
   with Humor 117

PART THREE: Tests and Exams

9. A Guide to the Skill of Essay Construction in History . 139

10. How Advanced Placement History Essay Questions
    Are Prepared—and How Yours Can Be Too 153

11. Bull's-Eye: A Teacher's Guide for Developing Student
    Skill in Responding to Essay Questions 163
12. Advanced Placement European History: An Anatomy
    of the Essay Examination, 1956-2000. 175
13. So Many Choices, So Little Time: Strategies for
    Understanding and Taking Multiple-Choice Exams in
    History 225
14. The Little ID: A Guide for Answering Identification
    Questions Effectively 245
Acknowledgments 251
About the Author 253

INTRODUCTION

"Boring!" is the most frequent response to a question I ask when I speak to middle school students about a subject that is to me, in contrast, excitingly alive, fascinating, and meaningful. It is a response, often spoken in unplanned unison, to my asking groups of these students to tell me what they would say if they were asked to use one word to describe their history class to a friend. This disturbs me, naturally, but I believe I understand why students respond this way; that is, history, to them, is all too often about a seemingly endless stream of names, dates, and facts to memorize when, instead, it should be about, among other things, both real people and solving the mysteries of the past; it is also about meaning and understanding and what history can teach us about the evolving human condition and experience: to know where we are going we need in order to know where we have been, individually as well as a race, that is, the human race. My middle-school scenario, visited many times over recent decades, has helped to motivate me—as a teacher, author, and speaker to K-12 classes—to seek ways to change students' perceptions of what history is, why they should care about it, and why they should study it with newfound or, sometimes, renewed interest and from various perspectives.

The articles and essays printed between the covers of this book are based not only on more than forty years of experience as a college and university teacher, coincidental with allied experiences through work with the Educational Testing Service, The College Board, and the American Historical Association (which I served as vice president in the early 1990s), but also on a quarter century of immersion in the subject-and-research area of history teaching and learning—a legitimate, if not universally prized (much less rewarded), area of pursuit that is also recognized as such by the American Historical Association, the foremost organization of professional historians in the United States.

My interest in this field for the joint purpose of research and writing, following after earlier published works in the areas of eighteenth-century English history and the interdisciplinary field of comparative revolutions, emerged from my responsibilities as Chief Reader of Advanced Placement European History (1976-80). Specifically, toward the end of my term in that position I decided to write a paper that would enable my colleagues and successors on the Test Development Committee to profit not only from what I had learned about constructing essay examination questions—based on my experiences overseeing the scoring of these highly competitive exams—but also from my analysis of all previous annual reports (dating back to the mid-1950s) that chief readers—in both European and United States History—write as part of their assessment of a given year's exam. Before that paper was circulated, only the previous year's report was distributed to committee members whereas all earlier reports were archived and effectively inaccessible (although they could be requested). That paper, in revised form, became available to a larger audience of secondary school and post-secondary teachers with the publication, in 1981, of "A Guide to the Skill of Essay Construction in History." In time, and over time, my interest expanded to other areas of history teaching and learning as well as to the teaching of writing, both within existing history courses and through separate courses on writing for upper-division students. Thus, it seems to me, I had found an area that was every bit as vital to the education of students, especially history students, as the traditional scholarship in which I was trained and to which I brought that training.

Because education theory does not ordinarily capture my attention, my focus has been on the practical side of teaching and learning, with an emphasis on: test construction; how students can improve the ways they respond to essay, identification, and multiple-choice questions; standard as well as innovative classroom techniques; and written assignments along with ways to improve student writing. These are all traditional and still standard subjects of interest for most teachers of history. Others may indeed practice what has for me been innovative, but few college professors have given the thought and time necessary to investigate these subjects and write about them. What is here, in other words, is personal and dear to my students and me, but it is also meant to be shared with and—one can only hope— inspiring to others.

These published articles and unpublished essays are separated into three parts: *Lecturing and Classroom Techniques*, *Written Assignments and Writing*, and *Tests and Exams*. My own preferred method of teaching is the lecture-discussion approach; as such, the four pieces comprising the first section are geared toward enlivening regular classroom presentations as well as engaging students more effectively, although there is much in those pieces that will interest teachers who prefer other teaching approaches. There are, nevertheless, no magic formulas here, only ideas, suggestions, and examples that with effort can be replicated and adapted—and, I expect, ultimately improved upon—by any history teacher.

Part II concentrates on written assignments, especially the critical book review,[1] and on ways to improve student writing, in history and other courses. In addition to devoting a lot of time to constructively directing and editing what students write in my

---

1. There are no articles here on the venerable research paper, a vital assignment for history students in upper-division and graduate courses. This is a notable but conscious omission that is based on the fact that I have nothing exciting and new to add to the many fine existing guides and short volumes that provide direction to students as they navigate their way through this rigorous and demanding assignment.

classes, the results of which are examined in two of the articles, another suggests ways in which humor can help to lower student anxiety as well as to improve some of their writing skills.

The final section is devoted to tests and exams, including how to write clear and unambiguous questions and how we can teach our students to make more effective use of what they have studied and learned for the inevitable essay, identification, and multiple-choice questions they will likely face during their school and college careers. There is also an article that surveys and analyzes the history of the AP European History essay examination that includes information—including trends with regard to the themes and subjects taught in history classes in the United States in the second half of the twentieth century and how the construction and types of such questions evolved—that should be of interest to non-AP teachers as well.

The collection that awaits you here certainly does not provide everything about history teaching and learning that teachers will need to know in order to be successful; I would be suspicious of any single collection that made claims along those lines. What it does do, however, is provide interested and motivated teachers with insights and suggestions about many of the key elements that are surely involved in, as well as integral to, effective history teaching.

PART ONE:
LECTURING AND
CLASSROOM TECHNIQUES

1. NEW WINE IN
OLD BOTTLES

Revitalizing the Traditional
History Lecture

Active learning...student-centered learning...interactive learning...collaborative education...student-directed learning... empowerment in the classroom.

The jargon of cognitive psychology and education make many of us historians cringe. While there doubtless are good educational techniques and substance lurking behind these terms, an underlying premise is that the traditional lecture[2] does not work, that by its very nature lecturing renders students passive learners, induces apathy, and runs a greater risk of boring them into not learning at all (e.g., much of the content presented via lecture "is not attended to by students and what is attended to may be distorted on its path from the lecturer's notes to the students"[3]). Although it is certainly possible that lecturing can contribute to a student's failure to learn, the contention here is that such results are not inevitable, that lecturing, especially

---

2. Our word "lecture" from the Latin verb *legere*, meaning "gather, choose," developed semantically to mean "read" when, during the Middle Ages, students did not have books readily available to them. John Ayto, *Dictionary of Word Origins* (New York: Arcade Publishing/Little, Brown, 1990).

3. Christopher Knapper, "Large Classes and Learning," in Maryellen Gleason Weimer, ed., *Teaching Large Classes Well* (San Francisco: Jossey-Bass, 1987), 9.

history lecturing, can be made to promote learning in a way comparable to any other technique. I myself learned a great deal—certainly more than just historical facts and dead-weight information—from several outstanding lecturers. And I have gotten enough feedback over more than a quarter century of teaching to believe that I have had at least some success as a lecturer and, as well, a positive influence on many of my students who have become teachers (but not all of whom lecture).

I would contend, for the following reasons, that no single approach to teaching history is absolutely superior to all others: (1) each of us is better at one technique or another; (2) our students are not always the same nor is the size of each class; and (3) with our goals remaining neither static nor uniform—both within a single course and from course to course—we inevitably determine the approach to use based upon how we see those goals being achieved optimally. Thus any number of methods can be used effectively, and several methods can, and should, be combined—which is part of what will be recommended here, although not that simply. That is, any method of teaching can become routine over time, and research has suggested that the attention span of students may start to wane after the first ten minutes or so.[4] Therefore, some energy, throughout a class session, ought to be indirectly devoted to reviving that attention, and even the best lecturers should regularly interrupt the spoken narrative with something a little different.

In essence, however, and fundamental to teaching—regardless of the way one teaches or the styles employed—is the ability to **engage** students, to get them involved intellectually. Some teaching techniques and styles may lend themselves more

---

4. Wilbert J. McKeachie, *Teaching Tips: A Guidebook for the Beginning College Teacher*, 8th ed. (Lexington, MA: D.C. Heath, 1986), 72; also see Peter Elbow, *Embracing Contraries: Explorations in Learning and Teaching* (New York: Oxford University Press, 1986), 182-94. Others suggest that attention starts to wane within 15 and 25 minutes. The number of minutes notwithstanding, the important distinction is that interest can start to slacken long before a class session ends.

readily to engagement, but virtually all approaches can be made to work, including the traditional history lecture. To be sure, a lecturer must avoid appearing to pontificate, or merely to pass along information and fact, or to repeat what is "in the book"; a lecture is not a paper delivered at a professional meeting, it is not a speech before a partisan audience. To present a straight, factual, chronological history is to trivialize our discipline and to transform the teacher into an abridged version of a talking textbook. Instead, success in lecturing involves interacting with students; the lecturer must make what goes on in the classroom engaging. The purpose of this paper, then, is to suggest a number of ways that can help make such success happen in history classrooms.

Goals and Philosophy

Let's start with a generalization. Regardless of the history we teach, as we approach each course we should have goals. Having goals means we should take time to be introspective, to reflect upon our courses in order to determine what we want our students to come away with at the end of the term; and when we reflect, we should think as well about how lecturing can contribute to those goals. For example, in my various history courses I have established three kinds of broad goals: First, that students come to possess some minimal knowledge base and an understanding of the subject in question. Second, that they become, at the very least, a little bit excited about the passion of history, that they come to acknowledge the importance of history for who they are and who they will become. And third, that they expand their reading, writing, and thinking skills under the heading of what can be called "thinking historically"; that is, I realize that whatever body of knowledge students may have absorbed, over time much of it will be forgotten.

So, what is it that I want them to learn over and above content? If I can help them to think in a historical way, if I can get them to ask certain kinds of questions and to challenge perceived wisdom, if I can encourage them to evaluate and analyze material, if I can stir their blood, if I can push them to become more sophisticated writers, thinkers, and speakers, then they will possess attitudes and skills—even if only in rudimentary form—that can be taken with them to other classes, and into the world beyond school.[5] Therefore, to know where we wish to take our students—to know how to forge a link between our sophisticated comprehension and their growing understanding—is a prerequisite for trying to teach them.

Related to our sophisticated comprehension and students' ability to understand is a Darwinian-like selection we must make with regard to what should be excluded from a lecture. There is always so much we might include, especially when we know a lot about a topic, but studies have shown what François Fénelon quipped three centuries ago: "the more you say, the less people remember."[6] Among the skills excellent teachers seem to possess are the ability to make these selections as per class level, to support these selections with sufficient examples, to make difficult material comprehensible, and to be aware that these skills are intertwined with one another.

Further, it should be remembered that we learn best when we acknowledge a need to know. Whatever method of teaching is employed, the teacher must "bring students to an awareness of their ignorance of a subject...[and since] students also learn best when they think for themselves,"[7] lectures should be more than

---

5. For an examination of ten different explanations of what it means to think historically and how that translates into practice, see "Teaching Innovations Forum: Thinking Historically," ed. by Robert Blackey. *Perspectives*, 33:7 (October 1995).

6. Quoted in *The Dictionary of Humorous Quotations*, ed. By Evan Egar (New York: Dorset, 1989), 73; the studies referred to are in McKeachie, *Teaching Tips*. And William E. Cashin, "Improving Lectures," in Maryellen Weimer and Rose Ann Neff, eds., *Teaching College: Reading for the New Instructor* (Madison, WI: Magna Publications, 1990), 59-63.

7. Patrick Malcolmson and Richard Myers, "Pooled Ignorance, Talking

a conveyor belt for the passage of knowledge from the producer to the consumer. Once we determine what it is we want our students to understand, we have to involve them in discovering this for themselves. Where, then, do we start to make the traditional history lecture work as a technique to engage and involve our students? The following suggestions are divided into two broad categories: first is a menu of vital actions and considerations, second is a collection of useful strategies.

Vital Actions and Considerations

The Human Dimension: Audiences do not connect well with intellectual abstractions; they do identify with people and feelings.[8] Concepts and events are more likely to come to life and to have meaning when they are related to the people involved. To the extent possible, therefore, humanize the people you talk about. Learn what you can about their human characteristics; it is easy enough to impress students with the sometimes superhuman or out-of-the-ordinary accomplishments of the important individuals who are highlighted in lectures and texts, but without conveying a sense of what these people were like behind the scenes or between the lines, without bringing them to life in a way students can identify with—warts and all—you run the risk of lower levels of understanding.[9]

Heads, and Socratic Dialectic," *College Teaching*, 42:1 (1994), 2.

8. William Zinsser, *On Writing Well*, 5th ed. (New York: HarperCollins, 1995), 175.

9. The following, in addition to standard and popular biographies, are useful for learning about individual historic figures: Anne Commire, ed., *Historic World Leaders*, 5 vols. (Detroit: Gale Research, 1994) [It contains some 620 biographical sketches of prominent figure throughout the history of the world.]; Ken Wolf, *Personalities and Problems*, 2 vols. (New York: McGraw-Hill, 1994) [It contains 21 essays that compare contemporaneous figures in world history.]; J. Kelley Sowards, ed., *Makers of World History*, 2nd ed., 2 vols. (New York: St. Martin's Press, 1995) [It includes biographical information, coupled with historical interpretation and documentary source material, on 28 historical figures.]; Dorothy M. Johnson and R.T. Turner,

In a comparable way, your presenting yourself in a human—as opposed to robotic—way should be more conducive to learning. By being enthusiastic, dynamic, and passionate you can become a model for promoting motivation, inspiration, and curiosity. Teachers who enjoy what they are doing are more likely to have students who enjoy being in their classes; enjoyment is contagious. "Enthusiasm is the most convincing orator. It is like an infallible law of nature. The simplest person, fired with enthusiasm, is more persuasive than the most eloquent person without it."[10] Explain why you are committed to your field, why a topic is important to you, and why it is essential to study history. As you read and do research in your subject, inevitably you learn something new. Why not demonstrate an eagerness to share it? Relate experiences from your research and travel: not just "war stories" but tales that convey the thrill (as well as the tedium) of research and the discovery that usually comes from perseverance and from travel to places you teach about. To me, each group of students is a new audience to be won over, to be convinced mine is the most important class they have ever had, and that I am their best teacher.

Be yourself and allow who you are to characterize your style and to free you from conventional and predictable boundaries. There is no single way that can work for all of us because none of us are the same. Each person's style is like a fingerprint, unique to that individual. Find yours and make it work. (In my first couple of years teaching, I recall imitating those of my own history teachers who left a lasting impression. In time, I adapted their styles to suit me, and I allowed who I was

The Bedside Book of Bastards (New York: McGraw-Hill, 1973) [It includes tales about the notorious activities of 36 figures in world history.]; Ronald D. Smith, *Fascinating People and Astounding Events from the History of the Western World* (Santa Barbara, Ca: ABC-Clio, 1990); *Dictionary of American Biography* (New York: Charles Scribner's Sons, 1973-94).

10. Richard L. Weaver and Howard W. Cotrell, "Lecturing: Essential Communication Strategies," in Weimer, ed., *Teaching Large Classes Well*, 63-64.

to evolve into the teacher I have become.) Analyze your own personality and learn to make use of your most positive and endearing characteristics, including your vulnerability, in order to help make what you do add to your appeal. Reduce anxiety—which can conceal passion and distort your public personality—by imagining and visualizing how you wish to be perceived, by reminding yourself that you are more knowledgeable than your students, by believing that you can and will improve, and by adequately preparing yourself.[11]

Teach By Example: Teach by example, critically approaching your subject. How does the way you lecture both teach and encourage students to think in the ways prescribed by our discipline? The history we teach should be argued, not simply narrated; whole courses, as well as individual lectures, should focus on problems and puzzles (some of the pieces of which have become distorted over time or are even missing) and not be a mere chronology of events, even when a course is designed to cover a set period in a country's or a region's history. During a lecture introduce various interpretations and alternatives or conflicting explanations (and not just one when several exist—although these should be limited for lower-division students, in order to make the point without overwhelming them). Similarly, it is crucial to emphasize periodically the difference between interpretation and fact in history (e.g., the United States' dropping atomic bombs on Hiroshima and Nagasaki at the end the World War II is a fact, whereas the reasons for our doing so is subject to interpretation). Knowing that something happened is generally easier to determine than why it happened, which is also different from deciding whether what happened was good or bad, right or wrong. "Students must be made aware that although there is an inescapable subjective dimension to the study of history, not everything is up for grabs or a matter of opinion."[12]

---

11. Ibid., 57-59.

12. Gerald N. Izenberg, "Teaching History," in Keith W. Prichard and

Motivate students by alerting them to problems and by challenging ideas they have previously taken for granted. Draw upon your own research and reading to show how alive and fascinating our discipline is. Demonstrate what is involved when you weigh and consider evidence and when you make connections and see relationships, especially unexpected connections and relationships. Surely we should all seek to demonstrate that there is not a single, unchanging version of history. Lectures should be used to create frameworks and expectations that might assist students as they read materials for your course, and this can be supplemented by providing students with a list of several questions to think about—some questions to help them understand the material and others to encourage them to think critically about it—as they do their assigned reading.

In class, ask rhetorical questions, and be relaxed enough in your presentation to allow for spontaneous discussion. Raise questions that challenge the subject matter, especially as it appears in textbooks, in supplementary readings, and among commonly-held beliefs; then model answers to these questions, eventually with students' involvement. Think out loud and walk them through your thought processes. Suggest to students that while they rarely have the opportunity to question the author of their textbooks, they do have regular access to you both in and out of class. (Incidentally, if you ask thought-provoking essay test questions, such modeling in class should eventually help students to respond more effectively on your exams.)[13] Also,

R. McLaren Sawyer, eds., *Handbook of College Teaching: Theory and Applications* (Westport, CT: Greenwood, 1994), 265; also see Samuel S. Wineburg and Suzanne M. Wilson, "Models of Wisdom in the Teaching of History," *Phi Delta Kappan* (September 1988), 50-58.

13. Robert Blackey, "A Guide to the Skill of Essay Construction in History," *Social Education*, 45:3 (March 1981), 178-82; Robert Blackey, "Bull's-eye: A Teachers' Guide for Developing Student Skills in Responding to Essay Questions," *Social Education*, 52:6 (October 1988), 464-66; John C. Bartul, "Teaching the Value of Inquiry Through the Essay Question," *Perspectives*, 27:8 (November 1989). These articles are reprinted in Robert Blackey, ed., *History Anew: Innovations in the Teaching of History Today* (Long Beach:

allow students to walk you through their thought processes as well; this is educational for you and for them.

The mention of modeling and textbooks calls to mind the once time-honored but now, I expect, little used teaching technique of textual analysis (*explication du texte*). We all may assign readings, but many of us no doubt devote insufficient attention to analyzing them thoroughly. It would be more instructive, however, for us first to model reading and analyzing passages out loud and then to encourage students to do the same—while providing constructive criticism in the process. Even in large classes students can follow their teachers in this act of modeling (of their books, with handouts, or via transparencies), and then be divided into small groups of three-to-five in order to try their hand and to provide their own feedback. This same approach can be used to teach analysis of graphs, charts, tables, political cartoons, maps, census data, parish rolls, and the like, as the important work of historians Peter J. Frederick and Robert F. Berkhofer, Jr. has demonstrated.[14] Our job, let us remember, is to help students to become more vital human beings, to teach them to learn and to think. And this means we must involve them in "analyzing materials, formulating problems, developing hypotheses, bringing evidence to bear, criticizing and evaluating alternative solutions."[15]

Modeling, not incidentally, is also a way to reveal ourselves as passionate, very human creatures, with deeply held beliefs and convictions that cannot necessarily be proven or disproven objectively. In turn, this becomes an opportunity for teachers to show themselves as subjective beings who can tolerate and respect alternative opinions. History is, in fact, not as objec-

University Press, California State University, Long Beach, 1993).

14. Peter J. Frederick, "The Lively Lecture—8 Variations," *College Teaching*, 34:2 (1986), 47-48. For detailed directions and guidance on how to teach textual analysis, see Robert F. Berkhofer, Jr., "Demystifying Historical Authority: Critical Textual Analysis in the Classroom," *Perspectives*, 26:2 (February 1988), reprinted in *History Anew*.

15. McKeachie, *Teaching Tips*, 77.

tive as we might like to believe, and realizing this can perhaps help us to be more honest with ourselves and with our students. More than a hundred years ago, Nietzsche reflected on this very subject, declaring that "History unsettles the feelings.... If the personality is once emptied of its subjectivity, and comes to what men call an 'objective' condition, nothing can have any more effect on it.... *You can explain the past only by what is most powerful in the present....* To take everything objectively, to be angry at nothing, to love nothing, to understand every-thing—makes one gentle and pliable."[16]

All of the above, then, is to say that being a lecturer does not preclude the use of other teaching techniques and a variety of postures. Discussion can be used with most classes, regard-less of size; all students do not have to participate, but the very act of discussion can encourage intellectual engagement if not vocal involvement. Ask questions, and ask for questions and comments. For this to be intellectually sound, however, instruc-tors must explain that they will only accept comments and reac-tions based on an assessment of facts and on interpretations, not simply on "personal feelings"—although feelings, which cannot be discounted, might instead be used as a basis on which to broaden understanding. As R.G. Collingwood wrote, "To the historian, the activities whose history he is studying are not spectacles to be watched, but experiences to be lived through his own mind; they are objective, or known to him, only because they are also subjective, or activities of his own."[17]

Similarly, an instructor's questions should go beyond the simple recall of facts to include the effects of learning what it means to think historically.[18] Call on students who look puzzled

16. Friedrich Nietzsche, *The Use and Abuse of History* (Indianapolis: Bobbs-Merrill, 1957), 32. 33. 40, 53. In these pages, and throughout the book, Nietzsche presents an intriguing discourse on passion and objectivity.

17. R. G. Collingwood, *The Idea of History* (New York: Oxford University Press, 1956), 218.

18. Even the Socratic method will be useless unless students are prepared with sufficient reading and understanding. "Socratic questions rarely evoke

in order to elicit questions from those who might be reluctant to volunteer. Questions form a bridge between the two techniques—of lecture and discussion—and will help you to gauge student comprehension. Good lecturing, especially when joined by discussion, can teach compassion, tolerance, and empathy.[19] Together they can also teach a love of words and for the poetry of language; and they can help you to improve your ability to think on your feet and to learn to be in command of your mind.

Organization and Connections: For any lecture to be successful the teacher must be organized, keeping in mind both the plan for each specific class session and for the entire course, and then thinking about how these are related. Lectures in which insights are scattered and not clearly connected make it difficult for students to assimilate the material, much less to understand and retain it. Even a great delivery cannot camouflage lack of preparation, whereas having one's lecture notes or outline organized will fail to help students if there is no pattern when the lecture is delivered. "Ideally students should be able to state the intended organization, and how one fact is broadly related to the rest, at any time during the lecture, firstly because they need to take notes if the amount of information to be retained exceeds the amount they can remember, and secondly because...these links are essential to understanding."[20]

Before a lecture, therefore, think of ways to forge links between new material and what students may already know or have learned, between lecture material and out-of-class

---

factual information because their intent is not to challenge the students' knowledge-base but to bring information already possessed into the student's conscious awareness and help him or her reason through difficult problems." James Overholser, "Socrates in the Classroom," *The Social Studies*, 83:2 (March/April 1992), 78.

19. An excellent work on this subject is John A. Williams, *Classroom in Conflict: Teaching Controversial Subjects in a Diverse Society* (Albany: State University of New York Press, 1994).

20. Donald A. Bligh, *What's the Use of Lectures* (Middlesex, England: Penguin, 1972), 76.

assignments, between one day's lecture and both the previous and following ones, between a main point and other subjects or other parts of the same subject or even other disciplines. One way to create such links is through the framing device of starting the lecture with references to the last session followed by a summary of the topic for the day. This places students on familiar ground, and it enables the instructor to indicate how one lecture's material follows from the preceding one.[21] In addition, you should determine beforehand what you hope your students will learn as a result of the lecture.

Not incidentally, the organization of a course also includes developing a detailed syllabus, complete with the subject matter to be covered each week (or each class session), course objectives, expectations (both yours of students and theirs of you), grading procedures, a definition of plagiarism (how to avoid plagiarizing[22] and the penalty for failing to do so), due dates for required readings, exams, and assignments, and with all assignments (including written, oral, and research projects) explained thoroughly, so that students know what to expect each week (or day) and what rules you expect them to follow—rules, say, about attendance, arriving late, talking in class. With regard to required readings, it is wise to introduce them and to explain why they have been chosen, both at the start of the course and, later, when they are about to be read, in order to peak students' interest and to explain their importance for the course. Also, plan in advance so that materials you require, such as audio-visual equipment and reading selections, will be ready.

At the start of each lecture pose questions, dilemmas, or

21. Heather Dubrow and James Wilkinson, "The Theory and Practice of Lectures," in Margaret Morganroth Gullette, ed., *The Art and Craft of Teaching* (Cambridge, MA: Harvard University Press, 1984), 26-27; John P. Murray and Judy L. Murray, "How Do I Lecture Thee?" *College Teaching*, 40:3 (1992), 109.

22. See "Note on Responsible Use of Sources," in *The Pop Culture Tradition: Readings with Analysis for Writing*, edited by E. M. White (New York: W.W. Norton, 1972), 194-96.

problems, or raise a controversial issue related to the session's assignment or to the material to be covered. Allude to this during the lecture, and again at the end of the lecture. Then solicit students' ideas about the degree to which the questions have been answered, the problem solved, the controversy resolved (or at least sufficiently addressed). This technique provides students with a framework for grasping and organizing the lecture. And responses at the end of class provide the instructor with feedback about student learning and thinking. In other words, allow students to see where you are heading, the main points to be covered, and the purpose behind your choices. In this way, if some students miss a point or a transition, they should still be able to follow the lecture.[23]

Variations on these lecture-launching techniques include the introduction of unusual or even alarming facts or statistics, the telling of an intriguing story, or the showing of a dramatic illustration, all connected, of course, to the day's material. These serve the same purpose as an introductory paragraph in an essay, the opening remarks of a speech, or a newspaper headline: they grab the attention of the audience and ease entry into the subject at hand. Remember, however, that attention does not last long. Thus not only must thought be given to the opening of a lecture, but to retaining attention throughout as well. (The suggestions included in the next section are meant to serve that purpose.)

Consider, as well, the use of handouts, especially in large classes and for lower-division students whose skills development is unsophisticated, because they may be the best way to ensure that everyone in the class receives at least some form of the most essential information. Handouts cannot substitute for elaboration of main points and for the use of examples, but

---

23. Richard L. Weaver II, "Effective Lecturing Techniques: Alternatives to Classroom Boredom," in Weimer and Neff, eds., *Teaching College*, 65. Weaver outlines a variety of ways to secure students' attention, hold their interest, and develop your own desire and actions to reinforce what you teach.

they can provide useful introductory information, they can serve to guide students through the lecture and, perhaps, reduce compulsive note taking. Later, they can help to guide students through their reading and/or reviewing.[24]

During the course of every lecture always make it a habit to explain—and to get students to explain—why something was or is significant: in the short run, in the long run, as it relates to other issues and events. Show cause and effect, the impact of something. Make it clear, as well, that events rarely have just one cause and one effect. And while inevitably we must engage in simplifying a topic for pedagogical purposes, students should always be left with a sense of the complexity of the history making process. Focus on change and the causes of change while also calling attention to continuities amid the changes. Explain how events and actions fit in with long-range trends, and how the role played, at times, by contingency or accidental factors must be considered. Similar connections must be made between those actions and an individual's, a government's, or a group's goals and achievements. All this is important to help develop students' ability to think historically, to make them aware that history "is concerned with the processes of life rather than with the meaning or purpose or goal of life,"[25] and to help them make sense of history so they can appreciate the discipline as being far more than a sterile chronicling of unconnected, perhaps mindless events, all of equal importance (or of equal insignificance).

---

24. Karron G. Lewis, "Teaching Large Classes (How to Do It Well and Remain Sane)," in Prichard and Sawyer, eds., *Handbook of College Teaching*, 336-37.

25. Herbert Butterfield, *The Whig Interpretation of History* (New York: W.W. Norton, 1965), 67.

Useful Strategies

Launching the Lecture: Begin courses by pointing to possible gaps in students' knowledge, or by challenging accepted beliefs, or by raising provocative questions, all of which will be filled, discussed, and possibly answered over the next several weeks. Each of these approaches can serve to raise curiosity and to grab attention. They can help students to know where you are headed and what is expected of them. I especially like to start each course—after I have reviewed the syllabus and other introductory items—with assorted material about the subject matter (e.g., aspects and anecdotes about the British for my courses on their history) and the distinctiveness of my approach that lets them know that both learning and sophisticated subjects can be fun and that I do not fit any preconceived stereotype of a history professor. I find this keeps them a little off balance—in a healthy way—and generates anticipation. Alternatively, it is useful to begin survey courses with a discussion of history as a discipline—perhaps building upon provocative quotations on what history is and means[26]—and the reasons for studying the particular period and places to be covered.[27] One could also anticipate and counter the anti-intellectual old saw, "What can you do with history?" with a brief response to the more insightful, "What can you do without it?"[28]

In launching a new topic or unit, one can make use of the interactive lecture, a technique involving brainstorming that has

---

26. In addition to useful reference books such as *Bartlett's Familiar Quotations*, computer CD-ROM disks, such as Microsoft Bookshelf, are convenient and speedy resources for quotations.

27. Izenberg, "Teaching History," 265.

28. In building a response to this question I use quotations from Polybius ("History offers the best training for those who are to take part in public affairs."), Cicero ("Not to know what happened before one was born is always to be a child."), Plato ("Those who tell the stories also rule the society."), and George Orwell ("Whoever controls the past controls the future.")

been advocated by Peter Frederick.[29] Students contribute to the creation of a lecture by participating in the process of structuring a topic into a rational pattern. The teacher begins by having students call out what they know about the topic at hand and, then, by writing on the board (or on a transparency) whatever is said. The teacher might arrange these responses in groups or have students comment on the accuracy and relative importance of the items. Either way, many students get to participate and to sense what their classmates already know (or don't know), the teacher gains a sense of the class' level of knowledge and understanding, and a jointly created, even coherent, understanding of the topic is begun. To be sure, the teacher must be a subtle director, making certain the appropriate material is included, but the teacher must also be open enough to deviate from his or her preconceived ideas. One way to keep this method on track is for the instructor to ask the class, now and then, to identify themes and patterns that have emerged from the brainstorming, to make connections between and among what is on the board (or transparency), and to determine what might be missing. In the end, while considerable time may be consumed in using this approach, it is probably time well spent since students tend to be more preoccupied with thinking than with note taking, and that ought to help them to understand better and to remember more. Of equal consideration, and what may determine the success of the interactive lecture, is the careful planning that will be needed beforehand in order for the teacher to be prepared to redirect the energy level that has been raised.

Attention and Imagination Techniques: Employing humor in the classroom was once thought to be unprofessional: it was unscholarly and undignified; it was frivolous and mere enter-

---

29. "Student Involvement: Active Learning in Large Classes," in Weimer, *Teaching Large Classes Well*, 47-48; Frederick, "Motivating Students by Active Learning in the History Classroom," *Perspectives* 31:7 (October 1993); Frederick, "The Lively Lecture—8 Variations," 45-46. Also see Alan Booth and Paul Hyland, eds., *History in Higher Education: New Directions in Teaching and Learning* (Cambridge, MA: Blackwell, 1995).

tainment, the antithesis of education, which was serious business. To be humorous was to court popularity.[30] In our own time, however, humor in teaching not only has received better press, it is seen as well as being compatible with learning, freeing creative thinking, and reducing social distance; it is also believed to increase attentiveness, interest, and the retention of material, and it can foster class discussion.[31] I like to use humor as a tool to motivate students, although utilizing humor does not presuppose that one is or should be a stand-up comedian or a clown. Humor should emerge from the subject matter and the setting, which means that the lecturer maintains control over the kind of humor and its occasion. Humor relieves anxiety, both the students' and the teacher's, it breaks the ice, it helps to build trust, and it joins students and teacher together in a more relaxed atmosphere. I allow my sense of humor to be spontaneous, but I also use humor in the form of cartoons (from magazine and newspapers as well as published political cartoons that can do double duty as documents) and howlers (or bloopers), both of which I have been collecting for years.[32] There is no

30. John Morreall, *Taking Laughter Seriously* (Albany: State University of New York Press, 1983), 88-89.

31. Debra Korobkin, "Humor in the Classroom: Considerations and Strategies," in Weimer and Neff, eds., *Teaching College*, 81.

32. For howlers in the form of essays, see Anders Henrikson, compiler, "A History of the Past: 'Life Reeked with Joy,'" *Wilson Quarterly* (Spring 1983), 168-171; "The World According to Student Bloopers," in Richard Lederer, *Anguished English* (Charleston, SC: Wyrick & Co., 1987), 7-15. As a long-time Reader of Advanced Placement examinations, for the Educational Testing Service, I have had access to an overflowing plater of howlers, but I only use them as if on a diet. A number of individual bloopers can be found in Richard Lederer, *More Anguished English* (New York: Delacorte Press, 1993), 15-17. For collections of history cartoons, which ordinarily must be found one at a time, patiently, in magazines and newspapers, see Burr Shafer, *Through History with J. Wesley Smith* (New York: Vanguard, 1950) and *The Wonderful World of J. Wesley Smith* (New York: Vanguard, 1960); also see Larry Gonick, *The Cartoon History of the Universe II*, vols. 1-7: *From the Big Bang to Alexander*, vols. 8-13: *From the Springtime of China to the Fall of Rome* (New York: Doubleday, 1990) and Larry Gonick,

harm in poking playful fun at your subject and at the blunders of those who study it, as long as it is clear to students that there is no intent to ridicule individuals.

Research suggests that students tend to remember principles and generalizations more than anything else,[33] but my own experience indicates they also remember anecdotes, oddities, and curious information as well. Therefore, I like to sprinkle these throughout a lecture as a way of keeping—or even piquing—students' attention, and of making difficult material more palatable.[34] Students frequently are curious where I find

The Cartoon History of the United States (New York: HarperCollins, 1991).

33. Cashin, "Improving Lectures," 61.

34. For selected sources for such material, see Tom Burnam, *The Dictionary of Misinformation* (New York: Thomas Y. Crowell, 1975); Tom Burnam, *More Misinformation* (New York: Lippincott & Crowell, 1980); Richard Shenkman, *Legends, Lies, & Cherished Myths of American History* (New York: Morrow, 1988); Richard Shenkman, *Legends, Lies, & Cherished Myths of World History* (New York: HarperCollins, 1993); M. Hirsh Goldberg, *The Blunder Book: Colossal Errors, Minor Mistakes, and Surprising Slipups That Have Changed the Course of History* (New York: Morrow, 1988); Paul F. Boller, Jr., *Not So! Popular Myths About America's Past From Columbus to Clinton* (New York: Oxford University Press, 1995); Paul F. Boller, Jr. and John George, *They Never Said It: A Book of Fake Quotes, Misquotes, and Misleading Attributions* (New York: Oxford University Press, 1989); Paul Kuttner, *History's Trickiest Questions* (New York: Henry Holt, 1990); Leo Rosten, *Infinite Riches: Gems from a Lifetime of Reading* (New York: McGraw-Hill, 1979); Reay Tannahill, *Sex in History* (New York: Stein & Day, 1980); Reay Tannahill, *Food in History* (New York: Crown Publishers, 1988); Maguelonne Toussaint-Samat, *History of Food* (Cambridge, MA: Blackwell, 1992); Sanche de Gramont, *Epitaph for Kings* (New York: Dell Publishers, 1967); Sanche de Gramont, *The French: Portrait of a People* (New York: G.P. Putnam's Sons, 1969); Elizabeth Burton, *The Pageant of Elizabethan England* (New York: Charles Scribner's Sons, 1958); Elizabeth Burton, *The Pageant of Stuart England* (New York: Charles Scribner's Sons, 1962); Elizabeth Burton, *The Pageant of Georgian England* (New York: Charles Scribner's Sons, 1967); Elizabeth Burton, *The Pageant of Early Victorian England* (New York: Charles Scribner's Sons, 1972); Daniel Pool, *What Jane Austin Ate and Charles Dickens Knew* (New York: Simon & Schuster, 1993); Otto L. Bettmann, *The Good Old Days—They Were Terrible* (New York:

such items, since they are largely absent from most textbooks and from other history books students have encountered, which conveniently allows me to tell them that I read widely and often, which in turn, I hope, encourages them to do the same.

Make the subject matter relevant to the contemporary world, where appropriate, and make it instructive by including references to news of current events that can be linked to what is being studied. The past is always with us at some time or in some way or other, and we have the potential to demonstrate the value of history to the present more accurately—if not more effectively—than TV news reporters or pundits or politicians. While some purists would argue against this suggestion as marginal (irrelevant?) to the study of history, as pandering to fashion and the short attention span of the public, it would be wise to recall

---

Random House, 1974); Thomas A. Bailey, *Presidential Saints and Sinners* (New York: Free Press, 1981); Thomas A. Bailey, *Probing America's Past: A Critical Examination of Major Myths and Misconceptions* (Lexington, MA: D.C. Heath, 1973); Ted Morgan, *A Shovel of Stars: The Making of the American West, 1830 to the Present* (New York: Simon & Schuster, 1995); Paul F. Boller, Jr., *Presidential Anecdotes*, new & revised edition (New York: Oxford University Press, 1996); Michael Olmert, *Milton's Teeth and Ovid's Umbrella: Curiouser and Curiouser Adventures in History* (New York: Touchstone/Simon & Schuster, 1996); Kwame Anthony Appiah & Henry Louis Gates, Jr., *The Dictionary of Global Culture* (New York: Alfred A. Knopf, 1997).

The role played by disease in history is a separate sub-category here for intriguing and by no means insignificant or trivial material. The following are especially useful: Hans Zinsser, *Rats, Lice, and History* (Boston: Little, Brown, 1963); Frederick F. Cartwright, *Disease and History* (New York: New American Library, 1972); Theodor Rosebury, Mic*robes and Morals: The Strange Story of Venereal Disease* (New York: Ballantine Books, 1973); William H. McNeill, *Plagues and People* (Garden City, NY: Anchor Press, 1976); Philip Ziegler, *The Black Death* (Wolfeboro Falls, NH: Allan Sutton Publishing, 1991); Ida Macalpine and Richard Hunter, *George III and the Mad Business* (New York: Pantheon, 1969); Arno Kaplan, *Man and Microbes: Disease and Plagues in History and Modern Times* (New York: Touchstone/Simon & Schuster, 1996). For general reference, see Roderick E. McGrew, *Encyclopedia of Medical History* (London: Macmillan, 1985); Kenneth F. Kiple, ed., *The Cambridge World History of Human Disease* (New York: Cambridge University Press, 1993).

that every age writes its own history—because our interpretations depend to a considerable degree on the times in which we live and the values prevalent at that time. For example, does it not make a difference to our understanding of the importance and course of the Bolshevik Revolution, and to the history of the countries of Eastern Europe as well, that the Soviet Union collapsed in our time?

Drawing analogies can be a constructive technique, but doing so should include a discussion of both their value and the pitfalls. We should especially be aware that "there are many examples of how political decisions and developments have been based on misinterpreting and misreading past events, and how historical myths have influenced statesman and politicians."[35] Analogies are a matter of interpretation, "proper" interpretation if you will, but since historians and other experts will not always agree on what is the proper interpretation of any series of events, our obligation is to acknowledge the fallibility of this approach while simultaneously using it (cautiously) to promote understanding. Or, as Herbert Butterfield advised, "the chief aim of the historian is the elucidation of the unlikenesses between past and present and his chief function is to act in this way as the mediator between other generations and our own."[36] Thus, to try to find lessons in history may be presumptuous of us, but this does not mean there is nothing to learn from such efforts; or, expressed in another way, history will not enable us to predict the future, but it can help us to anticipate it more intelligently, as long as we remember that our responsibility is not "to dogmas or creeds, but to truth and humanity."[37]

---

35. George O. Kent, "Clio the Tyrant: Historical Analogies and the Meaning of History," *The Historian*, 32:1 (November 1969), 102. Kent's essay (covering pages 99-106) is especially useful for its sober assessment of analogies as a historian's tool, especially for events of the twentieth century.

36. Butterfield, *The Whig Interpretation*, 10.

37. Hans Kohn, *Reflections on Modern History* (Princeton: Princeton University Press, 1963), 9-10.

The imaginations of students can be stimulated in a variety of ways. Crisp quotations from documentary sources and literary works[38] as well as from the writings of other scholars can be included periodically to enliven and enrich the spoken narrative. Likewise, there are recordings of written and spoken documents that might be utilized to punctuate lectures with a dollop of aural you-are-there authenticity.[39] The use of pictures, slides, and postcards from travel, museum exhibits, and published catalogues make it easier for students to visualize the places, events, and people being discussed; in addition, I regularly pass around illustrated books, along with photographic material from the likes of *National Geographic, History Today, Smithsonian, American Heritage*, and from newspapers and travel magazines. Where appropriate, maps—and not just political maps and those that illustrate physical features—should be integrated into lectures, as both primary and secondary sources and as texts drawn to transmit information, ideas, and values.[40] Recorded

---

38. One of my favorites, which I use to convey a sense of what it smelled like in early modern times, comes from the murder mystery, *Perfume*, by Patrick Süsskind (New York: Alfred A. Knopf, 1986). It begins: "In the period of which we speak, there reigned in the cities a stench barely conceivable to us modern men and women, The streets stank of manure, the courtyards of urine, the stairwells stank of moldering wood and rat droppings, the kitchens of spoiled cabbage and mutton fat" (3).

39. For example, Edward R. Morrow and Fred W. Friendly's *I Can Hear It Now* (Columbia Masterworks, ML 409, 4261, 4340) captures the recorded voices of earlier in the twentieth century, and they also recorded interviews with Marian Anderson, Gamal Abdel Nasser, David Ben-Gurion, and Winston Churchill; the Royal Shakespeare Company's *The Hollow Crown: The Fall and Foibles of the Kings and Queens of England* (London records, A4253) offers dramatic readings of letters, commentaries, and trials in English history; *Great Speeches of the 20th Century* (Rhino Records, R4 70567) is a collection of 68 speeches, mostly from American history, but also relating to events in world history, spanning the years 1906 to 1991.

40. Of great value for direct classroom use are the following collections prepared by Gerald A. Danzer: *Discovering American History through Maps and Views* (New York: HarperCollins, 1991); *Discovering Western Civilization through Maps and Views* (New York: HarperCollins, 1991);

songs and music—which can be used, in fact, as melodic documents—are available in order to broaden our understanding of cultures from other times and places in ways that two-dimensional representations and written words cannot; plus they add unexpected excitement.[41] (Many of us even have colleagues who occasionally break into song—or we had teachers who did so—although we need not pretend to have such talent in order to turn up the volume of student interest.)

All this can help teachers and students to feel as if they were there, or at least closer to wherever there was; and all this can be used to create images, moods, and emotions. Just as trial lawyers know that what jurors retain is enhanced and complemented by other sensory input, lecturers should be aware of the comparable impact these can have on students. There are also

---

Discovering World History Through Maps and Views (New York: HarperCollins, 1992). For general guidance and further bibliographic suggestions, see Gerald A. Danzer, "Maps, Methods, Motifs: Cartographic Resources for Teaching History, *Perspectives*, 33:9 (December 1995). In addition to the sources recommended by Danzer, much can be learned from Anthony Grafton, *New Worlds, Ancient Texts: The Power of Traditions and the Shock of Discovery* (Cambridge, MA: Belknap Press of Harvard University Press, 1992).

41. For example, see Roderic H. Davison, "Teaching History with Song and Doggerel," *Perspectives*, 28:8 (November 1990), reprinted in *History Anew*; Alex Zukas, "Different Drummers: Using Music to Teach History," *Perspectives* (September 1996); *Folk Songs in the Classroom*, a newsletter, published 3 times a year (contact Diana Palmer, Assistant Editor, 433 Leadmine Road, Fiskdale, MA 01518). *The Instructor's Resource Kit to Accompany World Civilizations: The Global Experience*, by Peter Stearns, et al. (New York: HarperCollins, 1992), includes a 60-minute audio cassette that contains 25 selections from different times and cultures in world history. And *History of Music: The Collection* is a four-disk CD-ROM (available for both Windows and Macintosh) of music from around the world (Zane Publishing, 1950 Stemmons, Ste. 4044, Dallas, TX 75207-3109).

political cartoons,[42] posters,[43] and reproductions of works of art. For example, the paintings of Peter Bruegel the Elder can form the centerpiece for a lecture on sixteenth-century social life in Europe, while the engravings of William Hogarth can do the same for politics and society in eighteenth-century England.[44]

42. For example, see Michael Wynn Jones, *The Cartoon History of Britain* (New York: Macmillan, 1971); Stephen Hess and Milton Kaplan, *The Ungentlemanly Art: A History of American Political Cartoons* (New York: Macmillan, 1975); Morton Keller, *The Art and Politics of Thomas Nast* (New York: Oxford University Press, 1968); *Thomas Nast: Cartoons and Illustrations*, with text by Thomas Nast St. Hill (New York: Dover Publications, 1974); Herbert Block, *Herblock On All Fronts: Text and Cartoons* (New York: New American Library, 1980); *A Cartoon History of United States Foreign Policy Since World War I*, by the editors of the Foreign Policy Association (New York: Vintage Books, 1968); *Bill Mauldin's Army: Bill Mauldin's Greatest World War II Cartoons* (Novato, CA: Presidio Press, 1983); Alice Sheppard, *Cartooning for Suffrage* (Albuquerque: University of New Mexico Press, 1994); Stephen Hess and Sandy Northrop, *Drawn and Quartered: The History of American Political Cartoons* (Washington, D.C.: Elliot & Clark, 1996).

43. For example, see Max Gallo, *The Poster in History* (New York: American Heritage Publishing, 1974); Peter Paret, et al., *Persuasive Images: Posters of War and Revolution from the Hoover Institution Archives* (Princeton: Princeton University Press, 1992); Maurice Rickards, *Posters of Protest and Revolution* (New York: Walker & Co., 1970).

44. For example, see Francis Haskell, *History and Its Images: Art and the Interpretation of the Past* (New Haven: Yale University Press, 1993); William Ayres, ed., *Picturing History: American Painting, 1770-1930* (New York: Rizzoli International, 1993); Robert I. Rotberg & Theodore K. Rabb, eds., *Art and History: Images and Their Meaning* (New York: Cambridge University Press, 1990); Shirley Wilton, "Art as Social History in the Western Civilization Survey," *Perspectives*, 25:9 (December 1987), reprinted in *History Anew*. A useful reference work is James Hall, *Dictionary of Subjects and Symbols in Art* (New York: Icon Editions/Harper & row, 1979); On Bruegel, see Margaret A. Sullivan, *Bruegel's Peasants: Art and Audience in the Northern Renaissance* (New York: Cambridge University Press, 1994) and Michael Gibson, *Bruegel* (New York: Tabard Press, 1989). On Hogarth, see Joseph Burke and Colin Caldwell, *Hogarth: The Complete Engravings* (London: Alpine Fine Arts, n.d.). For use directly in the classroom, see *History of the World: World Art Transparencies and User's Guide* (Boston: Houghton-Mifflin, 1992).

Reference can be made to feature films and television programs students have seen in recent years in order to support accurate portrayals and to correct errors; use film settings to build lessons that take advantage of those big-screen visual images. The films thus can become not history per se, but vivid points of reference if you make them work for you.[45] (A colleague has told me, for example, that he has even had success referring to the Arnold Schwarzenegger science-fiction time-travel adventure, *The Terminator*, when discussing Sidney Hook's *The Hero in History* with regard to the importance of individuals in the making of history. Another uses a short clip from *The Wizard of Oz* when she teaches about Populism in her introductory U.S. history course.)

For the more ambitious—but not much more—try to synchronize and coordinate two of these media supplements. Slides, say, might be matched with music, songs, speeches, literature, or other spoken words. (For example, along with my slide

45. For example, see Robert A. Rosenstone, "The Historical Film: Looking at the Past in a Postliterate Age" in Lloyd Kramer, et al., eds., *Learning History in America* (Minneapolis: University of Minnesota Press, 1994); Donald Mattheisen, "Finding the Right Film for the History Classroom," *Perspectives*, 27:9 (December 1989), reprinted in *History Anew*; John E. O'Connor, *Teaching History with Film and Television* (Washington, D.C.: American Historical Association, "Discussions on Teaching" pamphlet, 1987); Martha J. Feldman, "Totalitarianism without Pain: Teaching Communism and Fascism with Film," *The History Teacher*, 29:1 (November 1995) 51-61; Mark C. Carnes, ed., *Past Imperfect: According to the Movies* (New York: Henry Holt, 1995); Robert A. Rosenstone, *Revisioning History: Film and the Construction of a New Past* (Princeton: Princeton University Press, 1995); Robert A. Rosenstone, *Visions of the Past: The Challenge of Film to Our Idea of History* (Cambridge, MA: Harvard University Press, 1995); Neil M. Heyman, *Western Civilization: A Critical Guide to Documentary Films* (Westport, CT: Greenwood, 1995); Robert Brent Toplin, *History by Hollywood: The Use and Abuse of the American Past* (Champaign: University of Illinois Press, 1996). In addition, *Perspectives*, the monthly newsletter of the American Historical Association, regularly publishes a "Film and Media" column, and the *American Historical Review* and the *Journal of American History*, annually publish reviews of history-related films.

lecture on the Industrial Revolution, in Britain, I play a book-on-tape selection from chapter 15 in Anthony Trollope's 1858 novel *Doctor Thorne* that vividly pulls from the past a glimpse of a village in transition, hurt by the railway that has passed it by.) One can allot five or fifty minutes to the activity; either way, it will help to capture and set an appropriate mood and tone. Sometimes such a presentation can be used to illuminate discussion and assist in textual analysis. At other times a media demonstration might be used to conclude a lecture by allowing the mood thus created to linger.[46] In either case, students are engaged and the lecture is enhanced—although I would recommend paying attention so as to make sure technology does not become intrusive, an end in itself.[47]

These, then, are just a few ways to encourage students to interact with history, to bring life to a subject so as to give it meaning and value to students, especially among those in survey courses whose main interest may lie elsewhere. These techniques also assist individual students in trying to make sense of, and thus to remember, new information in terms of what they know; that is, "students use their own existing knowledge and prior experience to help them understand the new material; in particular, they generate relationships between and among new ideas and between the new material and information already in memory."[48] What must be remembered, too, is that it is the use of a variety of techniques that works best to capture and hold attention.

Delivering the Lecture: When lecturing, movement should be the shadow of speech, even if it only means your shifting from one side of the desk to the other. If you can be aware of how the television camera never stays fixed on a single image,

---

46. Frederick, "The Lively Lecture—8 Variations," 49.

47. Saul Cornell and Diane Dagefoerde, "Multimedia Presentations: Lecturing in the Age of MTV," *Perspectives*, 34:1 (January 1996), 1, 8-10.

48. Alison King, "From Sage on the Stage to Guide on the Side," *College Teaching*, 41:1 (1993), 30.

but instead shoots the same individual or scene from different angles, then you will know why it is important to provide some movement, including hand gestures and shifts in body position. Also, do not disdain the use of a little dramatics. Evidence of being a student of Stanislavski need not be demonstrated, but an occasional theatrical gesture or over-emphasis can be good for grabbing flagging attention. In addition to actions, the use of emotion-enhancing words creates reactions, and as long as the content of the lecture is of an appropriate quality such words should achieve the desired effect. These suggestions are especially important if you teach large lecture classes, where several factors will work against you: the distance between teacher and students, especially those in middle and back rows, is not readily conducive to interaction or discussion; the seating arrangement usually transforms the student into the role of a spectator, a passive observer who expects to be entertained and informed, not involved; large-size classrooms create an atmosphere that is impersonal, one in which students are especially reluctant to speak and where the instructor appears remote; and large numbers of students make individual participation difficult.[49]

While in the act of lecturing, it is wise to pay attention to your audience and to try to think yourself into students' minds in order to reach them more effectively, remembering that they do not possess the same depth of understanding or level of sophistication as you do. Look for non-verbal signs that might suggest confusion or lack of attention. Make eye contact with students, and do not be so wedded to notes that you fail to look up so as to get an on-going sense of how you are being received. You should be able to sense when they are with you, or are confused, or angry, or bored. Try to adjust as you proceed. If there is any doubt about your success here, it would not be a sign of weakness to ask students for suggestions; on the contrary, such a request is more likely to be seen as a reflection of commitment

49. Joel Geske, "Overcoming the Drawbacks of the Large Lecture Class," *College Teaching*, 40:4 (1992), 151.

and conscientiousness. In addition, build repetition of important points into the lecture (more than you would in your writing), in order to reduce the possibility of confusion, and pause at appropriate moments so as to provide students with an opportunity to think and catch up.

Also while lecturing, try to listen to yourself and to use a conversational delivery, and then try to eliminate what could distract your students, such as a pace that is consistently too slow or too rapid, or pauses that are too long, or the frequent use of "a-a-a-a," "you know," "okay," or "I mean," and the like, or ticks such as tugging at eye glasses or jewelry, or jiggling change or keys in a pocket, or regularly clearing your throat. As a speech teacher once told me, a speech defect is anything that calls attention to itself. (Viewing an occasional lecture you have had videotaped will enable you to see yourself as others do and, in time, to work on eliminating those distractions.) The pace at which you lecture should be adjusted according to what students are expected to be doing. For example, your words and ideas might be spoken somewhat rapidly if only listening is required from students. But if they are to take notes and to reflect on various points of the lecture, then a slower pace is necessary. Also, the introduction of new, complex, or unfamiliar material (or vocabulary) suggests that more time is needed by students for absorption and ordering.[50]

Be aware, too, that students look for cues that will suggest what it is the teacher has determined is important. Speak loud enough to be heard at the back of the room, and vary the speed with which you talk, slowing and providing emphasis in order to stress a key point, increasing the pace as you move on. But delivery is not just tempo and inflection; it is also alternating between "general information and detail, difficult concepts and easy ones, gravity and humor. You can overdo the use of any:

---

50. Marilla Svinicki, "How to Pace Your Lecture," in Weimer and Neff, eds., *Teaching College*, 71-73.

the trick is to keep all in proportion."[51] Delivery is also how you carry yourself, how you stand and move about; therefore, adopt a posture that conveys a sense of the importance of what it is you are doing.

Your attitude toward students, your demeanor, will likely affect their attitude toward you, your course, and eventually their ability to learn. We all have colleagues who are learned, bright, and capable, but who turn students away from—rather than toward—the discipline. By appearing in class on time, by being prepared and attentive we are quietly telling students they have our respect and that we are there to further their education. When students speak, we respect what they express even when we must correct them; we offer praise when it is warranted and encouragement for an honest effort made. We develop rapport with students. To intimidate students, to try to impress them with our credentials or with an air of superiority, and to appear unapproachable is only to call attention to our own inadequacies and to create obstacles to learning.[52] Seek a comfortable balance between formality and familiarity.

A Potpourri of Strategies: Explode myths in a dramatic way to call attention to the mystery and the propaganda of history, to its being alive and changing, in order to create curiosity and interest.[53] For example, I start my lecture on Martin Luther and the Reformation by asking students to visualize a movie screen, to see on that screen a sixteenth-century town square in the German city of Wittenberg, with its large castle church appearing at the top-center. The day is October 31, 1517, All Hallows' Eve, the day before All Saints' Day; it is a festive time, and town folks are setting up booths and stalls as many others are milling about. Suddenly, I say, we see an intense monk

---

51. Dubrow and Wilkinson, "The Theory and Practice of Lectures," 30.

52. Murray, "How Do I Lecture Thee?," 112.

53. For good background on debunking myths and on forged and dubious documents, see Allan Nevins, *The Gateway to History* (Garden City, NY: Anchor/Doubleday, 1962), especially chapters V and VI. For specific works that debunk such myths, see the first half dozen sources in note #33.

walking across the square, toward the church, carrying a rolled parchment, a hammer, and some nails. No one pays him much attention as he passes by until he mounts the steps to the church, whereupon he unravels the parchment, tacks it to the church door, and leaves the way he came. On the parchment is printed Luther's 95 Theses on Indulgences. People gather in front of the door, read the theses, and start talking among themselves, with increased levels of agitation. The scene then changes to a map of Europe, with Wittenberg highlighted in bold Gothic print. We stare at the map for a moment as a crackling sound is heard and a small flame breaks through the parchment at Wittenberg. Soon all of Europe is ablaze with the challenge of Martin Luther, and the Reformation has begun. This was a very dramatic moment, I tell my students, but the problem is that in spite of what they have read and heard, this posting of the 95 Theses never really happened![54] I do not tell them what, in fact, did happen until later, after we have gone into the Reformation's background. Not only does this little dramatization enable me to explode a myth and rouse curiosity, it also allows us to talk about literacy and the use of Latin versus the vernacular, historiography and historical interpretation, how events can be manipulated, and why it makes a difference where a position is argued. A gimmick or theatrics, therefore, need not be anti-intellectual. If truth be told, effective lecturing inevitably must involve some theatrics, whether it be an intimate variety associated with smaller classes or the more pronounced for larger classes.

During the course of a lecture, repeat important points several times, each in a slightly different way, from a different perspective, or with altered language; thus, build repetition into what you do. This gives slower note takers a chance to catch up, it calls attention to particularly important points, and it enables those points to be digested. Understanding will also be increased if key points are illustrated with examples—frequent examples—

54. Erwin Iserloh, *The Theses Were Not Posted: Luther Between Reform and Reformation* (Boston: Beacon Press, 1968).

especially with examples that involve student participation. By way of illustration, a theme that is woven into my week-long lecture on the Italian Renaissance, in a survey course, is that that period was not simply a cultural phenomenon but rather the result of the interrelationship among economic, political, social, and cultural factors. As each of these factors is discussed and supported with examples, I call attention to the theme; after a while I ask students to identify the ways in which all the factors come together. By the end of the unit, the point has not only been made but understood as well.

Develop a sense of the student body you teach. Where possible, try to link aspects of the lecture to their collective interests, to utilize examples that are vivid, curious, and intriguing, to build suspense as you advance toward resolving conflicts, and to call attention to resolutions that will create future problems. Such methods need not compromise the integrity of a subject, whereas they can serve to draw students in and secure their attention. Having a sense of one's students also means being aware of what they know and do not know; therefore, as new words, names, or concepts are introduced, be alert to the need to explain or to have students take over this task and thus involve them further.

We are all asked questions periodically to which we do not know the answer. When that happens, turn the question back to the students, to get one or more of them to look it up and report back at the next class session—but make sure you look it up too. Or use the revelation of your temporary ignorance to demonstrate that both you, and the discipline, do not have all the answers, and that professionals and experts do not always agree. Also, be prepared to learn from your students, and acknowledge that phenomenon, and be prepared as well to build on students' ideas; you will likely earn their respect, and everyone profits.

In a related way, if you blunder, stumble, or make an obvious mistake—which we all do from time to time—try to use that to your advantage; turn an apparent weakness into a strength. Acknowledge your own limitations, your humanity. Do not be afraid to make fun of yourself in order to reveal this human side; your students will likely think more highly of you and be able to identify with you. Just as we cannot know it all, we also cannot be flawless.

On the practical side, provide specific directions to yourself, in your lecture notes, of any actions you would like to take, such as moving forward toward the class or using a prop. Likewise, know the classroom in which you will teach in order to figure out—in advance—how to use it to your best advantage. For example, know where audio-visual materials might, or must, be used; make sure equipment as well as outlets work; test acoustic potential and problems; determine noises that might be made by lights, equipment, student movement, desks, entrances, and exists. In other words, know what you are up against and prepare accordingly.

There are times when something you say or is written in one of your required readings will be challenged by a student. Not all challenges will be intellectual; some will be emotional. Rather than get defensive and spoil for a fight, learn to reinterpret challenges to what you say in order to give them an intellectual basis.[55] Make it a learning experience.

Just as in writing we instruct students to employ transitions as they move from point to point, so too as we lecture we should be aware of a comparable need. Comprehension will improve if students can see and understand how where you have come from is connected to where you are going. Since connections that are logical to us may not be so to all students, it is generally wise to articulate these transitions explicitly, especially when they are not merely chronological. That is, it may make sense to move from the revolutions of 1830 to those of 1848, but more care should be taken to explain the links, say, between Romanticism and Liberalism.

Note-taking seems to go hand-in-hand with lecturing, and since note-taking is an aid to memory, plan and organize your

---

55. Williams, *Classroom in Conflict*, 163-69.

lecture in such a way so that as you speak you are able to think in terms of the relative ease (or difficulty) that may be involved for students as they take notes. This is where an outline (on the board or with an overhead)—so students can always see where you are relative to the lecture as a whole and where you are headed—and your regularly writing all names and terms on the board will help students to know (and how to spell) what you expect them to remember. Plus the act of writing on the board is a welcome and helpful break in the flow of the lecture, which means it is best to cease speaking as you write.

Summarizing and Reviewing: Learning is also enhanced when a lecture is interrupted by periodic summaries of the material just presented. Students can then catch up and correct misperceptions or errors. Such summaries also serve as transitions from one topic or theme to another, which in turn helps students to see your organization and improve their own.[56] Similarly, conclude a lecture by recapitulating key points, by putting the subject in perspective relative to what the course has covered and what it will cover. Then leave students with a question or two that will help them to think about the material and, possibly, to anticipate the next class session.

Some review before exams is appreciated by students. In addition to highlighting major topics to be covered on the test and to indicating the readings for which students will be responsible and the weighting and type of the questions to be asked, I devote time to practical advice about preparing to take the exam. I distribute a list of directive word meanings (e.g., describe, analyze, compare),[57] and I discuss what it means to analyze the significance of something—which is appropriate for both essays and identifications—and why listing is different from comparing. I address what it means to analyze a question

---

56. McKeachie, *Teaching Tips*, 81.

57. Such a list is included in the Course Description booklet for Advanced Placement History (published annually by The College Board), but with the use of simple dictionary definitions and sample questions incorporating the words you use, you can easily make up your own list.

and the value of brainstorming and clustering related information before beginning to write; I speak to the importance, for responding to an essay question, of organization, of an introduction and a thesis statement, and of a conclusion (which is different from a summary).[58] I offer suggestions for ways to study the material to be covered on the exam, and I make good use of sample essays that I comment on in such a way that students are able to know what to expect from me. When I use multiple-choice questions, I also distribute samples, and I use them in order to discuss the structure of the questions (e.g., whether I offer them four or five options for each question, the extent to which the stem and these options include such phrasing as *all of the following except, all of the above, A and B only*) and the types relative to difficulty (e.g., recall, analysis, connections). Even the brightest of students can profit from this instruction, and what they learn about test taking can be utilized easily in other courses.

Conclusion

We should be attentive to and critical of the way in which we lecture, just as we should scrutinize any method or technique used to teach. What we should most certainly not do is abandon the lecture method in favor of new, essentially yet-to-be-proven methods (such as straight interactive learning) or technologies (such as those connected with distance learning). Assertions that the new is superior to the traditional are just that, assertions. A lecture that engages students—involves them *and* informs them—is a truly rewarding experience for all concerned.

Among the clear advantages of the lecture method[59] are that

---

58. Blackey, "Bull's-eye."

59. For a balance sheet on the advantages and disadvantages of the lecture method, see William J. Ekeler, "The Lecture Method," in Prichard and Sawyer, eds., *Handbook of College Teaching*, 88-90; Frederick, "The Lively Lecture—8 Variations," 43-50; Cashin, "Improving Lectures," 59-60. The following are some of the disadvantages, and lecturers should at least be

it provides a good opportunity for the knowledgeable teacher to present background material and/or great sweeps of history to students (especially to large numbers of students), or material they do not ordinarily have access to (e.g., new research or interpretations), or subject matter that is more sophisticated and complicated than they may yet be ready to handle on their own or among themselves. The lecture can promote critical thinking by calling attention to easily overlooked relationships, by raising thought-provoking questions, and then by drawing students into the process through some means of their active involvement. It may be the preferred method when the teacher wishes to define terms, to motivate students to do research, to provide students with a logical and structured approach to a subject, to organize a subject in a special way, to maintain maximum control over what happens in class, or to model a particular thinking process. At its best, the lecture can inspire a reverence for learning, and it can convey an interest in and enthusiasm for a subject. When it does most of these things well, the lecture can, according to Emerson, "set the hearts of youth aflame."[60]

Critics of the lecture method have argued that a major flaw is the lack of immediate feedback[61] (with examinations as a form of feedback usually not serving as a learning experience

---

aware of what they are and then work to counteract or minimize them: (1) The lecture method tends to be inferior to other methods in developing students' problem-solving and higher order thinking skills (e.g., analysis, synthesis); (2) it focuses more on factual or problem-solving than on conceptual learning; (3) it fails to account for differences of interest, knowledge, skills, and intellectual ability among students (i.e., one size/approach fits all); (4) immediate feedback as to its effectiveness is difficult to ascertain; (5) all students do not "receive" equally what the lecturer imparts (i.e., students do not learn at the same pace or level of understanding); (6) it is too easy for too many students to remain passive and thus to do little to discover things for themselves; (7) it does not readily promote long-term recall of subject matter; (8) if the teacher is not an effective and skilled speaker, the lecture method will not succeed.

60. Quoted in Frederick, "The Lively Lecture—8 Variations," 44

61. Bligh, *What's the Use of Lectures?,* 11.

for students). The same flaw, however, is also a characteristic of books and articles, but this does not seem to keep us from publishing or from assigning such works by others.

Besides, we can learn from and build upon the feedback that comes from student evaluations; and just as we, as writers, profit from the suggestions of good editors, lecturers would be wise to have experienced colleagues observe them in action and offer constructive criticism. In addition, lecturers, by having a class videotaped, can be their own observers, to help them see and feel what works. It is also recommended that instructors seek permission to visit the classes of colleagues who are known to be effective lecturers; alternatively, there are videotapes available of skilled lecturers that can be viewed, and studied, to good effect.[62]

Finally, there is indirect feedback in the form of audience reactions (e.g., facial expressions)—if we pay attention to those reactions. Moreover, as we have seen, direct feedback can be built in if the traditional lecture is expanded beyond traditional boundaries. In fact, it may be that the greatest opportunity for the lecturer is interacting with an audience. Good lecturing, like painting and music composition, is part art, part skill, and a lot of planning; we can learn a certain amount by reading, but ultimately we must practice, practice, practice.

Author's Note: For their advice and suggestions, I am grateful to my colleagues Ward McAfee, Lanny Fields, and Robin Balthrope, to James Lorence (University of Wisconsin-Marathon Center), and to Carol Pixton (Polytechnic School, Pasadena, CA).

---

62. Lectures on videotape, including by historians, are available from the Derek Bok Center for Teaching and Learning (Harvard University, One Oxford Street, Room 318, Cambridge, MA 02138); Stanford Video and Electronic Media Group (Stanford Alumni Association, Bowman Alumni House, Stanford, CA 94305-4005); The Teaching Company (7405 Alban Station court, Suite A107, Springfield, VA 22150-2318).

2. TO ILLUMINATE HISTORY
Making Teaching Picture-Perfect

Teaching can be improved dramatically if we use images creatively and in a way that was not possible until recently. As a student, I was fortunate to be in the classrooms of several extraordinary teachers who inspired with their words, stories, and insights, but I had to use my imagination to supply the visual content inherent in what they said, much as I did when reading. This was not a bad thing; I eventually wondered, however, whether it was something to build upon, not to be satisfied with. At the start of my teaching career, several decades ago, I launched a collection of history-related cartoons to circulate in class—for both their perspective and the light touch they provided—and, almost immediately thereafter, I began to include occasional pictures from books and other sources. I also made use of art slides and others from my travels to historic places. But passing materials among students sometimes distracted as much as enlightened, and by the time everyone had a chance to examine a given image, the class was usually onto another topic. And using slides served—and sometimes still serves—a purpose, but mostly as separate and distinct presentations. In contrast, transparencies and/or PowerPoint give teachers greater flexibility.[63] What I want to suggest here, however, might very well be

---

63. When using overhead projectors, it is best to have a spare bulb handy; a burned out bulb is, effectively, the only malfunction to anticipate. PowerPoint allows for smoother transitions from one slide to the next, but

perceived as a more imaginative and educational way to employ these images, or what can be called *Illuminated Teaching, Learning, and Understanding.*

Textbooks include illustrations, as do some monographs and other histories, but never enough of them, and hardly ever more than one on a given subject. Yet modern technology has made it possible for teachers to find and employ visual images in class in creative ways that both illuminate history and enhance our educational goals; by involving students—by asking them to describe what they see, by asking questions of the material we show, by introducing them to the intellectual possibilities inherent in many images—we have the potential to improve their communication skills and their critical thinking abilities. Scanning paintings, photographs, drawings, maps, and cartoons (political and otherwise) into our computers and downloading them from web sites gives us access to an almost unlimited variety of images—sometimes in concert with music, poetry, literature, and film clips—that we can then use to bring the past to life in ways not possible earlier. What follows are a number of examples taken from the courses I teach (European, English, and world history) that, I hope, will inspire other teaching historians to follow suit.

Perhaps here I should stress my belief in the power of visual images to enhance the spoken word. Students today are especially visual, and what we enable them to actually see, coupled with our descriptions and questions to draw them further into the subject matter, helps to develop their skills to think histori-

---

the hardware is sometimes known to not always work as advertised. There are also overhead projectors that include cameras that enable teachers to project images directly from books. As long as a room is not lighted too brightly, all of these technologies can be used in typical classrooms; I usually dim or turn off some of the lights closest to the viewing screen. Teachers will also have to decide how much time to expend in pursuit of images; finding them takes time and energy, but the effort stimulates my creative juices, and my experience in seeking and then incorporating them into my class presentations has broadened my enthusiasm for teaching.

cally. Thus I employ the verb *to illuminate* in the title to suggest not merely *to illustrate* but *to shed light on* as well. Further, it is not merely the use of images that is being advocated here but the use of sequences of images (potentially in conjunction with other means of learning). This is what is novel, this is what stimulates students through several of their senses, this is what has the potential to engage more of them more effectively.

Art and architecture play a prominent role when my class examines the Pazzi Conspiracy of 1478, a plot to kill Lorenzo de Medici; the plot is an example of the violent nature of the political side of the cultural center that was Florence, and it reveals why princes (or despots) needed the tacit consent of citizens in order to rule. The conspiracy was hatched by a rival business family, the Pazzi, and had the support of Pope Sixtus IV (after whom the Sistine Chapel would be named). Ironically, the attack came while Lorenzo and his brother, Giuliano, were attending Mass in the recently completed Cathedral of Santa Maria del Fiore (Duomo). After projecting a contemporary image of a drawing of an assassination, complete with daggers being wielded and bodies fallen, I show Florence as it appeared in a painting from 1480, with the Duomo dominating the skyline. Next come images of the Duomo itself, from afar and up close, as I talk tangentially about the special qualities of Brunelleschi's dome and how the architect's study of the Roman Pantheon (pictures of which I also project, exterior and interior, complete with the hole in the dome's center) helped him to design a structure that Europeans had lost the ability to replicate for a thousand years.[64]

---

64. To find a wealth of pictures and other images, use the image function in a search engine such as Google (http://www.google.com) and/or use websites such as Artcyclopedia.com and Artchive.com. Most textbooks today, for courses in world, Western, and U.S. history, include excellent color and black-and-white images which can be scanned into a PowerPoint program or made into transparencies, with each new edition of these texts including many new pictures. In addition, the following offer quality text to accompany their many images: Gloria K. Fiero, *The Humanistic Tradition*, 2 vols., 4th ed. (New York: McGraw-Hill, 2002); Mary A.F. Witt, et al., *The Humanities*, 2 vols., 7th ed. (Boston: Houghton Mifflin, 2005); Robert C.

As I relate the story of the attack, students view portraits of Lorenzo and Giuliani, the latter by Botticelli. Although Giuliani was killed, a wounded Lorenzo escaped and sought protection in the city. The people rallied to his side, rounded up the conspirators, and hanged them. Finally, I show Leonardo da Vinci's sketch of one of the hanging men and a photograph of the Palazzo Vecchio from which he was hanged. And, to draw a modern reference from popular culture, I remind students of *Hannibal*, both the book by Thomas Harris and the motion picture,[65] where the evil title character, living incognito in present-day Florence, is pursued by a detective named Pazzi who soon meets a fate similar to his forebears.[66]

Students are thus led through an episode visually via images of art and architecture, with scenes from two cities, as they

---

Lamm, *The Humanities in Western Culture*, 4th ed. (New York: McGraw-Hill, 2004); Roy C. Matthews and F. DeWitt Platt, *The Western Humanities*, 2 vols., 5th ed. (New York: McGraw-Hill, 2004); H.W. Janson and Anthony E. Janson, *History of Art: The Western Tradition*, 6th ed. (Upper Saddle River, NJ: Prentice-Hall and New York: Henry N. Abrams, 2001); F. David Martin and Lee A. Jacobus, *The Humanities Through the Arts*, 6th ed. (New York: McGraw-Hill, 2004); Martin Kemp, *The Oxford History of Western Art* (New York: Oxford University Press, 2000); Hugh Brigstocke, ed., *The Oxford Companion to Western Art* (New York: Oxford University Press, 2001).

65. Thomas Harris, *Hannibal* (New York: Dell, 2000); *Hannibal*, VHS/DVD (MGM, 2001).

66. For more on the conspiracy, see Lauro Martines, *April Blood: Florence and the Plot Against the Medici* (New York: Oxford University Press, 2003); the bibliography will direct readers to many other sources. Interested readers should be aware of a new twist to the conspiracy. On March 6, 2004, *The New York Times* (first section, p. 17) reported that, according to Marcello Simonetta, a professor of Italian history and literature (and based on his research in a private archive in Urbino), the mercenary Federico da Montefeltro, duke of Urbino, played a pivotal role in the assassination plot. Mr. Simonetta's findings, recently published in *Archivo Storico Italiano* and in a new book, *The Secret Renaissance* (2004), point to the duke's desire to eliminate the Medici brothers and that he would support the effort with 550 soldiers and 50 knights. It remains to be determined, it would seem, why those soldiers were not sent.

learn about more than just the dark side of Renaissance politics. Students tell me that these visuals help them to remember and understand the conspiracy more effectively, along with its historical significance. Not incidentally, teaching it this way is also more fun for the instructor; I enjoy seeing these images, mentally revisiting places I've been, and sharing my enthusiasm with students. Another example from the same period involves a discussion of the causes of the Italian Renaissance, one of which is Italy's being the site of the old Roman world. This point is emphasized via the projection of photos of the remains of the Roman Forum, the Coliseum, Circus Maximus, a section of the wall that still encircles much of old Rome, and Piazza Navona, whose oblong shape reflects the racing arena (Domitian's Stadium) that once occupied the site.[67]

In teaching world history I find it instructive to give some attention to *dehumanization*, the act of rendering opponents something less than human in order to justify inhumane actions against them. This can be demonstrated visually in a variety of compelling ways, with drawings, propaganda posters, modern journalism, photographs, film, and music serving as guiding lights. For example, a machine gun, patented in England in 1718 and illustrated by a contemporary drawing, included two different magazines: One containing round shot, for use against "civilized" Christian enemies, the other with square shot—which caused more devastating wounds—for "uncivilized" non-Christians.[68] More recently, in the United States we have dehumanized Japanese and Vietnamese, among others, when

---

67. In addition to picture-filled guidebooks (purchased when visiting Rome and other historic sites) that can be used as sources for images, most of these Roman sites, and more, are featured in the various humanities books cited in footnote #1.

68. *TimeFrame: The Enterprise of War* (Alexandria, VA: Time-Life Books, 1991), 73. This book is part of a 23-volume TimeFrame series that offers reasonably sound general-audience text accompanied by excellent visual materials. Another, equally useful Time-Life collection is the more recent (1998-2000) 18-volume *What Life Was Like* series.

we were at war, which in turn made it easier to try to kill them. The point is driven home, first, through the projection of three posters from World War II of caricatures ridiculing Japanese as rats, apes, menacing creatures, or comic characters with over-size teeth and glasses,[69] and then, with the viewing of the unintentionally humorous guide, "How to Tell Your Friends from the Japs," published in *Time* magazine in 1941. Among the "few rules of thumb—not always reliable" for distinguishing between our Chinese friends and Japanese enemies are: "Chinese, not as hairy as Japanese, seldom grow an impressive mustache"; "Japanese walk stiffly erect, hard-heeled. Chinese, more relaxed, have an easy gait, sometimes shuffle"; "Most Chinese avoid horn-rimmed spectacles."[70]

There are many images of Jews, Africans, and African Americans that demonstrate the twisted creativity behind the forces of dehumanization (and of racism and nationalism). An illustration from one of Julius Streicher's children's books works well here, such as the one that shows blond Germanic pupils rejoicing as grossly-caricatured Jewish children and their teacher are expelled from school so that discipline can be restored. Useful companion pieces include a Nazi "race-identification table," used to portray typical German heads, and a photograph of the width of a man's nose being measured to determine racial origin.[71] A useful addition is an excerpt (about halfway into the film) from *Europa Europa* in which a

---

69. Peter Paret, et al., *Persuasive Images: Posters of War and Revolution* (Princeton: Princeton University Press, 1992), 198. This is a rich topic that can be pursued further on the Internet where several sites show World War II posters.

70. *Time* (December 22, 1941), 33.

71. *Shadow of the Dictators: TimeFrame AD 1925-1950* (Alexandria, VA: Time-Life Books, 1989), 36-37. A parallel avenue to pursue along these lines of race and discrimination, but this time in Latin and Hispanic parts of the Western hemisphere, concerns race mixing. See Ilona Katzew, *Casta Painting: Images of Race in Eighteenth-Century Mexico* (New Haven: Yale University Press, 2004).

German Jewish teenager, who had been surviving World War II by passing himself off as a Christian, is brought to the front of his class to have his head measured in order to demonstrate his Aryan features.[72] I also find it telling to then show a map (published in newspapers in November, 2002)[73] of the African origins of all human species. Finally, the playing of military songs or aggressive national anthems, such as the *Marseillaise*[74] (including the sanguinary words in translation), to promote nationalism expands the subject ever more vividly.

Monarchs, especially those who reigned for a long time, often had their portraits painted (or, in more modern times, photographed) at various stages in their lives and in a variety of settings. Louis XIV on horseback at a military siege might look like Frederick the Great under similar circumstances, but a lesson in comparative rule can be more instructive when accompanied by their painted images, as Frederick actually directed his troops while Louis only appeared at a battle site in time to be painted at the moment of victory.[75] Flattering the subject notwithstanding, artists provide us character studies that reveal a great deal about the looks and nurtured images of, say, Henry VIII and his daughter, Elizabeth I. Students can be shown Henry metamorphosing from a physically impressive Adonis to a bloated, diseased, angry, and disappointed man; the increasing dimensions of his several surviving suits of armor, when projected on a screen, underline the point.[76] We know less

---

72. *Europa Europa* (1991; VHS/DVD, MGM, 2003).

73. *The New York Times* (November 12, 2002), Section F, p. 3.

74. http://www.marseillaise.org/audio/mireille_mathieu_-_la_marseillaise.mp3

75. Examples of such illustrations can be found in A.G. Dickens, ed., *The Courts of Europe: Politics, Patronage and Royalty, 1400-1800* (New York: McGraw-Hill, 1977), 255; Nancy Mitford, *The Sun King* (New York: Crescent Books, 1966), 33; Nancy Mitford, *Frederick the Great* (London: Hamish Hamilton, 1970), 278-79, 284. An Internet search will yield other relevant images.

76. In this case, seeing is believing, but it isn't always: see David King, *The*

about Elizabeth's appearance, especially as she aged, lost her hair and smooth skin to the ravages of smallpox, and had her vanished beauty made over with the fawning words of courtiers, but there at least two portraits that show her as an older woman,[77] while the backgrounds, as well as the costumes, of the earlier portraits reveal much about the queen and her times. Catherine the Great and Queen Victoria are two other monarchs whose lives, in part, are illuminated in both individual and family portraits over long periods.

Artists who painted for royalty and for social and political elites sometimes offered subtle messages that we can use in class to demonstrate the personalities of subjects and thus the success or failure of a project. For example, when the thrice-married-but-now-bachelor Henry VIII sought a fourth wife, he sent Hans Holbein the Younger to the courts of Europe, where eligible princesses resided, in order to relay to him as much about these women as possible to help him make his choice. Henry was sent the portraits of Christina of Denmark and Anne of Cleves, but the artist wanted his patron to know something about each woman's personality, as well as her appearance. (Wanting to know something about a prospective spouse was not unusual. In fact, Henry's father, the widowed Henry VII, sent a secret memorandum to his ambassadors concerning a proposed marriage between himself and the Queen of Naples. The first Tudor monarch asked about "the features of her body... whether she be painted or not...the fashion of her nose...[and whether] her breasts...be big or small." A wonderful recording of this, and other documents from English history, *The Hollow Crown*, was made in 1962.[78])

Commissar Vanishes: The Falsification of Photographs and Art in Stalin's Russia (New York: Metropolitan Books/Henry Holt, 1997).

77. Neville Williams, *A Royal History of England: The Tudors* (London: Cassell, 2000), 77.

78. Royal Shakespeare Company, *The Hollow Crown: The Fall and Foibles of the Kings and Queens of England* (London Records, A4253). The print version of the performance, including the exchange between Henry

The clever Holbein painted the lively, intelligent Christina in subdued clothes that do little to distract attention from the woman herself. In contrast, we see the rather sweet but dull Anne in an elaborate jeweled headdress and colorful dress, both of which are more interesting than her face.[79] I have students tell me what they see as they compare the two works. Christina looks directly at us with an air of confidence, while Anne's eyes are downcast; Christina's hands gracefully hold a pair of gloves, while Anne's are folded submissively. As it turned out, Christina refused to be enticed to share Henry's bed, whereas the more obedient Anne accepted. But upon seeing her, Henry initiated divorce proceedings that had political consequences as well.

An already-dramatic and significant episode in the history of the early modern world can be given added dimension with the use of art, music, maps, and photographs. During the height of the Ottoman Empire (fifteenth and sixteenth centuries), the ruling sultans made effective use of their Janissary corps of foot soldiers. The Janissaries were slaves, recruited mainly from conquered Christian peasant villages in the Balkans. Taken as young men as a form of tax, they were drilled in military tactics, converted to Islam, and educated to become obedient, disciplined agents of the sultan's will; they also comprised what some have called Europe's first standing army. Showing contemporary images of the recruitment of those Christian boys and of Janissaries in their colorful uniforms and headgear,[80] while also playing "Gneç Osman" ("Young Osman"), a Janissary march,[81] melds vivid illustrations with the vibrant sounds made

VII and his ambassadors, can be found in John Barton, *The Hollow Crown: An Entertainment by and about the Kings and Queens of England* (London: Samuel French Ltd & George G. Harrap & Co Ltd, 1962), 24-26.

79. Helen Langdon, *Holbein* (London: Phaidon Press, 1976), 110-13.

80. The following web sites offer relevant images: www.humanities. ualbert.ca/ottoman/tur2pict.htm; http://www.siue.edu/COSTUMES/ PLATE67CX.HTML.

81. Mehter Band of the Asker Müse, Istanbul, Lyrichord Discs, Inc.

by ensembles of drums and double reed wind instruments. The Ottomans marched to battle to the accompaniment of music, which at first terrified the Europeans but was subsequently imitated by them.[82] Later western composers, such as Mozart and Beethoven, were influenced by this Turkish music, and we today can often hear its echoes in marching bands.

These same Janissaries[83], in 1453, played a crucial role in the Fall of Constantinople (the Conquest of Istanbul for Muslims). The story of this pivotal event fascinates, starting with Sultan Mehmet II's building a great fortress—in a mere five months—across the Bosporus from an existing castle built by his grandfather, which enabled him to control the strait's narrowest point; it still survives. With entrance to the Golden Horn—an inlet that forms the inner part of the city and where the city's walls were most vulnerable—blocked by a huge chain with links close to eleven feet long, Mehmet developed an audacious idea. He had his men build a wooden ramp laid with metal tracks (starting at the waterfront site where the Dolmabahçe Palace

---

Excellent suggestions for ways to use music and where to find a wide variety of selections can be found in Alex Zukas, "Different Drummers: Using Music to Teach History," *Perspectives* (September 1996), pp. 27-33. Also see Joseph Machlis and Kristine Forney, *The Enjoyment of Music*, 9th ed., shorter version (New York: W.W. Norton, 2003); in addition to a history-friendly narrative and discussions of specific pieces of music, information is provided about relevant CDs and cassettes; also available is the *Norton Digital Music Collection*, featuring six hours of music that were selected to enhance the core repertory of the 9th edition (see www.wwnorton.com/college/music/ndmc).

82. According to Machlis and Forney, *The Enjoyment of Music*, 59, 234-35: Janissary bands originated in Anatolia/Turkey in the fourteenth century as an elite corps of mounted musicians. They accompanied soldiers to war, playing their brass and percussion instruments from horseback and their fifes and drums from among the ranks of foot soldiers in order to spur the troops into battle.

83. For more on the Janissaries by one of their own who served during this time period, see Konstantin Mihailovic, *Memoirs of a Janissary*, trans. B. Stolz. Michigan Slavic Translations no. 3 (Ann Arbor: Michigan Slavic Publications, 1975).

now stands) from the Bosporus overland so that some 70 Turkish ships, hauled out of the water by pulleys and placed on wooden cradles made by the sultan's carpenters and fitted with iron wheels, could be pulled some three miles by oxen up a 200-foot hill and down the other side into the Golden Horn. An analysis of this episode becomes especially meaningful, and memorable, when accompanied by a map showing the region around Constantinople (including the Black Sea, the Bosporus, the Sea of Mamara, and the Dardanelles), a picture of the Golden Horn and immediate surroundings and another of the ships being hauled, along with a portrait of the sultan, photographs of the fortress, the restored walls around parts of the old city, and those extraordinary chain links.[84]

A monarch every bit as splendid and central to his empire's success was Louis XIV of France. A veritable recreation of his court, complete with photographs, paintings, music, and film can give students a heightened sense of what it must have been like to be in the presence of the Sun King. Ingredients include images of what Versailles looked like in 1668 and 1722 (i.e., the difference between a palace not much larger than the original chateau of Louis XIII and that which Louis XIV had quadrupled in size), a portrait or two of Louis (such as those by Claude Lefebvre and Hyacinthe Rigaud), a photograph of the Hall of Mirrors, pictures of seventeenth-century French nobles in all

---

84. For many of these and other relevant images, see: J.J. Norwich, *Byzantium: The Decline and Fall* (New York: Alfred A. Knopf, 1966); Nurhan Atasoy, *Splendors of the Ottoman Sultans* (Memphis, TN: Wonders, The Memphis International Cultural Series, 1992); Ilhan Aksit, *The City of Two Continents: Istanbul* (Istanbul: Aksit Kültür Turizm Sanat Ajans Ltd. Sti., 1995). For the most thorough history of the event, see Steven Runciman, *The Fall of Constantinople, 1453* (London: Cambridge University Press, 1965). According to Runciman (pp. 104-05), and based on a then-recent action undertaken by the Venetians, "it was probably an Italian in his [Mehmet's] service who suggested to him that ships could be transported overland." No source is provided for this speculation, but even if the initial idea was this Italian's, it was Mehmet who had to adapt it to the specific circumstances and terrain and who had to oversee its successful execution.

their finery, the music of Jean-Baptiste Lully (especially the brief Ouverture to his court opera, *Atys*[85]), and a little imagination by both instructor and students.[86] Not incidentally, Lully, an Italian immigrant, defined the essence of French opera for years to come; his music is filled with nationalistic overtones and flattering tributes to the king while reflecting the grandeur and confidence of the royal court.

After projecting the portraits of Louis and talking about his appearance and demeanor, as well as his desire to dominate those about him, the discussion moves to the ways in which the king made enjoying life at court the goal of the nobility—as opposed to their attempting to emasculate the monarchy, as had been the norm earlier, especially when the crown was weak. In time, the great object of noblemen was to keep themselves in the king's eye, with Versailles being center court. With the sounds of *Atys* filling the room, I show, in succession, those images of Versailles, drawings of the dress of the nobility, and the Hall of Mirrors, which I describe (i.e., the dimensions, the crystal chandeliers, the painted ceiling and generous use of gold leaf, the parquet floor, the seventeen windows and the seventeen identically-shaped mirrors). I ask students to visualize in their mind's eye the light of the sun piercing those windows, darting every which way as it passes through the crystal chandeliers, bouncing off the mirrors—it had to be dazzling. The Hall is filled with nobles on display, eager to be noticed by the king. He passes among them, nodding to several deemed worthy of his recognition, even exchanging a word or two with a select few, which separates them from their peers and, surely, engulfs their bodies like few other experiences. This was all part of a great game Louis played; it is perhaps why he created Versailles, and

85. Jean-Baptiste Lully, *Atys*. Les Arts Florissant, Harmonia Mundi Fran. 3 compact discs, HMC 901257.59.

86. Mitford, *The Sun King*; Dickens, *Courts of Europe*, 233-61; John Adamson, ed., *The Princely Courts of Europe* (London: Weidenfeld & Nicolson, 1999), 67-93. Also useful for several film clips is *The Rise of Louis XIV* (1966, directed by R. Rossellini; VHS, Hen's Tooth Video, 1990).

this brief presentation [i.e., the audio-visual part takes only about five minutes] seems to capture its essence in a way students can appreciate at another level than if described with words alone.[87]

In teaching about nineteenth-century industrialization and especially the coming of the railway, I focus first on the inaugural run of the initial line from Liverpool to Manchester in 1830 and then on the impact of trains on towns that were once regular coach stops but were thereafter bypassed; primary sources and literature supplement a number of valuable visual images. Along with projecting an image of "The Rocket," the first commercial locomotive, and a print of the opening day ceremonies,[88] I have students read an eyewitness description by one of the passengers, who was as exhilarated as her mother was terrified by the speed (approximately twenty-four mph) with which "we flew by" the many people who lined the parallel road. Among the dignitaries on the train were William Huskisson, a prominent politician, and the prime minister, the Duke of Wellington. When the train stopped to take on a supply of water, Huskisson, among others, exited to look about and greet the Duke in his carriage. Just then another engine, demonstrating its speed on an adjacent track, came "upon them like lightning." Poor Huskisson froze, "looked helplessly to the right and left, and was instantaneously prostrated by the fatal machine, which dashed down like a thunderbolt upon him."[89] This account of the first railway fatality can also be accompanied by other images of the carriages provided for the different classes of travel and cartoons (from *Punch* among others[90])

---

87. Ibid. for paintings and photographs of Versailles and the Hall of Mirrors.

88. *The Pulse of Enterprise: TimeFrame AD 1800-1850* (Alexandria, VA: Time-Life Books, 1990), 60-61; John Langdon-Davies, ed., *James Watt and Steam Power* (Amawalk, NY: Jackdaw Publications, 1965).

89. John Carey, ed., *Eyewitness to History* (New York: Avon Books, 1997), 304-06.

90. Ralph Harrington, "The Neuroses of the Railway," *History Today* 44:7 (July 1994), 15-21; Lionel Lambourne, *Victorian Painting* (London:

depicting the anticipated horrors of this newfangled form of transportation.

There's a particularly telling print, from 1859, that reveals the price of progress by contrasting a passenger train, an impressive new station, and a growing new town, in the background, with an abandoned, decaying stagecoach and broken-down inn from the previous era in the foreground.[91] A perfect accompaniment is to read the first couple of pages from Chapter XV, "Courcy," in Anthony Trollope's *Doctor Thorne* (1858), which describes, in narrative and dialogue, the negative impact a neighboring railway has been having on a once-thriving town at which the stagecoach no longer stops;[92] it is as if the picture had been composed specifically for the novel, and having students read it is a way of demonstrating the value literature can have for historians. Needless to say, there are many other images that can be used effectively to help students comprehend the significance of the Industrial Revolution, including an excerpt or two from Charlie Chaplin's classic film, *Modern Times*.[93]

There is virtually no limit to what can be done to illuminate the subjects we teach, and appealing to students through more than just one of their sense organs has positive results for teaching and learning. By way of some quick takes: In teaching about the Reformation, I talk about the role played by relics. The discussion gets a boost from images of, say, what the Catholic Church accepts as a piece of the True Cross or a nail used during the Crucifixion, or of objects linked to saints, such as the chains used to bind St. Peter or the shoes of St. Teresa of Avila. The Church is supposed to be in possession of what was once believed to be the footprint of Jesus, but it is not displayed (I indicate why). In contrast, a mold of the footprint of the Prophet

---

Phaidon Press, 1999), 265, 267-68.

91. Ibid., 18.

92. Anthony Trollope, *Doctor Thorne* (New York: Oxford University Press, 2001).

93. *Modern Times* (1936; VHS, Twentieth Century Fox, 1992).

Mohammed is on display in Topkapi Palace in Istanbul. Teaching about the Chinese civil service examinations hits closer to home with students when accompanied by images of the settings and cubicles in which the exams were taken, along with a recitation of sample questions. A discussion of foot binding, a practice that was once an integral part of the lives of millions of Chinese women, comes to life through drawings showing how feet were bound, photographs of the tiny shoes as well as of deformed naked feet, and an authentic pair of such shoes that students can actually see and touch. And poetry always adds an effectively lyric touch, whether combining it, say, with a study of Italian humanism (e.g., Dante's *The Divine Comedy*) or analyzing the role of women in China and Latin America (e.g., *Book of Songs*, for the poem beginning, "When a son is born"[94] or "Woman" by Fu Hsüan[95] and "To Be Born a Man" by Bolivian poet Adela Zamudio[96]). There is also a plethora of poetry associated with World War I.[97] Siegfried Sassoon's "To a Childless Woman" is given a brilliantly poignant reading by the English actor Jeremy Irons, to the accompaniment of documentary footage, at the conclusion of PBS's first-rate series, *The Great War*, which can be used to good effect in class.[98]

And on and on it can go: Thomas More's trial is brought to life by a film clip from *A Man For All Seasons*[99] and then can be followed up by showing how the site of the trial, Westminster

94. http://china.tyfo.com/int/literature/ancient%20poems/i990817literature.htm.

95. http://www.wsu.edu:8080/~wldciv/world_civ_reader/world_civ_reader_1/chinese_poetry.html.

96. http://coloquio.com/coloquioonline/0206jbzamudio.htm.

97. For example, see Jon Silken, ed., *The Penguin Book of First World War Poetry* (London: Penguin, 1997) and Carolyn Forché, ed., *Against Forgetting: Twentieth-Century Poetry of Witness* (New York: W.W. Norton, 1993).

98. *The Great War and the Shaping of the 20th Century*, VHS (PBS Home Video, 1998).

99. *A Man For All Seasons* (1966; DVD, 2004, Columbia/Tristar).

Hall in London, was for centuries the location of as many as four separate courts, some in session simultaneously: with the use of early nineteenth-century illustrations of the hall and the courts by architectural draftsman Augustus Pugin in collaboration with caricaturist Thomas Rowlandson.[100] The Great Depression is buttressed with photographs, a song by Woody Guthrie (e.g., "I Ain't Got No Home in This World Any More" [1940]),[101] and an excerpt from John Steinbeck's *The Grapes of Wrath* (1939).[102] Examples of African art, and thus a part of African culture, can be projected to demonstrate the skills involved, the way that art gave voice to African reactions to the coming of Europeans, the way it exerted an influence on later European art—say, on Picasso and Matisse—and to dispel Western myths of African backwardness. Teaching about Africa and the slave trade will benefit from maps, music (such as *griot* songs and slave shout songs), and a host of images of, among other things, African cities and village life, slave forts, European, Arab, and African traders, the Middle Passage (including a powerful film clip from *Amistad*[103] and a reading from Olaudah Equiano's description of his experience aboard a slave ship[104]), slave life in the Americas, North and South, and the propaganda that led to the end of the slave trade. And examples from the art of the great twentieth-century Mexican muralists, Diego Rivera, José Clemente Orozco, and David Alfaro Siqueiros, can be shown to demonstrate how they made use of history to educate, to promote their political and social ideas, and to mobilize the population at large.[105]

---

100. Fiona St. Aubyn, *Ackermann's Illustrated London* (Ware, UK: Wordsworth Editions, 1985), 66-75.

101. *Dust Bowl Ballads* (Audeo 2000, Buddha/Bmg, #99727).

102. John Steinbeck, *The Grapes of Wrath* (New York: Penguin, 2002).

103. *Amistad* (1997; DVD, Dreamworks Skg, 2003; VHS, Universal Studio, 2000).

104. *The Life of Olaudah Equiano* (New York: Dover, 1999).

105. Desmond Rochfort, *Mexican Muralists: Orozco, Rivera, Siqueiros*

Images, in short, help students to understand and remember events and ideas, just as words coax deeper meaning from images. When images and words are used together—with images serving words—they help to promote more effective teaching and learning. The following comments from some of my students might serve, at least anecdotally and representatively, as evidence of my claim: "We learn by building on what we know, but with an unfamiliar subject sometimes there isn't enough background knowledge to facilitate learning. Using images gives students a visual tool useful for retaining new information because they are able to link an image with a person or even a concept." Images help "to contextualize the student with the period. They place you geographically. They set you within the culture....[They also make] the class more interactive....It allows us to get a more in-depth view of [the teacher's] perspective on history." "Because I am a visual person, images bring the content to life, and I understand the subject better." The presentation on seventeenth-century Dutch art "was a terrific integration and visual demonstration of societal change in Dutch society....[Getting] a sense of the culture is sometimes more important than a little more factual data."

In addition, and as a result of my using images, some students are incorporating within their research papers images that they themselves have discovered (e.g., engravings of women, men, and families for a paper on Luther's views on these subjects); others, in critical book reviews, are evaluating the effectiveness of visual illustrations. I also have constructed a few essay exam questions that require students to integrate into their responses what they have seen and discussed in class with required course readings.[106]

(New York: Chronicle Books, 1998).

106. For example: "The unity that was the 'United' Netherlands was based upon political and economic success and upon a distinctive civilization." With this quotation as a point of reference, describe and analyze the nature of 17th-century Dutch life and society. Support your answer with examples from and direct references to J.L. Price's *The Dutch Republic in the 17th*

A great variety of images are housed in textbooks, with each new edition offering additional opportunities to the searcher. Some monographs and other histories laden with illustrations, along with art books, especially those in color, are another helpful source. The potential of the Internet for finding resources, including images, is increasingly being appreciated.

As you, fellow teachers, review class notes and the subjects you will be addressing, imagine the kind of images that might be useful to augment and improve what you do; then look for them. Reviewing images in books, on the World Wide Web, and elsewhere will often suggest ways in which they might be used, e.g., to expand a story or to compliment music, poetry, litera- ture, and film. In other words, when I determine that a lecture or discussion subject would profit from illustrations, I search for them; when I come across images while reading I think about ways I might be able to incorporate them into what I do in class. Not every idea pans out, not every image proves useful. Either way, the process keeps me thinking about my teaching effec- tiveness. Before long, this process takes on a life of its own: the art of teaching surges to new heights and, like medieval manuscripts, history is illuminated. But let me be clear: this approach is not simply a more advanced version of show-and- tell. It is, instead, a means to improve student thinking skills and learning by melding and integrating words, concepts, and ideas with visual stimulation. Following my lead will take time, but used selectively it is an approach that can be effective in drawing students more deeply and broadly into the material, in getting more students more involved.

It was said of Petrarch that he lived by and for writing, with no interest that could not be converted into a literary form. In a comparable way, so it is with historians who take pride in their teaching and who see in what they read, observe, hear, and experience possibilities for use or adaptation in their classes.[107]

Century and the art shown in class."

107. For example, the articles, books, and book reviews I read generate

ideas for what might be integrated into class lectures and discussions (and often for the need for a possible visual accompaniment as an added stimulant). And my travels to both historic and natural sites I instinctively see through the tripartite lens of being a teacher, a historian, and a tourist. Can I use this in class, I ask myself, and if so, to what educational advantage?

3. EARLY BIRD SPECIALS
SOME THOUGHTS ON USE OF CLASS TIME BEFORE CLASS BEGINS

Please read no further if you are a teacher who, for whatever reason, is rarely able to arrive in class early. But if, instead, you routinely appear at least five minutes before class begins—to set up materials, to be available to students with questions, to set an example, or to demonstrate a genuine concern for students—then the suggestions below for using those few minutes constructively might whet your creative appetite.

I have recently begun my fifth decade as a full-time university professor of history. Not surprisingly, I have found that just as our discipline continues to evolve and expand, so have the possible topics and areas to teach in each of my courses, as they surely have, or will have, for most teachers. Yet class time is not part of an expanding academic universe, and the number of minutes we spend in class—each day and each term—ordinarily does not increase from year to year in order to accommodate a potentially fuller, more thorough, and inclusive course syllabus. This dilemma inevitably involves us in reevaluating what we do and cover in class and more so when we factor in changing technologies that enable us to be innovative in new ways. Most of us, I expect, add and drop some subjects and expand and contract others, but not without some considerable deliberation and regret for topics we have had to abridge or even eliminate altogether.

In recent years I have been integrating significant numbers of projected images—along with a little music—into classroom presentations, which in turn has inspired—if not pushed—me to be creative in nontraditional ways.[108] Although students both enjoy and seem to profit from these visual stimuli—many of which can function as documents and primary sources, as they draw students more fully and effectively into the subject at hand[109]—they most surely take additional class time to show and discuss. As a result, I have chosen to marginalize rather than cut some of this visual material by showing and describing it during the three-to-five minutes before the official start of a class session. None of this pre-class material is considered when I prepare course examinations, so students who merely arrive on time are not penalized, but by giving a few extra minutes of my time I am able, in turn, to give much more to my students, who now, not incidentally, have an incentive to arrive early as well. As some students have noted in their course evaluations: "The pre-class materials made getting there early very enjoyable"; "He provided visuals and music before class which made me want to come early"; "The way you taught the class enhanced

---

108. Robert Blackey, "To Illuminate History: Making History Picture-Perfect," *Teaching History: A Journal of Methods*, 30:2 (Fall 2005), 59-71. Also see Robert Blackey, "New Wine in Old Bottles: Revitalizing the Traditional History Lecture," *Teaching History: A Journal of Methods*, 22:1 (Spring 1997), 3-25. For more on using images see Anna Pegler-Gordon, "Seeing Images in History," *Perspectives* 44 (2006), 28-31 and Joseph Coohill, "Images and the History Lecture: Teaching the History Channel Generation," *The History Teacher* 39:4 (August 2006), 455-65.

109. For example, in describing the changes that took place in written English, from the sixteenth through the eighteenth centuries, I project samples of handwritten letters from early, middle, and late parts of those centuries (some of which, not incidentally, come from my own research) and, in each case, then have students take turns trying to read them aloud. Whether it is in the use of words, phrases, or the actual physical form the letters of the alphabet take, this lesson in paleography—and working with documents—has never failed to capture students' attention. Paintings, too, become primary sources when they are used to augment aspects of social history, as I do, for example, with seventeenth-century Dutch art.

my learning experience and made me want to get to class earlier because I did not want to miss any of the pictures"; "Those first five minutes or so before the start of class—with the pictures of places and the stories about them—were related to the topics we were going to cover that day and were so interesting"; "I always looked forward to coming to class early because the images served as a way to transition from class to class, to focus on the subject at hand, and to 'travel' the world"; " One of the things I appreciated about Dr. Blackey's teaching style was the five or so minutes leading into the class. He set the tone by projecting images of different locations that I never would have known about if it were not for his class. These images started off class on the right foot and inspired me to think outside the normal curriculum. It was truly a benefit to my learning experience."

The genesis of this practice is to be found in my lower-division large-lecture World Civilizations course, wherein I launch each class session with music from a different part of the globe.[110] In doing so, I highlight the important role played by music in civilizations past and present. Not incidentally, students generally respond well to music, but the realization that it plays an historical role is something of a revelation to many. In my class, in addition to integrating music selections and excerpts into the narrative of the course, I arrive in class ten minutes prior to its start and play music that is usually linked to the content, continent, or thematic subject of that day's lecture. For example, I play Antonin Dvorak's *New World Symphony* when I introduce the unit "Global Expansion and Encounter, 1450-1750," which is appropriate, because Dvorak composed the symphony in order to capture some of the spirit of America; ceremonial music from Dahomey precedes a lecture on the African slave trade and thus calls attention to the cultural side of one African people; music from the Balkans provides sounds from that explosive part of the world in the early twentieth century and thus provides back-

110. I am especially grateful for inspiration from Alex Zukas, "Different Drummers: Using Music to Teach History," *Perspectives* (September 1996), 27-33.

ground for a presentation on World War I. To accompany the pre-class music, I project one or more complementary images, all of which I elaborate on as the actual session is about to begin. For example, when the subject is Asian history, at the start of one class session, I play Cambodian music recorded at Angkor Wat, which I complement with several projected images of this well-preserved temple as well as others from around the Angkor complex, and of the ubiquitous, ever-encroaching jungle, along with a little background history. When imperialism in Africa is the subject, I play a recording of music of the BaBenzéle Pygmies while projecting photographs of pygmy people at work in their village. Before a class session devoted to World War II, I play music and project images specific to that global conflict, just as for the preceding class session on the Great Depression era, I play period music to the visual accompaniment of appropriate images from the 1930s. For the final class session I show scenes from the film *Koyaanisqatsi*, directed by Godfrey Reggio, while students listen to the mesmerizing score composed by Philip Glass; the Hopi Indian word *koyaanisqatsi*, meaning "life out of balance," seems an appropriate way to end the course as well as to reflect the contemporary state of world affairs.

Virtually all the music and images function as primary sources, about which I pose questions and encourage students to offer commentary. By the time the course is over students have been exposed to select and diverse samples of music and accompanying images of places and peoples from the major continents. Here is what a few students have observed: "I loved the projections and music. He really helps different styles of learners apply themselves in this course"; "The pre-class materials were one of the most interesting parts of the class. The music was incredible and showed that there is much more to music than Lil' Wayne and The Jonas Brothers"; "The music, especially when combined with the images, helped me hold interest not only in the class but outside of class too! I would search to find out more about a certain piece or the culture that the music was from"; "I found that it was enjoyable to listen to world music that would otherwise be lost to me. If I did not particularly care for the style of music, I would try to picture what kind of people sat around listening to the music. Did they listen to phonographs, were they smoking opium and relaxing, was this music only accessible through concerts?"

This practice in my World Civilizations course has worked effectively to interest, and sometimes to inspire, students, which in turn encouraged me to think about what I might do for my other courses. During the previous several years I had been using the few minutes before the start of each class session to encourage or spark in students an interest in words and language use and to tickle them with unusual historical facts or anecdotes. For example, in one of my English history classes, each day I project the spellings of a couple of place or proper names and challenge students to pronounce them correctly, such as Leicester (Lester) and St. John (Sin Jin). Doing so served, and still serves, a function comparable to that played by the people who warm up audiences that attend television programs taped before actual audiences: It helps to establish a positive atmosphere. In my case, it also helps to ease students into the subject at hand. Then during the winter term 2006, I added another pre-start-of-class activity linked to what I was already doing during regular class time.

As a history undergraduate and graduate student in the 1960s, my teachers never made use of images, projected or otherwise, but I appreciated their value when I came across them during my own reading and research: portraits of historical figures, photographs and paintings of historically relevant places and documents, works of art, and even cartoons on history-themed subjects.[111] Collectively, they helped me to visualize places and

---

111. The first cartoon I ever cut out was from a mid-1960s issue of *The New Yorker*, by cartoonist James Stevenson, that showed two peasants walking away from a castle, one saying to the other: "What do you think will be next—a period of spiritual rebirth, with renewed inquiry in the sciences and a humanistic resurgence of the arts?" As a student of European history

to comprehend the role they played in events, to put faces to names (especially as those faces and forms reflected personality), to add depth and character to subjects, to value the artists and paintings that were otherwise mere names and titles, and to learn that there often was insight embedded in humor. In other words, images can be used not simply as mere illustrations of historical experience but rather as another dimension of that same experience. When I began to teach, I circulated among students books that included such images as well as the occasional cartoon for comic-history relief, and I showed slides of works of art and from my travels as well as the occasional filmstrip or video clip that provided useful images to supplement course narratives. But passing books and other printed images around the room takes time for each student to examine them, and more often than not by the time a given book or image reaches the last student I have already moved on to another topic. The problem with old-fashioned slides is that they cannot be used easily for every topic. Now, however, the same technology that enables us to search the Internet for countless images and to make transparencies and PowerPoints has changed the way we can teach, and it also adds, with mind-boggling potential, to the material that we can weave into class sessions. Compelled to drop some images rather than compromise more traditional content, I came up with the idea to use pre-class time constructively.

It's all rather simple: Interested teachers can make use of the types, number, and variety of images appropriate to their subjects and students. The best way to illustrate this is with examples from several courses. But I should note first that in addition to what can be fished from the Internet and from visual records of personal travel, potential images for class use can also be secured from different types of books, including history textbooks that change some of their illustrations with each new edition and others in art, architecture, or photography, including

I was hooked, and I have been collecting cartoons relevant to historical events ever since.

"from the air" books.[112] In addition, you can draw from books that focus on travel, national heritage sites, histories of cities, and museum exhibits, and from illustrated encyclopedias, cultural atlases (e.g., Facts on File), history-related series,[113] and unusual books that offer nontraditional images of places.[114] All you have to do is seek, as there is much to find.

I first experimented with projecting images before class in a course on Tudor and Stuart England. I had already been using projected images that included portraits, documents, and both paintings and photographs of the historical sites and artifacts that are integrated throughout the course narrative. One detailed example should suffice to illustrate how I have made this work during regulation class time: To discuss and analyze the trial of King Charles I in 1649, which follows an examination of the Rump Parliament, I project an image of Oliver Cromwell, who led army officers in pushing for the trial. I then turn attention to the king who, though strong in spirit, was looking older than his 48 years, as attested to in a portrait by Edward Bower, who observed Charles throughout the trial. The trial itself took place in Westminster Hall, which can be shown as it survives today but can also be seen as it looked from the outside in the mid-seventeenth century in an etching by Wenceslaus Hollar and on the inside during the trial itself in a couple of other contemporary engravings. The red velvet chair on which Charles sat

112. For example, see Georg Gerster, *The Past From Above: Aerial Photographs of Archaeological Sites* (Los Angeles: J. Paul Getty Museum, 2005); Guido Rossi & Franco Masiero, *Venice from the Air* (New York: Rizzoli, 1988); Guido Rossi & Franco Lefevre, *Rome from the Air* (New York: Rizzoli, 1989); Annabel Walker, *England from the Air* (New York: Harry N. Abrams, 1989); Mick Aston, *Interpreting the Landscape from the Air* (Charleston, SC: Tempus, 2003).

113. Some useful ones are *Treasures of the World* (Chicago: Stonehenge Press, 1982-83), *Time Frame* (Alexandria, VA: Time-Life Books, 1987-91), and *What Life Was Like* (Alexandria, VA: Time-Life Books, 1997-2000).

114. For example, those interested in British history will find some gems in Julian Calder & Alastair Bruce, *The Oldest: In Celebration of Britain's Living History* (London: Cassell Illustrated, 2005).

has survived, as has the specially made reinforced hat of John Bradshaw, who presided over the trial; seeing photographs of these artifacts adds authenticity to previously shown images and helps students to visualize the event in some detail. To add further dramatic verisimilitude, I play a recording of a performance of an exchange between the king and Bradshaw, based on the actual trial transcript, wherein they debate the meaning of treason and the degree to which Charles was an "ordinary" prisoner. I then lead students into exploring the arguments of the opposing sides. Other projected images include the death warrant signed by 59 judges, complete with waxed seals; a painting by Canaletto of the Banqueting House as it looked in the eighteenth century and a photograph of the way it looks today (i.e., Inigo Jones' Banqueting House is where Charles waited before stepping outside onto the scaffold erected especially for the occasion) along with photographs of its brilliant ceiling by Peter Paul Rubens, installed in 1635 and with its center panel representing, with unintended irony given that Charles virtually passed under it, the apotheosis of his father, King James I; one of the two shirts worn by Charles at his execution, so he would not shiver on that cold January morning and perhaps convey the impression of fear; and John Weesop's painting imagining the execution and the reaction of the crowd.

Considering the extensive use of images I already employed in that course, and given my desire to give students a still broader impression of the British Isles, even as I lacked additional class time to do so, I had something of an epiphany when I realized that a useful way around this dilemma would be to project a few images as part of what I was doing already in the several minutes before the start of class. To augment this new approach, I keep at the ready historical maps of the British Isles and of London so as to be able to identify the location of what will be viewed each day; this has the added benefit, therefore, of enhancing students' awareness of the geography of both the British Isles and England's capital city.

I launch this course's "early bird special" with photographs of Stonehenge and a brief summary of the site's significance, along with news of recent nearby excavations (2003-06) of the remains of what archaeologists say was probably the village of the workers who erected the monoliths on the Salisbury Plain. Other images of the early history of Britain that I project and discuss at the start of successive class sessions include Hadrian's Wall, Tintagel, the ruins of the abbey church at Glastonbury, a twelfth-century bridge in Lincoln to which still-surviving houses were added in 1540, Bury St. Edmunds, the scant remains of Old Sarum (eventually an infamous rotten borough), and Salisbury Cathedral, along with photos of its Magna Carta—one of four surviving copies—and a clock mechanism from 1386 and still functioning, purportedly the oldest in Europe.

Throughout the term I also show images from around England, e.g., Dover Castle and the White Cliffs, Windsor Castle, Oxford and Cambridge Universities, Bath, Coventry Cathedral (the new one and the remains of the old destroyed during World War II), York, the Major Oak (in Sherwood Forest) and the Bowthorne Oak (among the last of the huge oak trees that are wide enough to house people in their trunks), Windsor Castle, and Leeds Castle; Scotland, e.g., the ruins of Urquhart Castle and a satellite view of Loch Ness, West Highland Cows, whose hides are coated with long auburn hair and are the oldest type of cattle in Britain, Edinburgh Castle, and Scone Palace and the Stone of Scone; and Ireland, e.g., a satellite view of the emerald island, Trinity College Library, Dublin along with pages from the Book of Kells, Blarney Castle, and a "beehive" house located on the Dingle Peninsula. In addition, I include images from around England that relate to Tudor and Stuart times but have not otherwise been incorporated into regular class sessions, e.g., Hever Castle, which was given to Ann Boleyn's father by Henry VIII and then later to Anne of Cleves, which in turn functions as a commentary of the politics of marriage, beheading, and divorce, St. James's Palace, Stratford-upon-Avon, the new Globe Theatre as well as a drawing of the original, the Monument to the Great Fire of London, Hatfield House, built by Robert Cecil, Earl of

Salisbury, Greenwich, and St. Paul's Cathedral along with a model of the earlier cathedral destroyed in the Great Fire.

Thus, by the time the course ends students have been exposed to a variety of images that add significantly to their experiencing and understanding sixteenth- and seventeenth-century England and the contemporary British Isles. Comments by students, some solicited by me and others as part of standard course evaluations, reinforced my expectation and in-class observations that my efforts were worthwhile and added a dimension to the course students otherwise would not have been exposed to: "The images, even those shown before class, make me want to travel more"; "I liked his use of visuals before and during class, including pictures of historical places which allowed me to visit them without ever going to Europe (but now more than ever I want to go)"; "I hate history, but he made it fun with his pictures, music, stories, artifacts, and more, even doing some really interesting stuff before class began"; "I am a history major and even though I am more interested in modern history, Dr. Blackey always has a way of sparking my interest. He is creative in the way he presents the material and it is nice the way he shows pictures before class in order to ease us into lecture"; "Your class turned me into an Anglophile! My hope is that one day I will travel to Britain and see the places you showed and spoke of. I will soak it all in like a sponge"; "This set up was unlike anything I had experienced before; in my other classes the instructors would show up and just begin the class. What you did before class made the class as a whole more enjoyable"; "It's a benefit to student to have something to calm their nerves before class starts and to lighten the mood"; "I find that a professor who takes the time to arrange pre-class participation made me feel like HE wanted to be there"; "The pre-class activities helped add depth to the course material; they provided visual stimulation at the very least and also added a cultural flavor to the course in that they helped to explain some of the peculiarities that are unique to different countries or time periods. They also help you remember that there is a lot more to the making of history than just wars and important figures; it is almost like looking through a kaleidoscope in that everything is made of the same material but at every turn it creates a different pattern, similar to the previous but always different."

I modify my pre-class approach in courses on the Renaissance and Reformation and on Europe in the Age of Absolutism and Enlightenment by including images, along with accompanying maps, from a number of continental European countries. Not surprisingly, for example, Italy is featured prominently in my course on the Renaissance and Reformation. But in addition to the images that are integral to an examination of the political, economic, social, and cultural history of the period, I use pre-class time to familiarize students with the rich variety of surviving sites. From Rome, for example, there is the Church of Immaculate Conception with its macabre Cemetery of Capuchin Fathers, which includes six chapels crowded with the symmetrically and artistically arranged bones of some 4,000 monks who died between 1528-1870; the Michelangelo-designed Piazza del Campidoglio along with the broken remains of what was once a rather large statue likely to have been a representation of Constantine; the Mamertino Prison, one of the oldest buildings in Rome, with its dark and forbidding subterranean stone cell and its upside-down cross, symbolic of the way St. Peter was crucified, as this prison may have been the last place of his confinement—an accompanying image of Caravaggio's "The Crucifixion of St. Peter," showing Peter on an inverted cross, creates an artistic link to the photograph of the prison cell; and the Pyramid of Caius Cestius, a marble-faced brick pyramid-tomb, built shortly before the birth of Jesus, that makes up part of a section of the Roman wall built in the third century C.E.

Like Rome and Venice, Florence is saturated with history and art. Some of the images I project include the Medici Chapel, the Cloister of San Marco along with one of Fra Angelico's angelic frescoes, Brunelleschi's Pazzi Chapel, and Basilica di Santa Maria Novella with Masaccio's "Trinity" fresco (1425), the first known painting to demonstrate linear perspective. I use the occasion of this Masaccio innovation to talk about the role churches have played as repositories of art. Other images come from landmark sites in Milan, Ravenna, and Assisi. Additional images used during pre-class minutes focus on Spain, e.g., the building that once housed the University of Alcalá, founded during the reigns of Ferdinand and Isabel by Cardinal Jiménez de Cisneros; the Mosque-Cathedral of Cordoba; the pilgrimage destination of Santiago de Compostela; and select locations in Salamanca, Toledo, Segovia, Avila, Seville, and Burgos, Germany, e.g., Cologne, Munich, and Nuremberg, and Belgium, e.g., Bruges and Brussels.

The end result of these pre-class activities is that whether students take one or several of my courses, they have not only been exposed to the history and scholarship of the countries and time periods involved but to a panoramic sweep of historic and cultural sites that help to reinforce and expand upon the history they are learning and, at times, the documentary sources they are reading. Naturally, it's not the same as their being there, but it does help to give their imaginations some added stimulation and direction. This, in turn, works for me as a teacher, both because it broadens what I teach and because I enjoy talking about and revisiting places I have experienced myself or have come to know through teaching and reading.

So it seems that technology—especially in the form of the Internet, scanners, and the different methods available for projecting and interjecting visual materials—presents us with both challenges and opportunities. How we take advantage of these technologies depends upon our willingness to be creative as teachers and on how we decide to use our time. In my experience, using pre-class time is time well spent. One bright and articulate student effectively captured what I hope all my student will experience: "The beginnings of Robert Blackey's classes were decidedly different from any classes I'd ever taken before. For one thing, they started five minutes early—which is not to say you'd be considered late if you happened to arrive merely on time, only that if you were already present with nothing to do but wait, you were in for a treat. Prior to each lecture, Dr. Blackey made it a habit to project a series of images that were relevant to whatever topic or geographic region he would be covering that day. Without any particular emphasis or objective he would display these pictures, giving brief commentary about location, time period, and significance. There was no need to take notes, no pressure to awaken from your pre-class reverie if that was your choice—it was truly just an added bonus to take or leave as one saw fit.

"As an early-arriving student to all my classes, my initial reaction to these pre-class visual feasts was one of simple relief: it was less time I had to spend staring at blank walls and the even blanker looks on the faces of some fellow students. In retrospect, however, my experience in the five minutes before class officially started had a richness and depth I would not have anticipated. When I think back on the Renaissance and Reformation—which was the subject matter of the class I took with Dr. Blackey—my mind is instantly filled with vivid images, in much the same way a particularly pleasant vacation evokes fond memories of the sites one has visited. In some ways this is strange, because I equate the images with the lectures—as if they were being experienced simultaneously—but the lectures were characterized by fast and frantic note-taking and the clamoring sense of urgency about getting down the most important facts in preparation for the inevitable exams. Yet my memory marries these separate events and manifests a symphony of color, architecture, landscape, time, place, perception, and information. I can recall seeing mosques, churches, palaces, statues, cottages, and fountains. In my head there is a map that connects these images to places: Cordoba, Granada, Venice, Rome, Florence. It is hard to imagine that this *experience*—for that is what I must call it—was made possible because the teacher showed us images on the overhead for five minutes before class even started, yet I know I must attribute it to this.

"Additionally, there were times when I would see an image of some unknown place and feel a subtle quickening in my spirit, an intangible tug of desire, like seeing for the first time the face of a person one will later come to love. In these instances, I would find myself in the grip of a strange passion that would no longer allow Spain to be the country I never noticed, or Italy to be the place I never cared to visit. Suddenly, there was about these places something irresistible, something not-to-be-over-looked, and I would rush home after class and look online for the Spanish Steps, or every picture I could locate of Cordoba, and with this the world became both smaller and grander. More accessible, more familiar, and also a great deal more beautiful and wondrous.

"While I cannot say that this is the effect that Dr. Blackey's unusual teaching method had on everyone, I am grateful that it had this effect on me. And though it is peculiarly egocentric to say so, I'd like to suggest that therein lies proof enough of its worth."

4. AND NOW FOR SOMETHING A LITTLE DIFFERENT
Constructive Breaks in the History Lecture

In 1996, Oxford University Press published *Europe: A History* by Norman Davies. In addition to its substantial text (i.e., more than 1,200 pages including notes) and a massive appendix that includes more than 100 valuable maps, graphs, tables, charts, and lists, the book is marked distinctively by the inclusion of 301 capsules. *Capsules*, as Davies notes in his preface, are intended to illustrate "narrower themes that cut across the chronological flow." They are boxed breaks both accompanying and interrupting the developing narrative, but they are purposely keyed, either directly or indirectly, to some event, person, object, concept, phenomenon, or other aspect of history being discussed; they offer a micro-history collection of intriguing and thoughtful commentary about many subjects that are either ignored or merely grazed in standard texts. For teachers and students of European history or, more broadly, just history, these capsules have the potential to fascinate and appeal to a broad spectrum of tastes: from *Altmarkt* and *Archimedes* to *Zadruga* and *Zeus*, from *Codpiece* and *Vlad* [Tepes] to *Rouge* and *Usury*.

What attracted me to Davies' capsules is that for more than a decade prior to his book's publication I had been including as part of my teaching my own version of capsules, or "breaks" as I have called them. I use these breaks to interrupt my lecture so as to offer a closer look at select subjects that are often ignored or, at best, treated summarily in course textbooks. Based on comments from students—after class, in my office, and on student evaluation forms—these breaks are welcome for a variety of reasons: they enliven class sessions on a different level and in unexpected ways; they satisfy and spike curiosity, and sometimes even encourage students to investigate further; and they pique students' attention, because breaks can't be anticipated while they can be introduced at virtually any time. Wherever possible—and these days the resources available to teachers make so many existing images accessible—I illustrate my breaks with projected images and, occasionally, with actual artifacts or physical items I have acquired.

Where does one find subjects relevant to the subject matter of one's teaching to include as breaks? Naturally, the Internet makes searches for all kinds of subjects relatively easy, especially if we allow our imaginations free reign, but I launched my collection before the Internet was available to a wide audience. [Actually, "launched" makes what happened seem like the inauguration of a master plan whereas the reality is it all happened by chance: without any prompting I decided one day before class to investigate more thoroughly a seemingly minor subject I had hitherto merely mentioned in passing; I sought out additional relevant information; and then I used that information to create a break for use in class. Student reaction was positive, I enjoyed presenting the subject matter, and over time this action spawned other breaks]. In reading—especially books, book reviews, and articles—I would come across mention of a subject that fell under the purview of one of my courses that I decided I wanted to learn more about or one I had not thought of as worthy of consideration but suddenly realized would make a good addition to one or another of my courses, and so I searched to fill in the gaps in my knowledge. Magazines such as *History Today, History, BBC History Magazine, American*

History, and the *Magazine of History*—current as well as back issues—sometimes offer notes and articles that can be the source or inspiration for breaks. And, naturally, there is, again, one's imagination that I now couple with the question I periodically ask myself: What subjects might students be interested in that can be tied to specific subject matter I am teaching but that are also simultaneously valid intellectually as they relate to that course?

Embedded in the question ending the previous paragraph is the important point that breaks be tied to the subject matter under consideration in some fashion. Doing so works effectively in Davies' book and it has worked well for me, too, as is explained below through a small sampling of the breaks I use.

A word of caution first: There are some sensitive, perhaps even controversial, subjects I include as breaks—and that Davies comparably introduces as capsules—that I am careful to treat academically as the serious, legitimate subjects they are even though they might appear to some as frivolous or perhaps not even as subjects that should be broached at all. Any potential humor is allowed to emerge directly from the historical subject itself, unembellished by me or my students, as I am especially careful to avoid appealing to or feeding prurient interests. Teachers also need to be aware of their audience in terms of grade level, maturity of students, and with regard to the nature of school and community standards as well. Whereas I do seek to inform and even enlighten via these breaks, I do not go out of my way to offend. Each teacher must find the balance that works best for one's self and one's students.

Let us now turn to a number of examples so that I might explain the kinds of breaks I employ and the context in which I use them. These, it is hoped, will encourage interested teachers to create their own breaks. [By the way, in two survey courses, one lower-division, the other upper-, let it be noted, for guideline purposes, that I scatter more than 40 breaks.]

So, in discussing Renaissance Venice I take a *Ghetto* break. I show a number of projected images of the city (e.g., old maps, paintings by Caneletto and others, modern photographs), with its many small islands, canals, and connecting bridges, and then proceed to describe how the word *ghetto* is derived from *Geto Nuovo*, which is the name of the Venetian island that, until 1390, had been devoted to iron foundering (its name coming from *gettare*, meaning to cast metal and from *nuovo* meaning new, ergo "new foundry"; there is also the adjacent *Geto Vecchio*, or "old foundry" island). In 1516, the city's Jews were compelled to move to and live permanently on the island (i.e., they were allowed to exit the island and conduct business during the day but had to return at sunset). Projected images from the island's main piazza show what parts of the ghetto look like today and how they have changed little over the centuries (e.g., at least two of five old synagogues continue to function, although because Venetian laws forbade the building of separate synagogues they were added to the top floors of existing structures). Further, relevant additional information is discussed: what being compelled to live in the ghetto meant for its Jewish residents; how the ghetto was monitored and how patrols were paid for; how the island was where Shakespeare's Shylock lived (i.e., *The Merchant of Venice* was published seventy-four years after the ghetto was established); how long the gates that locked the Jews in for the night stayed in place (until 1797); how and why Rome, a few decades later, developed its ghetto for Jews; and then how all this connects us to the development of twentieth-century ghettos, not only for Jews—say, for example, in Warsaw or even in Venice's ghetto itself where there is a memorial commemorating the city's Jewish victims of the Holocaust—but for other minorities as well.

Jousting is a break that emerged from a lecture on the sixteenth-century French Civil Wars of Religion. The king on the eve of these wars, Henri II, was in good spirits in 1559, following the marriage of two of his daughters and the signing of a peace treaty with the Habsburgs that improved France's security. Henri, vibrant and athletic, decided a joust was an appropriate activity to celebrate these occasions. At this point

I describe the primary purpose of a joust—which was to break one's lance on the chest of one's opponent, with victory going to the competitor who amassed the most broken lances at the end of the day—while projecting a contemporary engraving that depicts this fatal joust as well as shows the soft-wood, hollow lance breaking. I also project an image of a stirrup, an Asian invention that reached Europe through earlier contacts and invasions and without which jousting would not have been possible. This particular jousting event proved fatal for Henri, because as his opponent's lance shattered on his chest a substantial splinter pushed up his visor, pierced his eye, and penetrated his brain. He lingered for eleven days, while court physicians decapitated four criminals in order to study their cranial anatomy in an unsuccessful effort to save the king. Another sixteenth-century image depicts Henri on his deathbed, with his wife (Catherine de Medici), his oldest son, and the about-to-be heir's new wife, Mary, Queen of Scots, anxious for his possible recovery but anticipating his imminent death. I conclude by projecting a few additional images: modern photographs of the Place des Vosges—today an upscale square on Paris' Right Bank which in Henri II's day was a park and the site of the joust; the Cathedral of St-Denis, where Henri and Catherine de Medici, as well as other French monarchs, were once interred (until, that is, during the French Revolution when the remains of the entombed royal couples were scattered to parts unknown); and another, inside the cathedral, of the agonized expression—reflecting the horror of the king's death—of the sculpted representation of a recumbent Henri atop his sepulchral monument.

The role of women in Chinese history leads to a break on *Bound-feet Shoes*. We discuss their purpose, not only their erotic role and why only Han women bound their feet but also their social function and the way such shoes made it difficult-if-not-impossible for women to work; this in turn enables me to draw a parallel to the role of the *Corset* in the West, which functions as yet another break in my world civilizations course. It's almost impossible for students not to be interested in bound-feet shoes, but I stimulate that interest with projected images: of the process by which the feet were bound; of shoes placed next to familiar objects—such as a tea cup or pack of cigarettes—in order to gauge how small they actually are; of a diagram comparing the shape and size of a normal foot with one that had been bound since childhood; of an X-ray of bound feet; and then of a series of photographs showing an elderly woman as she unwraps one of her feet until it is bare. And if that is not enough to leave a lasting impression, I then display for viewing a genuine pair of previously owned bound-feet shoes that are in my possession. I also read a poem, "Woman" by Fu Hsüan, whose first line is, "How sad it is to be a woman!" Although foot-binding decreased as the twentieth century unfolded, and was eventually outlawed after the Chinese Communist Party came to power, in 1949, ironically, in the twenty-first century some young Chinese women have been undergoing the Ilizarov surgical procedure in order to lengthen their legs and thus become taller but which can also lead to difficulties in walking normally. (I project a photograph from *The New York Times* that illustrates this procedure—while the caption describes the physical difficulties incurred by these women; similar images and information are available on the web).

When I introduce a break on *Forceps* during the discussion of the above-mentioned French Civil Wars of Religion, some students surely must wonder where that comes from and where it will take us. After I provide a brief look at birthing in early modern Europe, accompanied by a projected sixteenth-century engraving, I address the often-fatal risks involved during difficult births. At this point I mention the barber-surgeon Chamberlen brothers and their surgeon father, Huguenots and natives of Paris who, in 1569, fled France for London in the face of the Roman Catholic onslaught during those very same civil wars. There, in about 1588, around the time the English were confronting the Spanish Armada, the brothers perfected their amazing invention, childbirth forceps—adapted, perhaps, from the use of spoons by midwives to facilitate some births.

Before this time there were no live deliveries of births in the face of significant difficulties. In order to save a mother's life, however, hooks and other instruments were introduced to break apart the child's skull, dismember it, and remove the tiny body piece by piece—although baptism *in utero* provided some spiritual consolation for the would-be parents. The brothers would be hired and paid their hefty fee in advance, whether or not it became necessary for their forceps to be introduced. Aside from the mother-to-be, no one else was permitted to be present in the delivery chamber, even though the custom was for several female family members to be in attendance. In fact, the brothers were so protective of their device that they covered the mother's eyes so she could not catch a glimpse of the forceps; one of the brothers also made loud noises—by ringing bells, rattling chains, and banging hammers—in order to divert attention from what they were doing. The Chamberlen forceps—which I reveal through a projected photograph—were kept in a locked case so as to protect its secrecy further. Curiously, this would-be boon to birthing and saving lives was kept a secret by the brothers and their descendants—apparently for the sole purpose of the family's singular enrichment—for about a century.

I provide breaks for *Selected Artists*, *Chapels*, and *Churches*. The paintings of Hieronymus Bosch (c. 1450-1516) are particularly fascinating both for the criticism of the Catholic Church they target and their surrealistic quality. I focus, among others, on his *Garden of Earthly Delights*, a triptych that depicts human innocence in the Garden of Eden, the myriad ways men and women—after the expulsion from Eden—sin, and then the fate in store for those sinners in Hell. In addition to projecting the complex and detailed collection of images I pass among my students a book that contains the painting along with a magnifying glass for closer inspection of its many details. Another break is devoted to the brilliant sculptures of Gian Lorenzo Bernini (1598-1680)—especially those that depict religious ecstasy ("The Ecstasy of St. Teresa" and "Blessed Ludovica Albertoni") and the way in which he made sculpted marble look like human flesh ("Rape of Proserpina")—and to his mathematically precise construction of St. Peter's Square in Rome—especially the way in which he positioned the four rows, one behind the other, of adjacent columns so that from certain spots on either side of the Egyptian obelisk in the center of the square only the front row is visible. Breaks are also provided for Artemisia Gentileschi (1593-1652) and Maria Sibylla Merian (1647-1717), the former for her emphasis on both abused and revengeful women (i.e., following her own rape, Artemisia painted at least five versions of the biblical story of Judith beheading Holofernas), the latter for contributions to science through her paintings and observations of and her experiments with insect metamorphoses. The Brancacci Chapel in Santa Maria del Carmine, in Florence, gets special attention because of the frescoes of Masaccio (1401-28): for his use of linear perspective and illusionistic techniques, his use of light and shade (*chiaroscuro*), as well as his influence upon a young Michelangelo—which can be seen by comparing his chapel frescoes with Michelangelo's in the Sistine Chapel. Among churches, I use Florence's Cathedral of Santa Maria del Fiore (i.e., the *Duomo*) to demonstrate the way architect Filippo Brunelleschi (1377-1446) gained his commission following his discovery of how a dome might be built and supported, as Europeans had forgotten this knowledge in the centuries after the fall of Rome. All of these breaks are amply illustrated.

Studying the "Age of Exploration" is an ideal time for breaks on both *Sugar* and *Food*. The introduction of cane sugar into the European diet and the increase in its consumption, down to the present time, can be illustrated, for example, with Dutch still-life paintings of sweets and confections but also with the few faces that are depicted with open mouths and, alas, rotten teeth; there are also paintings of dentists extracting teeth, horrified patients, and interested, even entertained, spectators as well as photographs of actual extraction tools, all of which help to bring the subject to life. It doesn't take much nudging to get students to draw the obvious parallels to their own experiences with dentists. The foods involved in the Columbian

Exchange along with the spices Europeans bought from Asians or brought back as part of their commercial voyages broaden these *Sugar* and *Food* breaks, all of which can be illustrated with contemporary engravings and paintings as well as with modern photographs; an ambitious teacher could bring—or have students bring—samples of such foods and spices to class. And a health-conscious teacher might consider talking about the role fast foods play in contemporary life and how so much of this stems from the corn that came from the Americas. Another food break I take involves bread and the central role it played in the European diet for centuries (including as gruel). There are paintings and engravings from across centuries that illustrate the sumptuous meals of the well-to-do as well as the bread sellers who sold what was the basic food for the masses (i.e., bread was virtually synonymous with food). Other related breaks treat *Coffee*, the *Japanese Tea Ceremony*, *Tobacco*, and the *Canning and Preservation of Food*.

And so it goes, with additional breaks including such topics as *Christmas*, the *Man in the Iron Mask and Louis XIV*, *Toilets and Toilet Paper*, the *Pencil*, *Habsburg Remains in Vienna* (i.e., upon entombment their hearts and entrails were removed and placed in urns; these organs and bodies are kept separately from one another and divided among three churches, each a short walk from the others), *Bloodletting*, *Bathing*, *Vaccination*, *Vlad Tepes*, *Syphilis*, *Children: Their Role in Society and the Games They Played*, *Blood Letting*, *Hysteria and Its Treatment*, *St. Brendan the Navigator*, *Walled Cities*, *Relics*, *Luther on Women*, *Marriage*, *Dutch Dikes and Windmills*, and more.

These breaks (which I see, more accurately, as relevant tangents) not only constitute an occasionally welcome *break* in the narrative of a course, they also are examples of small-scale micro-histories, close-up looks at topics that often escape both the history teacher's attention and students' radar when they think about what history encompasses. Thus they serve the dual purpose of greasing the wheels of the narrative flow and creating interest in areas about which there is often much ignorance. They have the potential to be one of those characteristics of a course that—although not as critical, say, as encouraging students to develop their skills to think historically and write effectively—students will remember fondly for a long time.

PART TWO:
WRITTEN ASSIGNMENTS
AND WRITING

5. WRITING IN THE MAJOR

A Novel Approach That Works

It is a truism among teachers of writing that the only way for their charges to improve is to write, rewrite, and write some more. Writing, of course, is not only valuable for its own sake, but as a vital educational tool as well: the best way to understand something fully is to write and rewrite what we think we know. "He who writes badly thinks badly," wrote William Cobbett. And, according to John Updike, "Writing and rewriting are a constant search for what it is one is saying." For their part, most teachers of history acknowledge the value of student writing and routinely assign term papers, book reviews, and other writing projects; most of us also utilize essay exams.

But how much written work can history teachers assign each semester? How much dare we assign? We usually have more than enough to keep us busy each day, so there is a clear limit to what we will require of our students and be able to grade constructively. Besides, we are not English teachers! Some of us might think twice, moreover, before asking our students to work significantly more than do our colleagues. We could, as an alternative, devote additional time to extensive written suggestions and criticism of fewer papers, but this solution too is fraught with problems, since both the amount and frequency of writing is vital for learning. So, to borrow Lenin's pre-revolution words, "what is to be done?"

At California State University, San Bernardino, we are engaged in what appears to be a novel and effective solution that goes beyond the domain or responsibility of a single department. The program at CSUSB has its origins in an April 1976 directive by the Board of Trustees of the twenty campuses of the California State University mandating that all graduates demonstrate writing proficiency prior to graduation. Each campus subsequently developed a method of defining and certifying that writing ability for all degree candidates.

CSUSB came to offer five courses, all numbered 495, through the Schools of Administration, Education, Humanities, Natural Sciences, and Social and Behavioral Sciences, which in 1981-82 became part of our upper-division general education requirements. Prerequisites for 495 are freshman composition and upper-division standing. Significantly, teachers from within the schools themselves teach most of the courses. And this is how I, a historian, came to teach Social Sciences 495 to history and other majors from the school.

Social Sciences 495 takes more time than any other course I teach, but I gladly offer a couple of sections each year, as do several of my colleagues, for one simple reason: it works! Most students leave the course improved writers, more aware of the relationship of writing to thinking, of language, nuance, style, grammar, and what generally makes for good writing. Those who begin the class with poor skills can, with effort, leave with minimum levels of competency, while those with ability have the opportunity to refine their skills.

Most students think of writing in superficial ways—consisting primarily of spelling, grammar, and punctuation. But I try to help my students become aware, both implicitly and explicitly, of the vital link between writing and thinking. They learn, I hope, that writing is thinking, which means that every time they write they have another opportunity to discover just how perceptive they are, or are not. That is, there really is no writing equivalent of 'the gift of gab"; we may be able to fool ourselves and others with our spoken words, but with writing, if no thought is in our minds, nothing substantial reaches the page.

My particular qualifications, apart from willingness and enthusiasm, include my own writing and publications (in several fields and to diverse audiences), seven years as editor of CSUSB's annual self-study and accreditation reports, current editorship of the "Advanced Placement Teaching" column in this newsletter, and my participation in a series of faculty seminars (funded by an NEH grant and supported by CSUSB's Writing Reinforcement Program) designed to assist college teachers in improving their own assignments and the written work of their students. A program coordinator trains other teachers with less writing and editing experience, and most of us exchange materials and ideas.

The course itself (four quarter units, meeting four hours per week, with class size limited to a maximum of twenty) is one in expository writing, and it emphasizes the techniques of analysis, summary, review, research, and argumentation. Students are instructed to consider the class a writing workshop where they write, edit, and rewrite their own work, criticize the writing of others, and discuss the critiques of their own writing. Grades are A, B, C, and No Credit, with the latter meaning that students must repeat the course.

Students are required to develop and complete four short papers (three-to-four typed pages) and one longer paper (about ten pages), as well as take midterm and final exams, which, like the other assignments, are geared to enable them to work in and think about their academic majors. Papers are initially drafted in class, criticized by fellow students, edited and rewritten at home, and then handed in for grading.

My comments and marginal markings are such that students can learn from them and rewrite their papers for a higher grade. (For example, I call attention to inconsistencies in the use of verb tenses and places where subjects and verbs or nouns and pronouns do not agree. It then becomes the student's job to correct the errors. Or, rather than scribble the overused but always vague "awkward," I specify why a sentence or clause needs rewriting. And where a paper is cluttered with unnecessary words, I write the abbreviation "EUW" in the margin next to the offending line, which students are instructed to recognize as "eliminate unnecessary word"; the student must then determine which word may safely be eliminated without altering the meaning. Other abbreviations and notations focus on problems with punctuation, clarity, and choice of words.) Assigned readings and a steady flow of handouts help round out the course, all of which is described in more detail below.

I require that students read for class discussion throughout the course *On Writing Well*, an extremely helpful and readable text by William Zinsser (Harper and Row, 1985). I urge them to make active use of a dictionary and a thesaurus, and I recommend Kate Turabian's *Manual for Writers* and J. Heffernan and J. Lincoln's *Writing: A College Handbook* (which is also required in our University's freshman composition classes). I expose them to other kinds of writing about writing, such as George Orwell's "Politics and the English Language" and Kurt Vonnegut's "How to Write with Style." And I encourage them to learn to recognize, appreciate, and emulate good writing—examples of which I distribute—as an additional route to the goal of improvement,

Before I assign the first paper to be graded, students write two short papers, one an autobiographical essay, the other a review of a film on the revolution in Nicaragua. With these ungraded tasks we go through the motions of what is about to become standard operating procedure. Further, all assignments are explained in detail so there are no misunderstandings (there is always time for questions) and students can budget their time accordingly. Students are also familiarized with a minimum number of editorial markings and instructed in what to look for as they criticize one another's papers. These first two ungraded essays give me a chance to become acquainted with my students so as to anticipate strengths and weaknesses, and it gives them an opportunity to learn how I will respond to their work. In other words, this is good practice for all of us.

In addition, students keep a journal in which they make entries for five to ten minutes at the start of each class. They can write about anything they wish, and I neither grade nor read them. The actual writing is what is important, and at the end of the quarter I have students compare early, midcourse, and late entries to determine whether they see any changes. Some observe few differences, but a comment by one student illustrates what I hope most will ultimately realize: "When I began these journal entries, I simply described what I had been doing, but by the end I was writing about what I was thinking."

As students in the course must be at least juniors, they have usually begun taking courses in their majors. I construct all graded assignments with that in mind. These include an essay comparing book reviews from a professional journal and the popular press, a review of a book read or being read in a course in the major, an interview in essay form with a professional in the student's field, and an essay analyzing a contemporary issue from the perspective of the student's major. These are short papers. The longer one, a research paper, is a bibliographic essay, an analytic review of the literature on a subject within the major. A tour of the library, designed to help with assignments, is conducted by a librarian during an early class session; most upper-division students, I have learned, profit from this, because few have used the library for more than checking out books.

In addition to detailed explanations for each assignment in the syllabus, I discuss all assignments in class before any work is actually begun, and I distribute handouts that provide the supporting information. For example, one handout suggests guidelines for writing summaries and critiques for book reviews. Students read about interview techniques and the use of interviews in their discipline, and they help each other prepare the questions they will ask. Other handouts suggest writing strategies and procedures (including organization and style), alert them to uses and abuses of paraphrasing and the dangers of plagiarism, instruct them in note taking, and call their attention to a host of common writing errors. And they have available, on reserve in the library, samples of successful student papers.

Despite what may sound to some as dry and methodical, to me is not. I also try to have fun in the class. For example, to demonstrate that even serious subjects can be entertaining, I distribute copies of satirical and humorous writing, including a short article I wrote on robots and the labor force. Integrating some of my own writing is a convincing demonstration that I practice what I teach; and, not incidentally, my writing has become more precise due to my now keener editorial eye.

But the course can be fun in other ways, especially by looking at the lighter side of writing that is in fact meant to be serious. The *Quarterly Review of Doublespeak* publishes some of the worst misuses of our language. Its editor, William Lutz of Rutgers University, spoke at CSUSB and provided these examples, among others: the military has referred to an invasion as a "predawn vertical insertion"; politicians pledge not to raise taxes but instead vote for "revenue enhancements"; the Environmental Protection Agency tries to pacify us by describing acid rain as "poorly buffered precipitation."

I am always on the lookout in what I read for anything that can help students approach writing more positively. Jack Smith, in his column in the *Los Angeles Times*, ran a series of bloopers collected by teachers (e.g., "When you put Roosevelt and Wilson side by side, you can see that they had few differences but their contrasts weren't that similar." "In the Middle Ages, the Black Pledge was going around."). William Safire's column, "On Language," in the Sunday *New York Times Magazine* frequently is useful. Dear Abby has devoted several columns to word abuse. I even use jokes and cartoons. Comedian Steven Wright says he once went to a place to eat that said "Breakfast Any Time," so he ordered French Toast in the Renaissance. A *New Yorker* cartoon shows one tycoon sitting by a fireplace at his club saying to another: "Feeling poorly? Thank heaven! I thought you said you were feeling *poor*." Another pictures an elderly couple looking down at a mat in front of an apartment door on which they are about to knock; the mat reads: "Not Unwelcome."

Another instructive technique is to examine the corrected drafts of a professional's writing. Zinsser's book reproduces two pages in manuscript form complete with all word and phrase changes and editorial markings. This is a helpful way for students to see that what appears effortless in print actually took time and concentration. As Samuel Johnson said, "Easy writing makes damned hard reading." Then I circulate a typed copy of a review I wrote for the *American Historical Review* with all my own editorial markings, which collectively represent some eight editing read-throughs. The effect of all this is salutary and enables students to conceptualize with greater accuracy what writing is—that it is a form of thinking, not merely a matter of grammar.

Most of my course time is devoted to evaluating papers. But I do not rewrite or correct spelling and grammar. Instead, as described above, all marginal comments and editorial markings are meant to enable students to make corrections themselves. Thus, I encourage students to eliminate unnecessary words, substitute suspect words with more effective ones, rephrase with more feeling or style, use punctuation properly, communicate an idea more effectively, express a view in grammatically correct English, and—most important—rethink their ideas. I might, for example, ask whether they have in fact connected evidence and arguments to conclusions. My written comments focus on major problems and strengths, and I do my best to provide encouragement and to note improvement, especially as the early going can be difficult, if not depressing, for many students.

The mention of grammar may discourage some readers form considering teaching such a course. A common reaction might be: "I know how to write well enough, and I even know how to spot many grammatical errors, but I am neither trained nor able to teach grammar." Actually, this was my initial response when first asked to teach the course. In fact, I still am not able to teach grammar, nor do I wish to. (The best writers in our English department, I am told, share this view.)

Good writing involves much more than grammar, and that is what I concentrate on. I assist students as they seek to restore life to writing that functions poorly, if at all, and I guide them in efforts to emancipate their energy, imagination, style, creativity, and a feel for a subject when these need an inevitable boost. I do, however, call attention to grammatical errors and help students to overcome problems with punctuation; I distribute handouts that provide both rules and guidelines along with specific examples on the use of the comma, semicolon, colon, dash, apostrophe, and hyphen. Further, I schedule two individual conferences with each student to review graded work, often page by page, and many see me more often.

Finally, some class time is devoted to the skills involved in writing essay exams. I focus on techniques for brainstorming, grouping related points, the use of notes and outlines, and the value of organization. I stress understanding directive word meanings, analyzing and addressing the question, and keeping within time limits.

I view Social Sciences 495 as I see the history I teach; it is a means to a larger end and serves a higher purpose. Just as history is instructive in the way it illuminates life, writing is both a potent means of communicating a subject such as history and a vehicle for individual development. My ultimate goal in teaching this course is to help students realize their potential as educated human beings through their writing, their thinking, and in finding their own writing voices. I want them to recognize that growth is possible, with effort, and that however much a chore writing may be—and it usually is—it can also be fun and rewarding.

6. UNIVERSITY STUDENTS' WRITING

Does the writing of students majoring in the social sciences differ significantly from that of their peers in other disciplines? I think not. A cursory mental review of the work of those in my writing classes during the last few years, coupled with a comparable review of my history classes, as well as conversations with colleagues, suggests that our students possess no unique writing problems.

Most social sciences majors who have completed several electives have had experience in writing research and other papers. Often, following the lead of their teachers and those they read, they seek—although many struggle—to sound profound, to have their writing appear to be professional in tone and word usage. Unfortunately, that sometimes results in writing that confuses, words used incorrectly, and unfounded assumptions. The result is that clear thinking, and thus clear writing, may be camouflaged.

A related writing problem, which is also not peculiar to social sciences students, is the difficulty of addressing the questions posed in essay examinations. As often as not, students are unable to follow directive word meanings, and they fail (or even refuse) to limit their responses to what questions ask.

Unless a teacher assigns more than one research paper or is able to devote the extra time needed to guide students through a couple of drafts, there is little that can be done by any single teacher beyond providing explicit instructions and, upon returning papers, feedback. Such instructions are also useful before examinations, as is feedback afterward, and these plus the experience that comes from writing at least midterm and final exam essays helps in this area.

Most instructive in improving all kinds of student writing is Cal State, San Bernardino's upper-division required general education writing course [Social Sciences 306]. Those of us in the social sciences who teach it are convinced it works. Because of the nature of the assignments (i.e., all within the student's major) and the time devoted to writing, rewriting, and critiques, improvement is usually evident before completion of the course. We try to teach students, in the words of William Strunk, Jr., to make "every word tell." We emphasize that simple, clear writing is the product of a good mind (not a simple one), and that they must work hard so their readers need not.

7. WORDS TO THE WHYS
CRAFTING CRITICAL
BOOK REVIEWS

"My favorite character is...." and "I recommend this book because...." are typical phrases that characterize the traditional book report, but they also epitomize the kind of direction that provides little preparation for the critical evaluation and review of books that often awaits students in many of their high school and college classes. How can we as teachers transcend the simplicity of book reports and their minimal demands upon our students' intelligence and abilities? How can we teach book *reviewing*, a task that encourages the development of the more sophisticated, higher order thinking skills (e.g., the full evolution of ideas and the explanation and justification of reactions— the *whys* in the title) that have an educational value beyond the dimensions of the assignment itself? What follows are some thoughts and practical suggestions for answering these questions.

Book reviews, whether for professional journals, newspapers, or our classrooms, generally have two aims in common: to inform the reader about the contents of the book and to provide an evaluation that presents the reviewer's judgment of the book's quality. This two-fold task is often none too easy for many students. Since the degree to which students succeed— or fail—as they complete assignments is due as much to the clarity of directions as to their intelligence or experience, I have devised—and here expand upon—a set of instructions (batteries not included) that is aimed to make composition and thought development easier. These instructions are an integral part of my course syllabi; that is, the section of my syllabus devoted to the book review assignment includes three parts: (1) a discussion of the nature of book reviews and the goals of the assignment, plus advice on how to proceed; (2) a description of what a summary is and how it can be composed; and (3) an elaboration upon the essence of a critique and the variety of possibilities (in the form of questions) that can be explored. Teachers can, and should, modify my suggestions both to suit their own needs and to adapt them to the perceived ability levels of their students. In addition, I always include in-class oral elaboration and time for questions, both when the syllabus is distributed and again a week or so before the assignment is due.

Discussion and Preparation: A productive way to prepare students for what is expected of them is to discuss the nature of book reviews. What is the purpose of a review? How should it inform the reader? I encourage students to exchange ideas about the kind of information that should be included in—or excluded from—a book review, the various ways a review might be organized, and the degree to which a review ought to be used to forward the reviewer's own ideas. Teachers will have to establish their own guidelines and boundaries here, but as much as possible I try to allow for significant latitude since diverse approaches usually can be taken to reach the same goal. We also talk about assumptions the reviewer should or should not make and about the audience (read: level of sophistication) for which we are writing. As a reader of a book review, I ask students, what would you like to know that would help you to make an intelligent decision about whether to read the book?

I also recommend that students sit with paper, pencil, and instructions close at hand as they read their book so they can note any and all reactions precisely as they are being formulated. Just as one who observes a crime will be a more credible witness if what is seen is recorded immediately rather than recalled later on the basis of memory, so students should have a clearer fix on their thoughts if they note them when they occur rather than wait to gather and organize them after the book has been completed. In this way ideas cannot be lost, forgotten, or abridged, and when the reading has been completed students ought to be in possession of a thorough set of notes from which to craft a review. Waiting to collect one's thoughts until after the book is read is likely to result in shrugged shoulders and a shortage of ideas. Instead, taking notes along the way should produce more material than is needed. The resulting harvest, inevitably, yields more of substance—and without the need for fertilizer.

Like any piece of writing, be it an examination essay, a term paper, or something else, a book review reads best when it is launched with an introduction. This can take a variety of forms, including a personal anecdote that can be related to the subject of the book, a brief story from the book itself that can be used to introduce the broader content, or even a clever quotation on which to build an introduction—all of which can serve the useful function of capturing a reader's attention. There is, however, simpler and more fundamental information that an effective introduction should minimally contain in order to prepare the reader for what follows: an overview of the book that incorporates both an encapsulated summary and a sense of the reviewer's general judgment. Thus armed with this equivalent to a thesis statement, the reader is prepared to wade into the body of the review.

The Summary: A successful summary consists of a discussion and highlighting of the major features, trends, concepts, themes, ideas, and characteristics of the book in as much detail as space limitations, established by the instructor, will allow. This can be as brief as a single sentence—if such brevity is what is desired (if not, the essence of such a sentence can otherwise be included as part of the introduction, say as a topic sentence)—or a paragraph, or it can go on for two, three, or more pages. I find that a three-page limit (or half the total length of the review) works best in that it allows students enough space to describe the book without their losing sight of the purpose of the review. Since shorter summaries tend to be more difficult to write (i.e., because so much more has to be coherently compressed into fewer words), it is probably a good idea for teachers to restrict their length as much as conventional wisdom and student abilities dictate.

In the actual writing of the summary, I instruct students to use their own words, to combine ideas and story line into new sentences and phrasing of their own. While quotation marks should be placed around words and sentences taken directly from the book, for the most part using the exact language of the author should be avoided because it undermines original thinking. That is, summarizing is a good way to learn and to assimilate and explain material, but the process doesn't work especially well unless what is read and digested is translated into the student's own language, and that it is done in a way that makes sense to the student.

In addition, it is often best for students to present the summary in a manner that reflects the organization of the book, to write it as if the entire book were to be viewed through the wrong end of a telescope. That is, since one of the purposes of a review is to demonstrate how effectively a book is organized, summarizing in such a micro-reflective way will help to achieve this. In other words, the presentation of a true but condensed picture of a book should include the way in which it is organized, although chapter-by-chapter summaries are to be avoided in favor of a unified essay that highlights significant features and narrative thrust.

Finally, summarizing a book, despite what some students might imagine, does not ordinarily enable the reviewer to provide a particularly incisive understanding of the contents as a collection of hypotheses or arguments based upon any number of suppositions.[115] Even our telling students that they must reach

115. For an excellent look at how to teach students to analyze works of history critically, see Robert F. Berkhofer, Jr., "Demystifying Historical Authority: Critical Textual Analysis in the Classroom," in *History Anew:*

beyond summary into the realm of analysis is not enough in and of itself. Instead, in something akin to the directions that often accompany children's toys in need of assembling, we must offer guidelines that constitute a methodology that will help them to turn up the volume of their thinking.

The Critique: Students tend to be wary of undertaking a critique for several reasons. First, because they are neither professional historians nor experts in the subject matter of the book they are reading, students often assume such an assignment is beyond their level of knowledge. "How can I be critical of something I know nothing about?" is a common response. Second, since they have little or no experience with critical writing, they do not believe they possess such ability. Third, too often they have been allowed to get away with a level of thinking that is superficial, that places few demands on their intellect, that doesn't pressure them into trying harder. One of our jobs as teachers is to lead students forward, to show them how to do what appears beyond them, and that is what I try to accomplish with these instructions and the questions that follow.

To begin with, I make it clear, in the introductory paragraph to this section of my syllabus, just what a critique consists of—thoughts, responses, and reactions to what is read. Such a critique is not expected to be of a caliber similar to a professional historian's or to reflect an expertise not likely to exist— although, with experience, one can learn to review a book on the basis of one's general knowledge and one's ability to follow an argument or to test an hypothesis. I also try to dispel the notion that all criticism must be negative. In fact, I assure students, there is nothing wrong with having only positive things to say; the "trick" is to justify and support whatever position is taken.

What I do expect from students is a reaction to the book, but since not knowing what to react to is part of the problem,

Innovations in the Teaching of History Today, edited by Robert Blackey (Long Beach: The University Press, California State University, Long Beach, 1993).

I present a significant number of questions that I encourage them to keep in mind before, during, and after the book is read. Collectively, these questions comprise the bait to lure students away from the security of inexperience and the easy way out, and toward developing their minds and critical thinking abilities. They are not, I insist, to be answered seriatim, taken like numbers in a store by customers waiting their turn to be served; in fact, there are many more here than any single review could hope to address. Instead, they are meant to prod, to prime intellectual pumps, to suggest avenues of exploration for those who are new to the domain of criticism. Teachers should review this list and choose to include as many as would be considered appropriate guides for their students. Students, in turn, should be instructed to select several of the most useful (say, five to seven for a three-page critique) on which to concentrate. Thus, answers to as many of the questions as are fitting should form part of a smooth-flowing essay, complete with topic sentences and transitions. Effective criticism, in other words, also involves writing that is clear and coherent.

1. What is your overall opinion of the book? On what basis has this opinion been formulated? That is, tell the reader what you think and how you arrived at this judgment. What did you expect to learn when you selected the book? To what extent— and how effectively—were your expectations met? Did you nod in agreement (or off to sleep)? Did you wish you could talk back to the author? Amplify upon and explain your reactions?

2. Identify the author's thesis and explain it in your own words. How clearly and in what context is it stated and, subsequently, developed? To what extent and how effectively (i.e., with what kind of evidence?) is this thesis proven? Use examples to amplify your responses. If arguments or perspectives were omitted, why do you think this might have been allowed to occur?

3. What are the author's aims? How well have they been achieved, especially with regard to the way the book is organized? Are these aims supported or justified? (Aims are usually

found in the preface or introduction to the book, or sometimes in the opening paragraphs of the first chapter. If they are not found, what does this tell you about the book and/or the author? Were you able to discern them anyway? If so, how?) How closely does the organization follow the author's aims, whether stated or implied?

4. How are the author's main points presented, explained, and supported? What assumptions lie behind these points? What would be the most effective way for you to compress and/or reorder the author's scheme of presentation and argument?

5. How effectively does the author draw generalizations from the material being presented? Are connections between generalizations and the supporting material and evidence made clearly and logically? Use examples to support your evaluation.

6. What conclusions does the author reach and how clearly are they stated? Do these conclusions follow from the thesis and aims and from the ways in which they were developed? In other words, how effectively does the book come together?

7. Identify the assumptions made by the author in both the approach to and the writing of the book. For example, what prior knowledge does the author expect readers to possess? How effectively are these assumptions worked into the overall presentation? What assumptions do you think should not have been made? Why?

8. Are you able to detect any underlying philosophy of history held by the author (e.g., progress, decline, cyclical, circular, linear, random)? If so, how does this philosophy affect the presentation of the argument? If not, what kinds of thinking or attitudes appear to drive the author?

9. How does the author see history as being motivated: primarily by the forces of individuals, economics, politics, social factors, nationalism, class, race, gender, something else? What kind of impact does this view of historical motivation have upon the way in which the author develops the book?

10. Does the author's presentation seem fair and accurate? Is the interpretation biased? Can you detect any distortion, exag-

geration, or diminishing of material? If so, for what purpose might this have been done and what effect does it have on the overall presentation?

11. Does the date of the book's publication vis-à-vis the content reveal anything about how the period in which it was written might have influenced its thesis? For example, books written during the Great Depression, or during World War II, or during the Cold War might be affected by prevailing attitudes or perceptions. In other words, since every age writes its own history, to what extent does the book reflect its time?

12. Does the author's nationality, gender, race, ethnicity, class, and/or age (to the extent these are known) affect the writing? Does the author acknowledge any obvious or not so obvious biases?

13. Does the material presented raise your curiosity about the subject, and is there anything especially distinctive about the book? Might the book have some impact upon the course of your education or other pursuits? What are you most likely to remember about it in a week, a month, a year? Here, too, elaborate upon your responses.

14. Is there enough information in the book? Is the subject treated thoroughly or summarily? If you were the author's editor, what would you add to render the book more thorough and well rounded? What would you subtract that might be extraneous or distracting? Explain why you would take these actions.

15. Where and how does the book fit in relative to the content of the course for which it was read? Does it add or contradict anything you read in other books or texts or what was discussed in class? How would you explain, and possibly resolve, these differences?

16. How well is the book written? If you wish to use quotations to illustrate a particular style or point, keep them short, preferably no more than one sentence.

17. If the book includes graphic material (e.g., pictures, charts, diagrams, appendices), how easy are these to follow or read? Are they referred to in the narrative? If so, are they used

to enhance both the text and your understanding? If you had difficulty utilizing this material, explain why.

18. How useful are the footnotes (or endnotes) to you as a reader? If you made use of them, explain how. If more than just source citations are included in these notes, what purpose do they serve?

19. What is the quality of the bibliography provided? With the book's date of publication in mind, does the author seem familiar and up to date with the literature in the field? Upon what kinds of sources does the author seem to depend? What kind of primary and secondary sources? To what degree are you impressed by the use of these sources, and why?

20. If you had occasion to make use of the index, how easy was it to use and how useful was it in finding what you were looking for? Did you find any subjects missing?

Armed with these questions—veritable written stimulants to reflection—students have more than enough direction with which to formulate and organize a critical book review. Ignorance as to how to proceed cannot be an excuse, and better students can use this direction to be creative. It even becomes possible for students to develop their skills whereby they are able to integrate summary and critique in a way that discourages these two components from being presented as separate and distinct.

Moreover, by being aware of and thinking about these questions, students can learn to read more critically and to think about what historians do and why they do it. Every bit as important, learning to think and write critically in history can be carried over into their work in other disciplines, just as it also can, in general, further their development as educated and thinking citizens.

Without the experience of writing critical book reviews, students are likely to think the task is beyond their ability. But with these signposts in the form of directions and questions to guide their thinking, many discover and develop in ways hitherto unknown to them. To the extent it works—and it has worked effectively for my students, especially as I have refined these instructions over the years—the experience becomes both a profitable and exciting exercise.

8. THE LIGHT SIDE

Being Serious About Teaching Writing With Humor

A funny thing happens on the way to class: some teachers lose their sense of humor. But surely, one might argue, to teach a serious subject we ought to be serious, and we should take ourselves seriously too. Or should we? There is an honorable tradition that points to the use of humor as a vehicle to educate. Erasmus' *In Praise of Folly* (1509)—a delightful sermon given by the goddess Folly herself in which she demonstrates how essential her contribution is to human existence—was written with wit, irony, and paradox. Jonathan Swift used humor in many guises, most effectively in his savage *Modest Proposal* (1729). From characters such as Touchstone, Feste, Lavache, and Lear's Fool, "Shakespeare created an unusual but important kind of character—an individual who used his function as professional funny-man to couch his expression of a wry, even sad wisdom."[116] Through his fools, Shakespeare was able to comment on whatever he wished, speaking the truth because he was, of course, joking. The comic element acts as a useful contrast to the serious. In *As You Like It*, "without the presence of Touchstone's cynical sharpness, the romantic fool would cloy and grow tiresome.[117] Similarly, it would seem, without humor the seriousness of writing instruction could become strained,

---

116. Gareth Lloyd-Evans, *The Upstart Crow: An Introduction to Shakespeare's Plays* (London, 1982), 161.

117. Ibid., 175.

tense, even tiresome; humor, like sweet jelly on dry toast, helps the student to ingest the myriad difficulties of learning to compose and rewrite essays.

According to Robert MacNeil,[118] language purists often discourage pleasure in language in the name of saving it. In my own teaching of writing I have found that language play adds a wonderful dimension to the classroom. I contend, therefore, that humor and serious teaching are not incompatible; they are harmonious—possessing a kind of Yin and Yang relationship—two aspects of a learning environment.

In the 1960s, as a graduate teaching assistant and, subsequently, an assistant professor of history with a newly minted Ph.D., I was mostly an earnest heap of (hoped-for) profound thoughts, a furrowed brow, and damp armpits, all fueled by an overactive nervous system. In time, however, I was able first to discover and, ultimately, to reveal my personality through teaching, and this led to increased acceptance of my lighter side. It probably began with an unintentional slip. I remember lecturing about Martin Luther and telling students about the mess he had caused the Catholic Church at the time he posted his ninety-five *feces*; students suddenly had a graphic image to trigger their memories. And that lighter side was boosted further by my being inspired by a cartoon in *The New Yorker* that both suggested humorous historical possibilities and supported what I had to say about the role of periodization. It showed two field hands leaving the confines of city walls on their way to work the fields, with one saying to the other: "What do you think will be next—a period of spiritual rebirth, with renewed inquiry in the sciences and a humanistic resurgence of the arts?" Later on, student writing (and some of my own, too) produced marvelous gaffes that I subsequently repeated in class as a demonstration of our collective fallibility and our propensity to make unintentional errors; this, in turn, helped to ease students' fears by showing that is was all right to laugh at ourselves. For example,

---

118. *Wordstruck* (New York, 1989).

one student wrote about Michelangelo painting the Sixteen Chapels, and another about Galileo discovering the laws of gravity by dropping his balls from the Leaning Tower of Pisa.

In the course of my teaching career humor has become an important component in my repertoire of course presentations and strategies. While I do not use humor primarily to keep a class lively or to capture the attention of students who might otherwise sink deeply into their seats, it can also serve these purposes. More importantly, humor helps me to make the past more palatable to some and accessible to all. It humanizes and makes less formidable what some students unfortunately see as a two-dimensional discipline unconcerned with the business of living. I do not always need to take myself seriously, I discovered, in order to be serious about my subject.

Some of the humor I use to teach history has an added benefit: it illustrates the use, and misuse, of language. This lesson served me well when I volunteered to teach a new upper-division writing course, Expository Writing in the Social Sciences, established in 1981-82 to meet a requirement of the then 19-campus California State University system.

The prospect of teaching expository writing, for which I had no formal training, was both frightening and challenging. I called upon my resources as an author and editor, and I made use of what I had learned about test construction and the grading of essays in my work for the Educational Testing Service and The College Board. I also summoned my own wit and creativity, at first as a defense mechanism, but then, to my surprise, as a means to promote improved writing.

Most students, it seems, approach required writing classes laden with anxiety and bathed in trepidation. But small doses of appropriate humor, doled out in anecdotal dollops, orally and in print, throughout a term slowly peel away the dread and enrich instruction in a variety of ways. Humor, for example, eases tensions and fears by helping students feel comfortable with words; it helps to eliminate some of the hesitation that comes from making mistakes by humanizing error. One caveat here is that any humor found in the errors of our own current students must be treated with sensitivity so as not to shatter delicate feelings. On the whole, however, it is easier for teachers to address and correct errors, and to encourage students to appreciate language and its possibilities, through humor. Perhaps we could define educative humor as cognitive dissonance made instructive.

Humor serves other invaluable purposes. Memory, whether for word usage and placement or grammar, can be improved through humor, as can sensitivity to effective writing. Humor is also an aid to pointing out superfluous words and keeping rules and guidelines in perspective. Thus it is a boon to improved student editing, for their own work and that of their peers. Above all, it can actually make writing fun. When language is seen as having a playful side, writing can be approached with less apprehension; significant improvement then becomes a real possibility, and an appreciation blossoms for the power and potential of words.

The sources of humor are diverse and can be found all around us; they only require an inquisitive mind and the will and patience to discover. I have found examples in newspapers and magazines, in books on language[119] and collections of quotations,[120] in books on writing[121] and in grammar texts,[122] in headlines and announcements, in advertisements and signs, in graffiti and student writing. I examine cartoons and comic strips, I listen to comedians and punsters, and I read advice columnists, language mavens, and assorted others. And, as the spirit moves me, I create my own humor. What follows are examples of what I use and how I use them in the context of

---

119. Gyles Brandreth, *The Joy of Lex* (Parkwest, NY, 2001); Richard Lederer, *Crazy English: The Ultimate Joy Ride Through Our Language* (New York, 1989).

120. Jon Winokur, *The Portable Curmudgeon* (New York, 1987).

121. William Zinsser, *On Writing Well* (New York, 2006).

122. R. C. Pinckert, *Pinckert's Practical Grammar* (Cincinnati, OH, 1986)

teaching writing.

Among the narrative sections and class assignments in my syllabus, I include quotations, most of which are meant to encourage a positive attitude and focus student attention on some of the primary course goals. These include such bon mots as William Strunk's charge to make "every word tell," William Cobbett's observation that "he who writes badly thinks badly," John Updike's admission that "writing and rewriting are a constant search for what it is one is saying," Samuel Johnson's wisdom that "easy writing makes damned hard reading," and Jacques Barzun's caution that "simple English is no one's mother tongue; it has to be worked for." But other quotations serve the purpose of relieving the almost inevitable apprehension with which students enter a required writing class. As William Styron has written: "I get a fine warm feeling when I'm doing well, but that is pretty much negated by the pain of getting started each day. Let's face it, writing is hell." Peter DeVries has declared: "I love being a writer. What I can't stand is the paperwork." And according to Red Smith, "There is nothing to writing. All you do is sit down at the typewriter and open a vein." A cartoon by Campbell in *Phi Delta Kappan* serves a complementary purpose; it shows two students at their desks, pens in hand, blank paper before them, with one complaining about their teacher: "Write me a sentence. Write me a paragraph. Write me a page. What are we? Her students or her pen pals?"

The significance of effective word usage can be emphasized by means of traditional examples, but also by use of a lighter touch. The comedian Gallagher has called our attention to the multiple meanings of words and to the contradictions between words and their meanings. He asks, for example, "Did you ever have a permanent?... Where is it NOW?" "Should a bankruptcy lawyer expect to be paid?" "Why do you have a pair of pants, but only one bra?" "And, why do they call them apartments when they're all stuck together?" A newspaper column by Dan Bernstein, titled "A word from the wise could make you happy as a clam," confronts the clichés that, like acne on adolescents, inevitably surface in student writing. The article begins: "Once in a blue moon, someone puts a bug in my ear to tell them the tricks of the trade. Why? It's a mystery to me." The piece continues in this vein for several hundred words and then concludes: "'Avoid clichés like the plague.' Whoever said [that] took the words right out of my mouth."

Cartoons serve a comparable purpose for illustrating the use of the most effective or correct words. A cartoon from *The Far Side*, by Gary Larson, is captioned: "Edgar Allan Poe in a moment of writer's block." It shows the poet with his back to us as he faces a window. On his desk and in his wastebasket are several discarded sheets of paper on which the following words are inscribed and also crossed out: "The Tell Tale Spleen," "The Tell Tale Kidney," "The Tell Tale Stomach," "The Tell Tale Duodenum." A *Bloom County* comic strip, by Berke Breathed, contains this exchange: Character A: "I dunno...I think Gorbachev is a wolf in sheep's underwear." Character B: "Clothing." A: "Irregardless, I'm worried." B: "Irregardless isn't a word." A: "You always mock my political insights and it makes me mad as a wet hatter." B: "Hen." A: "Mad as a hen wetter...Goodbye and good day. Thppt."

Gallagher has also called our attention to words whose sound and meaning clash. For example, why are "hemorrhoids" called hemorrhoids and "asteroids" called asteroids? Wouldn't it make more sense if it were the other way around? But then if that were the case, the doctor you went to see wouldn't be a proctologist, he'd be an astronaut.

There are also other words that have been abused so badly they have lost their original meaning. Oliver Wendell Holmes called this *verbicide*. As Gyles Brandreth has reminded us, "There is no feeling of awe or terror or wonder in *awful* and *terrible* and *wonderful* anymore. And it's a long time since *fantastic* and *fabulous* conjured up the magical words of fantasy and fable.[123]" I myself have lost a sense of the meaning of the words *interesting*

---

123. *The Joy of Lex*, 64-65.

and *nice* and *very*. Verbicide is also rampant in the entertainment industry where failures are routinely described as "hits," or where, Brandreth notes by way of example, the 1976 remake of *King Kong* was billed as "the most original motion picture of all time." This brings to mind other adjectives that are incomparable, absolute, and not modifiable, but which we nonetheless often find modified, words such as *complete, contemporary, everlasting, indestructible, meaningless, omnipotent, perfect, supreme,* and *unique.* We must allow for exceptions, however, when it is clear writers know what they are doing, such as those who wrote, "We the people of the United States, in order to form a more perfect Union...."

Clever graffiti, literally and figuratively the handwriting on the wall, can be used to create a lighter touch in order to teach an appreciation for the power and effective use of words. The following appeared in response to a competition in *New York* magazine: "Dyslexics of the world, untie!"; "Life is a sexually transmitted and terminal disease"; "To understand fundamentalism, it helps to know what 'fundament' means"; and "Latin is a real angina gluteus maximus." Puns can serve the same purpose, witness these: "Lenin's tomb is a communist plot"; "A guillotine is a French chopping center"; "A fanatical computer data collector is an infomaniac"; and "A cemetery is a bury patch." Gyles Brandreth gives credit to Alan F.G. Lewis for these: "A Puritan is a man who noes what he likes"; "The guru refused to let his dentist freeze his jaw because he wanted to transcend dental medication"; "A pessimist is a person who looks at the world through morose-colored glasses"; and "Atrophy is a reward for long political service."[124] Puns such as these no doubt once prompted Fred Allen to declare: "Hanging is too good for a man who makes puns; he should be drawn and quoted."

Finally, the importance of word selection is addressed in a brief essay, titled "What Not to Name Your Dog," reprinted in an Ann Landers advice column. The author had named his

---

124. *More Joy of Lex* (New York, 1982).

dog *Sex*, which subsequently caused him a great deal of embarrassment. The essay concludes: "Last night Sex ran off again. I spent hours looking around town for him. A cop came over to me and asked, 'What are you doing in this alley at 4 o'clock in the morning?' I told him that I was looking for Sex. My case comes up on Friday."

Effective use of punctuation is a companion to good writing, but teaching punctuation is not something I am able to do well, except perhaps by example. In addition, I find eloquent support for the value of punctuation in a beautiful essay by Pico Iyer, which includes the following lines: "Punctuation is the way one bats one's eyes, lowers one's voice or blushes demurely. Punctuation adjusts the tone and color and volume till the feeling comes into perfect focus…. Punctuation, in short, gives us the human voice, and all the meanings that lie between the words."[125] A cartoon in *The New Yorker*, by Maslin, makes the same point through another medium and with a different kind of delicacy. It shows a motorcycle police officer filling out a citation for the driver of a van on the side of which is printed: "Me and Wallys Produce." The officer says, "Sorry, but I'm going to have to issue you a summons for reckless grammar and driving without an apostrophe."

The following stories are also illustrative of the importance of punctuation, and like fables they have heuristic value. Comedian George Kirby recalls an incident in Florida where an elderly Jewish gentleman was arrested for trespassing and brought before a judge who says, rather apologetically: "Sir, I'm afraid I'm going to have to fine you for using a private beach. After all, the sign clearly states, 'Private Property No Swimming Allowed.'" But quickly, in his own defense, the gentleman responds (note: using a Yiddish accent when telling this story makes it more effective): "Excuse me, your honor, I beg to differ with you. That's not how I read the sign." Well, then," responds the judge, "how do you read it?" "To me, your

---

125. "In Praise of the Humble Comma," *Time* (June 13, 19880, 80.

honor, it says, "Private Property? No! Swimming Allowed." Then there is the anecdote about the American art collector who sends his assistant to a London auction house to bid on a much-desired painting. As the price approaches the limit imposed by the collector, the assistant sends a telegram asking for instructions: should he bid higher? The response, without punctuation, reads: "No Price Too High." And we have all seen advertisements that proclaim: BIG SALE LAST WEEK. Without punctuation it appears as if the advertiser is spiteful, as we have obviously missed the sale. Thus punctuation, to paraphrase Iyer, enables us to affect a desired tone and reflects our attitude, which also plays a decisive role in our writing.

Just as a "winning attitude" might make the difference between success and failure in athletics, our behavior as writers may be indicative of what we can hope to accomplish. Saying we cannot write something can become self-fulfilling. Three cartoons put such behavior in perspective and serve to illustrate some of the difficulties in our approach to writing. One, from the *Drabble* strip, by Kevin Fagan, shows Wendy and Norman in the library. "Well, Wendy?" asks Norman, "What do you think of my term paper?" "To be honest, Norman," responds Wendy, "it's a bit disorganized, hastily written, and poorly researched. The pages are numbered incorrectly, it's carelessly typed, and you stapled the wrong corner." To this Norman asks, "Is everything else okay with it?" A Jim Davis comic strip shows Garfield, pencil in hand sitting before a stack of paper, thinking: "That's it! I have just come up with a cure for writer's cramp! Writer's block." Finally, a cartoon by H. Martin, in *The New Yorker*, titled "Writer's Block," depicts three sides of a building block, one with the letters "A, E, I, O, U" on them, another with the rule "i before e, except after c," and the third side containing various punctuation marks. Cartoons like these work best when used in conjunction with developing the writing process, say after returning a first draft; they can thus help relieve some of the sting that accompanies criticism.

Understanding formal grammar was always difficult for me

when I was a student of writing; I would have rather entered Orwell's Room 101 than diagram a sentence. In time, however, I developed an ear for correct usage, but grammar is something I do not try to teach; in fact, research in composition has demonstrated that it is not necessary to teach formal grammar as a prelude to writing.[126] To me, grammar is what Ambrose Bierce once defined as "a system of pitfalls thoughtfully prepared for the feet of the self-made man, along the path by which he advances to distinction." To supplement a traditional text on writing I distribute a distinctive collection that appears in a chapter titled "How to Write Good."[127] A sampling includes the following: "Subject and verb always has to agree"; "It behooves the writer to avoid archaic expressions"; "A truly good writer is always especially careful to practically eliminate the too-frequent use of adverbs"; and "Mixed metaphors are a pain in the neck and ought to be thrown out the window." Teaching by the use of obviously incorrect examples may be unorthodox, but it can also be an effective demonstration of reverse psychology.

One misperception about grammar (i.e., to never end a sentence with a preposition) can be dispelled with a story that reinforces the development of sensitivity to language. A freshman, looking as if he had just left the farm, arrives at Harvard. He stops a pipe-smoking, tweed-jacketed upperclassman and asks: "Excuse me, could you please tell me where the library's at?" Instead of directing the new student politely, the upperclassman, nose in the air, responds indignantly: "At Harvard we do not end a sentence with a preposition!" Humbled in this fashion, the freshman thinks a moment and then carefully rephrases his question: "OK, then, could you please tell me

---

126. R. Braddock et al., *Research in Written Composition* (Urbana, IL, 1963), 37-38; George Hillocks, Jr., *Research on Written Composition: New Directions for Teaching* (Urbana, IL, 1986), 133-51; Edward M. White, *Developing Successful College Writing Programs* (San Francisco, 1989), 70-75.

127. Alan Dundes & Carl R. Pagter, *When You're Up to Your Ass in Alligators* (Detroit, 1987), 121-22.

where the library's at, asshole?" The proscription that inspired this story once prompted Winston Churchill to declare: "That is the kind of pedantry up with which I will not put."

Words can be used to conjure powerful images, and students in all disciplines should be alerted to this potential. Einstein said it was imagination, not knowledge, which led to his theory of relativity: he imagined himself riding on a beam of light, and that image was the key to his discovery. Think of the imagery, as comedian George Carlin did to create his humor that accompanies the idea of a proctologist with poor depth perception. Steven Wright, another comedian, has offered us many good images that can be used to demonstrate the importance of accuracy in word usage. He said he once went to a restaurant at which a sign was posted offering "Breakfast Any Time," so he ordered French toast in the Renaissance. Another time he walked into a general store, but they would not sell him anything specific. And he also wondered whether illiterate people get the full effect of alphabet soup. Gallagher has asked some equally image-provoking questions that can be employed to stimulate discussion about the literal meaning of words or their apparent contradictions: If the world is getting smaller, why are postage rates going up? Why is it called "rush hour" when traffic moves at a snail's pace? If you see a sign ordering you to "keep this door closed at all times," why did they put a door there in the first place? And he has seen another sign that said, "Fine for Littering," but it is not fine; litter and it will cost you. In the spring, 1988, a newspaper headline announced: "Healthy breakfast tied to higher student test scores." All I could think of was the raisins in my cereal bowl flexing their muscles and puffing their chests to eliminate wrinkles as they prepared themselves to be tied. Images work in cartoons, too. One by Handelsman, in *The New Yorker*, captioned "Dickens' First Encounter with a Martini," depicts an incredulous author being asked by the bartender, as his drink is being poured: "Olive or twist?"

Clear definitions teach an appreciation for language and

help to build vocabulary playfully. Those by Ambrose Bierce[128] and by Gordon Bowker[129] are among the best. For example, according to Bierce, a *brain* is an apparatus with which we think we think; a *debauchee* is one who has so earnestly pursued pleasure that he has had the misfortune to overtake it; *genealogy* is an account of one's descent from a man who did not particularly care to trace his own; and *marriage* is the state or condition of a community consisting of a master, a mistress and two slaves, making in all two. According to Bowker, a *body-builder* is one who is fit for nothing; a *celibate* is a member of a union opposed to the union of members; a *hooker* is a fisher of men; a *Marxist* is a prophet of doom who predicts the doom of profit; and a *thief* is a businessman who does not issue receipts. Why not ask students to try their hand at this? Having fun with language can only have a positive impact on their approach to writing.

The need for precision in the use of language can be illustrated by its absence in everyday examples from newspapers and advertisements, examples of which can be found periodically on the Internet. I was shocked, therefore, to read a *Los Angeles Times* headline (January 8, 1986) proclaiming: [baseball commissioner] "Ueberroth to Begin Meeting on Drugs." It was with disbelief that I read in a Sunday supplement magazine that "Last week 21,000 high school boys got a girl pregnant." It was with aroused anticipation that I considered bringing my car to a dealer's service department that announced, on the radio: "We service the customer as well as the car." When CNN described a group of demonstrators as "not large but noisome," I thought: *descent* of man. It was with confusion that I read of the relief felt by airline passengers at the increase in the number of "near misses" in our skies. And it was with disappointment and genuine concern that I read, in 1988, how the National Council of Teachers of English was offering a "15 percent off discount" on its member-nomination form. The redundancy aside, that

---

128. *The Devil's Dictionary* (Franklin Center, PA, 1980).

129. See G. Brandreth, *More Joy of Lex*, 160-62.

same form asked teachers of English to sign below the statement: "I understand neither me, nor any of the colleagues I've recommended above, are obliged to accept NCTE membership."

We all may know what it is we mean by something we write or say, but ambivalence or imprecision sometimes exists that can be understood only by a reader or listener who also possesses our particular mindset or preconceptions. I make use of a number of clever cartoons that illustrate this as well if not better than any direct cautionary advice I might give to fledgling writers. For example, one in *The New Yorker*, by Lorenz, shows a couple staring at the mat in front of an apartment door on which they are about to knock; the mat reads "Not Unwelcome." A Handelsman cartoon, in *The New Yorker*, shows Charles Dickens being scolded by his publisher, who is holding a manuscript: "I wish you would make up your mind, Mr. Dickens. Was it the best of times or the worst of times? It could scarcely have been both." Another by Handelsman, again in *The New Yorker*, shows two businessmen in easy chairs in front of a fireplace in their club, with one responding to the other: "Feeling poorly? Thank heaven! I thought you said you were feeling *poor*." Finally, one by Gerberg, in *Playboy*, shows a man in a restaurant reacting to a waitress' question: "I'd *like* fame, fortune, love and understanding; I'll *have* a tuna on rye with lettuce and mayonnaise, a side of potato salad and tea with milk."

Ann Landers published summaries of accident reports received by insurance companies that inadvertently demonstrate the importance of writing with precision. The following are among what is no doubt a seemingly endless collection: "A pedestrian hit me and went under my car." "The guy was all over the place and I had to swerve a number of times before I hit him." "I was on my way to the doctor's with rear end trouble when my universal joint gave way, causing me to have an accident." "Coming home, I drove into the wrong house and collided with a tree I didn't have." "An invisible car came out of nowhere, struck my vehicle, and vanished." My students and I laugh at this blend of twisted English and convoluted imagery just as we might when witnessing someone slip on a banana peel: we are glad it did not happen to us and we will tread with greater vigilance. The same purpose can be achieved by reading the following excerpts, also from an Ann Landers column, from letters to a public assistance office by applicants seeking financial aid: "This is to let you know that Mrs. Jones has not had any clothes for a year and has been visited by her minister regularly." "In accordance with your instructions, I have given birth to twins in the enclosed envelope." "I am very annoyed to find that you have branded my son as illiterate. This is a lie. I was married to his father a week before he was born."

Euphemisms in language can be useful and appropriate when, according to columnist William Safire, they lessen pain and do not deny truth, as when we use *impaired* to describe the handicapped. But he chooses to expose where euphemism conceals reality from people who ought to be able to take their vocabulary straight: "*Local prostitutes* is a phrase that is clear and direct, but is never used by the United States Government. In the welcoming packet issued to our Embassy employees in Budapest, there is the phrase: 'It must be assumed that *available casual indigenous female companions* work for or cooperate with the Hungarian Government security establishment'.... [And] let us recoil in unison from *tube steaks*, the misleading new name for frankfurters."[130]

There is, however, another side to euphemisms: they can be useful in making a harsh point without seeming to be crude or cruel. The British use of understatement often serves this purpose. For example, a Member of Parliament catching an opponent in an untruth would be censured if he called his foe a "liar"; instead, he is likely, and more effectively, to say, "I believe the Right Honorable Member has unwittingly lapsed into error." Or consider describing someone as "having an open mind" when you mean to suggest he has a hole in his head. And

---

130. "On Language," *The New York Times Magazine* (January 10, 1988).

is it not kinder to say, "When you see his face time stands still," instead of "he has a face that would stop a clock"? For me, I have coined a phrase to be a polite substitute for the graphic, and perhaps offensive, *bulls__t*, when I wish to characterize a paper that is nonsense or of little worth: *toro excremental writing*.

One assignment I use to promote thinking skills as well as good writing is the critical book review. Along with a carefully developed and detailed set of guidelines, I provide a number of brief witty reviews (of books, plays, films, etc.) that act as hors d'oeuvres to whet students' appetites for the longer papers they will write, that will prompt them to go beyond the typically vacant, meaningless, "I liked the book because it was interesting," which tells us neither why the book was liked nor why it was interesting. About a book she read, Dorothy Parker wrote: "This is not a novel to be tossed aside lightly. It should be thrown with great force." About a play she saw, the same Dorothy Parker quipped: "*The House Beautiful* is a play lousy." Heinrich Heine wrote about a book by observing: "I fell asleep reading a dull book, and I dreamed that I was reading on, so I awoke from sheer boredom." About a two-line poem Comte De Rivarol said: "Very nice, but there are dull stretches." I believe it was a film reviewer for *The New Yorker* who summed up his opinion of the 1950s epic *Ben Hur*: "Loved him, hated Hur." The music of Richard Wagner, according to Mark Twain, "is better than it sounds." And writing to a would-be author, Samuel Johnson noted: "Your manuscript is both good and original; but the part that is good is not original, and the part that is original is not good."

Clever cartoons can complement caustic curmudgeons, and the following, distributed before students begin to write and as supplements to my guidelines, serve as friendly cautions on how *not* to proceed. A *Peanuts* strip by Shulz has Sally writing: "Tess of the d'Urbervilles by Laurel N. Hardy." "That's 'Thomas Hardy,'" corrects Charlie Brown, who then adds: "I can't believe you read this whole book." Responds Sally: "I read the first word...'on.'" "How can you write a book report," questions Charlie, "if you've only read the first word?" "No problem," says Sally as she starts to read her report: "Right from the first word I knew this was going to be a good book." Says Charlie, "I can see you're going to be a lover of great literature." Concludes Sally, "Those who can't do, fake it." There is also a lengthy *Shoe* strip, by Jeff MacNelly, showing Shoe laboring at a desk, reading his assignment: "Write a 200-word book report comparing the themes of *Tom Sawyer* and *Treasure Island.*" What he writes is an elaborate rephrasing of the question and an assessment of the task, which concludes: "In fact, such a question as comparing the themes of *Treasure Island* and *Tom Sawyer* is so difficult and complex a question that it certainly can't be properly discussed in a book report of only two hundred words of which this is the two-hundredth."

Revision and editing are complementary steps in the writing process that students tend to resist, as if they possess a gene that renders them reluctant to write something more than once. The folly of such a posture is noted with brevity in a *Frank and Ernest* comic strip, by Bob Thaves, that shows a frustrated Noah, in the process of naming the ark he has just built, having written and crossed out *ARG*, underneath which is written *ARCK*. He turns toward the heavens and, impatiently, asks, "*Now* what's wrong?" The delight of humor helps to allay the difficult truths it can reveal, including our own inadequacies and shortcomings. Indeed, students must be persuaded that if the need for revision and editing is perceived as a burden, it is one that is universally shared by writers. I supplement the cartoon with a heavily edited sample from my own writing, complete with the same kind of editorial markings I use on their papers. (If such a personal sample is unavailable, William Zinsser's *On Writing Well* reprints two pages of text as edited.)

Other aspects of the revision process can be approached from a different angle. Dear Abby once devoted a couple of columns to people sounding off about their pet peeves in language abuse. These are gems for instruction and focus attention on such abuses as substituting *goes* or *like* for *says*, misusing *basically*, *hopefully, totally, myself, further* and *farther,* using redundancies such as *irregardless, free gift,* and *true fact,* and substituting *between you and I* for *between you and me.* Headlines can assist in calling attention to unnecessary words, such as one that reads: "Long Beach Symphony Cancels Out." A jingle might be helpful in pointing out the writers' usual preference for active rather than passive verbs, such as *is, are, was,* and *were*: "Is-y was-y was a verb,/ Is-y was-y has no verve./ Does is-y work or is-y fuzzy?"

Some of the so-called rules of spelling might be put in perspective with an avalanche of exceptions. We have all been taught at least one such rule: use I before E except after C. That works fine for words like *receive, piece,* and *receipt.* But it does not work at all well for words such as *ancient, being, caffeine, either, glacier, leisure, neighbor, policies, their,* and some 50-to-60 more of which I am aware. Perhaps what we need is a special hotline, attended by unemployed English majors, to respond to queries about writing. If one were ever established, I would recommend it be called the *Grammar-Phone Line.* Perhaps, also, we need a set of rules to guide us in following rules. If so, I propose the following: (1) rules are made by fallible human beings; (2) rules have exceptions; (3) rules are sometimes meant to be broken; (4) rules should not be followed if they do not make sense; and (5) rules that make sense should not have to be rules in the first place.

Two cartoons poke fun at the student who is less than precise in spelling. One, by Campbell, in *Phi Delta Kappan,* shows two boys on a park bench looking over the results of a spelling test one of them just had returned. Comments the boy whose test it is: "She could've given me a point or two for originality." A *Herman* cartoon, by Unger, shows a job interviewee before the desk of a "personel" [sic] officer, who says: "Your resume says you spent 'fore years at collej.'"

Spelling errors help to direct our attention to the value of proofreading which, because it usually is a concern only at the end of the writing process, is more often than not minimized or ignored. But careful proofreading will also pick up punctuation and typographical errors that deform the meaning of a text. The addition of humorous anecdotes, such as the following, is a painless way to emphasize such value. A staple of *The New Yorker*, usually filling in the occasional small space at the end of a column following a story, are the typos and misprints that appear everywhere, like blemishes on the printed page. From a church newsletter, for example, came this announcement: "The ladies of the church have cast off clothes of every kind and they can be seen in the church basement on Friday afternoons." In another example, a furniture store, in advertising a bedroom set, indicated that the buyer would receive a "triple dresser, framed mirror, Queen-sized headboard and one night stand." And then there are student malapropisms that careful proofreading might have caught. Jack Smith used to print some enlightening ones in his column: "In 1957, Eugene O'Neill won the Pullet Surprise"; "A horse divided against itself cannot stand"; "A virgin forest is a place where the hand of man has never set foot"; and "Soldiers of high rank wear opulents on their shoulders."[131]

In addition to malapropisms (including those by Mrs. Malaprop herself: "allegories live on the banks of the Nile"[132]), language appreciation can come from spoonerisms (e.g., "The Lord is a shoving leopard," and "When the boys come back from France, we'll have the hags flung out"),[133] oxymorons (e.g., "civil wars," "make haste slowly," and "military intelligence"), and goldwynisms (e.g., "A verbal contract isn't worth the paper it's written on," "I'll give you a definite maybe," and "In two words: im-possible").[134] In the same ballpark but, so to

---

131. *Los Angeles Times* (February 18, 1985).

132. Richard Sheridan, *The Rivals* (in which the character of Mrs. Malaprop made her appearance) was first performed in 1775, in London.

133. Named after the Reverend William Archibald Spooner (1844-1930), Warden of New College, Oxford, who became famous for switching consonants, vowels, or morphemes.

134. After Samuel Goldwyn of Metro-Goldwyn-Mayer (MGM).

speak, a horse of a different color, are those misheard words and phrases that can illustrate the need for careful listening while writing. Emily Litella, the character portrayed by Gilda Radner in the early years of *Saturday Night Live*, became enraged, for example, by the excessive attention in the press being paid to "endangered feces"; she was also upset at our preoccupation with "violins on TV"; and she failed to see the public concern over "Soviet jewelry." It would be wise to use gems like these as periodic friendly reminders, say a few each time a new assignment is introduced.

Another linguistic affliction that can be treated with humor is the jargon that, like an endemic disease, is spreading among Americans and drives some of us to scratch our irritated intellects. A cartoon in *The New Yorker*, by Handelsman, shows a couple holding hands in a restaurant with the woman saying, "I do like you, Peter, but interfacing is a very serious step." The *Quarterly Review of Doublespeak*, a publication of the National Council of Teachers of English, collects and publishes some of the worst of these misuses in our language, and they, too, help us to develop an appreciation for precision in language use as well as for the way language can conceal meaning. Past violators include the military officer who referred to an invasion as a "predawn insertion," and another who stated that American troops are never ambushed but instead "engage the enemy on all sides"; the politician who pledged not to raise taxes but instead voted for "revenue enhancements"; the Environmental Protection Agency which labeled acid rain as "poorly buffered precipitation"; the Cadillac dealer who did not sell his used cars as *used* or even *pre-owned* but as *experienced*; the government official who referred to a recession as a period of "advanced negative economic growth"; and the hospital official who referred to deaths in his institution as "negative patient care outcomes." Thus, if Benjamin Franklin were alive, he would no doubt quip: Nothing in life is certain except negative patient care outcome and revenue enhancements.

Collecting all these materials has been fun, educational, and stimulating. In fact, the act of collecting becomes contagious, and I have had students and colleagues who periodically bring me cartoons and articles, which, to some extent, demonstrates my point that humor boosts language awareness. The above represents just a few years of serious collecting and sharing, so it is never too late to start. That which is collected, however, must be categorized and then used only to spark interest, to inspire, and to open creative doors. The use of bits of humor ought not to be strained but instead should fit like missing pieces of a puzzle; they should not be pasted on, as afterthoughts, but made to flow with the rhythm of a course. Teachers who see the possibilities this kind of humor has for their classes should collect and use materials appropriate to the grade or class level of their students, and teachers will need to adjust such material to their own levels of perversity. But if learning can be fun, why not make it so? And if the fun can promote learning, then there is all the more reason to have a (calculated) good time.

PART THREE:
TESTS AND EXAMS

9. A GUIDE TO THE SKILL OF ESSAY CONSTRUCTION IN HISTORY

Many teachers of history, at both secondary and college levels, invariably devote insufficient attention to the essay examinations they prepare for their classes. Typically, on the eve of an examination date, they dash off questions that are believed to deal appropriately with the subject matter they wish tested. Knowing the kinds of responses they expect, the questions seem clear enough; after all, teachers are cognizant of what their questions demand, and therefore they have no difficulty interpreting or seeing the implications of the words they have chosen. Unfortunately, not all students are blessed with such insight, and whether or not they respond as the teacher hopes—assuming they have studied properly—is often a matter of chance. Equally unfortunate is the failure to acknowledge that a student's misinterpretation of an essay question may be the teacher's fault, and thus teachers continue to repeat errors and handicap some among each new wave of students entrusted to their care.

From 1976 to 1980 I was Chief Reader for Advanced Placement European History. In that capacity I served on the committee that wrote the examinations, a process that involved, for each separate test, the deliberations of at least six secondary and college teachers over a period of about a year. I also supervised the annual grading of the thousands of student responses, after which I provided the Educational Testing Service with a report evaluating the performance of the questions. Further, I had access to twenty-five years of such reports from both European and United States History. What follows, then, represents the collective assessment and reaction of literally hundreds of teachers, all of whom benefited from experience and hindsight. In spite of the fact that a great deal of thought and deliberation have gone into AP essay construction, all too often the best and poorest questions are not discovered until after an examination has been administered and graded. Only then can the least obvious subtleties, which determine the success or failure of a question, be known. Nevertheless, approaching essay construction with a sense of what has or has not "worked" may help avoid past mistakes; in this fashion we can practice what we teach. (The sample questions included below are from past AP examinations.)

Essay Construction

Goals: All good essay questions, from a grading perspective, should be able to elicit responses of a varied caliber, roughly analogous to students' abilities and preparedness. Questions that can be answered by simple recall of facts should be avoided; they reveal nothing more than a student's skill at memorization. Machines can store and retrieve facts better than we can, so it is pointless to train students to compete with them. Instead, good questions test the student's ability to use historical facts in order to explain and interpret important developments and, by extension, to come to a better understanding of life. For example, the following question offers students an opportunity to exercise historical skills by integrating late-medieval developments with those of the Renaissance and Reformation periods, while it also requires them to integrate political and religious forces, as well as to observe national differences as they confront a significant theme: "How did the disintegration of the medieval church and the coming of the Reformation contribute to the development of nation-states in Western Europe between 1450 and 1648?"

Language/Wording: Appropriate language is a vital ingredient in any essay question. Vaguely worded and loose and unstructured items should be avoided. For example, the following question may be provocative, but it deals with concepts that likely are beyond the capacity of even superior students; moreover, it is poorly constructed and too open-ended: "It has been said that, from 1450 to the present, European life and institutions have been shaped by the existence of a world-wide frontier. Describe the main influence of this 'frontier' on the Europe of two of the following periods: the Elizabethan Era, the Age of Louis XIV, the Age of Reason, the Victorian Age, the period between the two World Wars." Also, by way of example, is the following question, which provided so much scope that it was relatively easy to go off in one direction and write, for instance, only on the revolution with the first clause ignored altogether: "'Although the thirteen American colonies were founded at different times by people with different motives and with different forms of colonial charters and political organization, by the Revolution the thirteen colonies had become remarkably similar.' Assess the validity of this statement." It is a useful practice to relate the purpose of a question to the goals of the course in such a way that students can appreciate it and, if necessary, discuss it afterwards. Considerable effort should be expended so that questions are well written, uncomplicated, and straightforward. Concepts, terms, and code words should be used with care, making certain they have already been noted in course texts or class and, therefore, are familiar to students.

Directions: Statements or quotations followed by the words "discuss" or "assess" (e.g., "The attempt of the Emperor Charles V to achieve the medieval ideal of a Christian European empire was doomed to failure from the start. Discuss.") usually unintentionally send students off in all directions; words like "discuss" and "assess" standing alone ask for nothing in particular. Make it clear what it is you wish to be discussed or assessed (e.g.,

"Discuss the origins and evolution of European liberalism as a political movement during the nineteenth century."). Similarly, students need to be led when asked to analyze or evaluate; state clearly what it is you want them to analyze or evaluate.

Questions that ask for the causes of something, or those that request students to explain why something happened, have worked well. Yet, those asking, "How do you account for" or "To what extent" frequently elicit vague and weak responses unless the rest of the wording is especially clear and direct. The phrase "In what ways" can be interpreted either as "To what extent" or "How," if, in fact, the former and either of the latter are actually desired, then join them together (e.g., "To what extent and in what ways may the Renaissance be regarded as a turning point in the western intellectual and cultural tradition?").

Instead of merely asking for the "effects" of something, ask for either the immediate or long-range effects, or both, whichever is desired. In a similar vein, when directing student to "explain and discuss the reasons" for something, and when several kinds of reasons are anticipated, your purposes will be better served if you request them to "explain and discuss the *several* reasons" or "the *variety* of reasons."

Essay questions should be structured so as to encourage or require that students go beyond mere accumulation of facts and textbook knowledge, and that they exercise critical judgment and show thoughtful interpretation.

Students tend to be weak on terminology; if some working definitions are desired, consideration should be given to asking for them as part of the question.

Avoid calling an event successful or unsuccessful (in a question that asks students why an event was or was not successful; e.g., "Why was revolution successful in France in 1789 but unsuccessful in the German states in 1848?") because it tends to stifle creative reflection and original judgment; students might prefer to challenge the assumptions within the question, but hesitate to do so given such wording. It is better to allow students to pass judgment and explain their reasoning. Similarly, when asking for an explanation of the success or failure (or other evaluative terms) of people or events, qualify it by stating the explicit criteria for success or failure, instead of leaving it open.

Finally, it is often wise for some questions to demand "evidence" to support a position or interpretation, even if such an implication is clear to you.

Sequence of Questions: Some attention should be devoted to the sequence of questions on any examination in which a variety of selections is offered. Given the pressure from time limitations, some students might not read all questions carefully and unload on the first one familiar to them. Although little can be done to prevent this, teachers might want to consider allotting more time, offering fewer choices, encouraging students to read each question carefully, and/or being certain that all questions are of near-equal difficulty. Where there is great disparity among questions, students choosing the more difficult ones are at a disadvantage. More specifically, the 1977 AP European History Examination offered two questions, among others, on the decline of the aristocracy in Western Europe and the industrialization of Eastern Europe. They were answered by more students than a traditional one on the origins and evolution of nineteenth-century liberalism. This unexpected result may have been due to the question on liberalism appearing as the last of six choices. Similarly, it has been suggested that had the first and sixth questions on the 1978 examination been reversed, the overall quality of the responses might have been improved. That is, question 1 concerned the Industrial Revolution, a topic that tends to lure less able students and/or result in inferior answers. Question 7 treated the political side of major revolutions, a mainstream subject, with responses being of a high quality. Thus while both questions were heavily answered, more chose question 1; had their order been reversed, more students might have elected the less troublesome topic. While this is speculation, to be sure, it is worth consideration in order to minimize the number of potential pitfalls.

Breadth versus Specificity: Questions should be constructed so as to be answerable in terms of time allotted and from the standpoint of a reasonable expectation of training for your students.

Questions with compound subjects (i.e., those that treat several variables, such as political, social, and economic factors, or several concepts) may be asking for more than can be reasonably expected; they also encourage students to wander and not focus on the question (e.g., "Estimate the roles of British sea power, French governmental weakness, and Prussian military strength in the relations among states in Europe, 1715-1789."). Similarly, some teachers think that a broad, generalized question gives students freedom. In practice, however, such questions often force students to use time and energy trying to guess what the teacher really wants.

Avoid questions that are either too general or too specific (or too specialized); a balance between the two should be the aim. Some structure is needed, but room for student initiative should also exist. Questions must be manageable.

Questions within Questions: Multi-part questions (e.g., "Discuss the extent to which early modern European society encouraged education for women. What criteria were used to evaluate women's education or its role, and women's potential for learning? What evolution, if any, can be seen in attitudes toward education for women from the Renaissance through the early eighteenth century?") become unnecessarily complex and should be avoided or kept to a minimum. If used, they should be well thought-out so they elicit only what is desired. Questions that ask for too many separate areas to be covered run the risk of some areas being ignored.

Compare and Contrast Questions: Unless phrased very carefully, questions calling upon students to compare and contrast (either explicitly or implicitly) usually, at best, evoke no more than separate listing. Teachers ought to consider offering examples of what they are looking for in such questions, or train their students beforehand in how they should be handled. For example, although the following question may have problems, it instructs students on what it is they should compare, and then on how they should apply that comparison to a broader issue: "Compare the economic, political, and social conditions in Great Britain and in France during the eighteenth century, showing why they favored the Industrial Revolution in Great Britain more so than in France." Comparative analyses are instructive, but even scholars employing such an approach often fail to achieve satisfactory results.

Another especially useful suggestion when planning to ask "compare" and "compare and contrast" questions is, instead, to ask students to describe and analyze "similarities" and "differences." The difference between these two sets of terms may appear to be insignificant—mere semantics, if you will—but experience indicates that the latter function more effectively in eliciting the desired comparisons.

Quotations in Questions: The use of quotations can create unintended and unnecessary pitfalls. Quotations are often interesting, snappy, and clever, but they can deprive students of clear directions; besides, quotations are also frequently subtle, imprecise, and sophisticated, and not necessarily understood or used as hoped. For example, "According to Lord Acton, 'The authentic interpreter of Machiavelli is the whole of later history.' Discuss this statement with reference to the history of modern Europe, concentrating on those periods with which you are most familiar." The Acton quotation is indeed provocative, but it is also too cryptic for most students. "Revolt is easier than reform" was the quotation that preceded another question, but such quotations could mean anything and nothing.

Quotations, when used, should not be ambiguous, and the quotation and question must be paired properly; that is, the question should be clearly and directly linked to the quotation. Quotations from historical figures should have the language modernized enough so as to be understood easily by contemporary students. Metaphors in quotations, like ghosts in old homes, will return to haunt teachers, or else they will be taken at face value.

Dates: Dates should not be chosen arbitrarily, as students read significance into them; care should be taken so that dates are used accurately and for specific purposes. When using a set of dates and a question that calls for reference to more than one country, the dates should be equally applicable to each country. The mention of centuries is often not enough to restrict the boundaries of a question, because even the best students occasionally become confused; specific dates should be included (perhaps parenthetically) as well, even though this may be obviously redundant. The use of date-phrases, such as 'by 1700" or "by the twentieth century," is misleading and should be avoided. "By 1700" can be taken to mean the sixteenth century, only 1700, the beginning of the eighteenth century, or all three. Clear chronological limits are important, because they confine responses within reasonable bounds: when it comes to dates, leave no room for doubt or variation.

Words, Concepts, Phrases: Words should be used to express precisely what is meant. Do not introduce words or esoteric concepts on an examination. As a test is being constructed, all words should be scrutinized in an effort to foresee their implications and to determine whether they coincide with the intention of the question. The list below does not comprise a collection of prohibitive words; instead, it includes examples that have caused problems for students. As such, it is intended to sensitize teachers and alert them to potential problems.

- *state* (could mean existing government, society, something else, or some combination of things)
- *administration/administrative* (could mean ruler, the government, or more)
- *Central Europe, the West* (these and similar expressions of geography are imprecise unless clearly defined beforehand; list or specify which countries/states are to be included or excluded)
- *art/literature* (unless it does not matter what type students might use, including music and film, specify the type

desired)

- *science and philosophy* (questions on intellectual history calling for a discussion of science and philosophy will often result in little or no differentiation between the two)
- *society* (could mean the governed, the government, both or something else)
- *Rationalism, Romanticism* (when these and similar words are used to refer to the societal movements that bear their names, they should be capitalized; otherwise, rationalism emerges as logical, pragmatic, wise, whereas romanticism is presented as dreaminess, emotion, unclear thinking)
- *social structure* (could be taken to mean any number of different things, including social conditions)
- *liberal, conservative, radical* (these words mean something different to United States and European history, and to different times during those histories)
- *aristocracy/nobility* (students generally see no difference between these words)
- *peasant, working class, middle class* (the first two are often used interchangeably; the latter is broad enough to include a wide range of social classes)
- *culture* (can be used to refer to literary and artistic factors, but also to sociological factors as well)
- *minorities* (can be ethnic, racial, religious, or other)

Right or Wrong Questions: These questions are phrased in such a way that a position is taken or a moral judgment appears to be rendered (e.g., "The European saw himself as a benefactor, carrying the blessings of Western civilization to Asia and Africa. The peoples of these regions viewed the Europeans as disruptive of their own valued traditions. Discuss the conflicting outlooks for the colonized regions of the world from the mid-nineteenth century to 1960.") Such questions encourage ideological rhetoric and, worse, often stifle open inquiry and historical analysis of historical processes. It would be more instructive to focus questions on, say, causation.

Current Events Questions: Questions that deal with or are related to present-day concerns frequently are long on polemics, rhetoric, and emotion, and short on historical analysis. For example, questions on war and military organization, such as the following, attract either military buffs who tend to ignore the question as they expound on their beliefs, or anti-militarists who use the question as a forum from which to make pronouncements about the evils of war: "Write an essay that relates the development of the large conscripted citizen army from its origins in the *levée en masse* to the emergence of the modern nation-state." Questions that deal with minorities and/or toleration tend to generate hot rhetoric about "human beings' inhumanity to other human beings," instead of historical analysis (e.g., "Unpopular minority groups have been a persistent historical dilemma. Explain and discuss the reasons why the Huguenots in seventeenth-century France, the Irish in nineteenth-century Great Britain, and the Jews in twentieth-century Central and Eastern Europe were unpopular with the majority and treated harshly." Or "'The leadership, organization, and programs of ethnic and racial minority movements after 1945 represented a fundamental departure from those which had existed from 1900 to 1945.' Discuss with reference to black Americans or Mexican American, giving equal attention to the periods before and after 1945.") Teachers should be aware of the pitfalls involved, and advise students beforehand of what is expected from them and/or word such questions with care.

Successful Questions for Study

There is no easy road to writing foolproof essay questions. Each new question has the potential to present a new array of problems. Nevertheless, by employing these guidelines, adapted and modified to suit specific needs, teachers should be able to avoid what have proven to be problems, and use what has worked with a greater degree of success. As a result, students should learn more efficiently and be treated more fairly, and teachers themselves will deserve and earn further praise. In addition, teachers should consider establishing preliminary expectations or standards for their questions: this can serve the function of a pre-test, and should be pursued, as much as is humanly possible, from the perspective of students so as to anticipate potential problems. That is, after being written, questions should be screened with regard to intent and the extent that they actually ask what is intended. If there is a colleague with whom you can work to achieve this result, so much the better.

Finally, if studying questions that have been successful (for both students and graders) will aid the reader further, the following are offered from recent AP European and United States History. (It should be noted that United States History AP questions all begin with quotations, whereas only some European History questions are constructed this way. The reader can determine which questions best adhere to the guidelines that comprise this essay.)

1. Discuss the various factors which enabled Europeans to achieve economic and political dominance over many non-European peoples between 1450 and 1750.

2. Explain how economic, technological, political, and religious factors promoted European exploration, from about 1450 to 1525.

3. In the seventeenth century, England and the Netherlands developed effective capitalist economies while Spain did not. Why did the economies develop so differently in England and the Netherlands, on the one hand, and in Spain, on the other?

4. What political and social changes in Western and Central Europe account for the virtual disappearance of revolutionary outbreaks in the half-century following 1848?

5. Discuss the extent to which nineteenth-century romanticism was or was NOT a conservative cultural and intellectual movement.

6. Assess the nature and importance of economic factors that

helped determine the race for empire among the major European powers in the late nineteenth and early twentieth centuries.

7. "Every age projects its own image of man into its art." Assess the validity of this statement with reference to two representative twentieth-century European works in either the visual or literary arts.

8. "The Treaty of Vienna (1815) was a more realistic accommodation to the post-Napoleonic period than was the Versailles settlement (1919) to the post-First World War period." Decide the merits of the statement above and in a well-developed argument support your decision with a carefully reasoned analysis of the events mentioned.

9. A favorite device of social critics has been to construct model societies to illuminate the problems and the shortcomings of their times and to project a possible blueprint for the future. Describe and compare the utopias of Jean-Jacques Rousseau and Karl Marx. What were the chief faults they found with their own societies and how were their utopias designed to correct them?

10. "Every successful revolution puts on in time the robes of the tyrant it has deposed." Evaluate this statement with regard to the English Revolution (1640-1660), the French Revolution (1789-1815), and the Russian Revolution (1917-1930).

11. "Both the Jackson Democrats during 1824-1840 and the Populists during 1890-1896 attacked and sought to root out special privilege in American life. The Jacksonian Democrats attained power and succeeded; the Populists failed." Assess the validity of this view. Give roughly equal attention to the Jacksonian Democrats and the Populists.

12. "Although the United States is widely regarded as the home of free enterprise, business values, and materialism, American fiction since 1865 has generally been critical of business behavior and values." Assess the validity of this generalization with reference to the work of at least TWO writers who have treated the behavior and values of businessmen in their fiction since 1865.

13. "Paradoxically, Darwinism provided a justification for both social conservatism and social reform in the period from 1870 to 1915." Discuss this statement.

14. "Ironically, popular belief in the 'self-sufficient farmer' and the 'self-made man' increased during the nineteenth century as the reality behind these beliefs faded." Assess the validity of this statement.

15. "From 1914 to the present, the main trend in the relationship between the central government and the states has been toward concentration of power in the federal government." Discuss with reference to such areas of government as regulation of business, social welfare, and civil rights.

16. "War has frequently had unexpected consequences for United States foreign policy but has seldom resulted in major reorientations of policy." Discuss with reference to the First and Second World Wars, giving about equal attention to both.

17. "Between 1776 and 1823 a young and weak United States achieved considerable success in foreign policy when confronted with the two principle European powers, Great Britain and France. Between 1914 and 1950, however, a far more powerful United States was far less successful in achieving its foreign policy objectives in Europe." Discuss by comparing United States foreign policy in Europe during the period 1776-1823 with United States policy in Europe during ONE of the following periods: 1914-1932 or 1933-1950.

18. "From 1790 to the 1870s, state and national governments intervened in the American economy mainly to aid private economic interests and promote economic growth. Between 1890 and 1929, however, government intervention was designed primarily to curb and regulate private economic activity in the public interest." Assess the validity of this statement, discussing for *each* of these periods at least TWO major areas of public economic policy.

19. "The term isolationism" does not adequately describe the reality of either United States foreign policy or America's relationships with other nations during the period from Washington's

farewell address (1796) to 1940." Assess the validity of this generalization.

20. "Presidents who have been notably successful in either foreign affairs or domestic affairs have seldom been notably successful in both." Assess this statement with reference to TWO presidents, one in the nineteenth century and the other in the twentieth century, giving reasons for success or failure in each case.

10. HOW ADVANCED PLACEMENT HISTORY ESSAY QUESTIONS ARE PREPARED—AND HOW YOURS CAN BE TOO

Essay tests are a means of collecting and then judging information and reflections from students, or at least they should be. On the Advanced Placement examination, for which secondary school students may receive advanced standing at hundreds of colleges, essays are one-half of the exam. That is why it is vital—both to us as teachers and to the whole educational process—to devote sufficient time to the preparation and evaluation of test questions to determine precisely what kind of information and reflections are meant to be retrieved. Questions that are inappropriate for your students' level, training, or ability will not tell you what they actually know. In turn, this diminishes your chances for successful judgment. Or, questions that ask only for a list of facts designed as essay questions are educationally pointless, except insofar as the test skills of memorization. Therefore, constructive and useful essay questions are built around a framework that automatically propels students to link and consider facts and ideas.

The men and women from colleges and secondary schools across the country who work for the Advanced Placement Program (AP) expend as much, if not more, time, thought, and energy as any teachers anywhere preparing the questions in AP United States and European history. The purpose of this paper is to explain how these tests are prepared. This should, it is hoped, be instructive to teachers at all levels and, further, it should demystify what need not be mysterious.

AP history examinations typically consist of two types of essay questions: the standard, free-response essay and the document-based question (DBQ). The standard questions provide an opportunity for students to demonstrate possession of a range of skills and information in a broad interpretive essay. The DBQ is different in that it does not seek to test students' prior knowledge of subject matter. Rather, it is designed to evaluate their ability to analyze actual historical (documentary) evidence and then formulate an answer. All essay questions are intended to reflect current trends in college teaching in terms of subject matter and approach.

Approximately a year and a half before the actual AP examination is administered, work is begun preparing those free-response questions from which students will make their choices. Members of the development committees (i.e., there are separate committees for United States history and European history, each usually consisting of five members, at least two of whom are from secondary schools, plus the chief reader—whose primary responsibility is to direct the grading of examinations—and an Educational Testing Service [ETS] consultant), working individually, compose several questions each. These are sent to Princeton where the ETS consultant places them in some kind of order (e.g., all political questions together) before the entire collection is mailed to all members of the committee for their careful scrutiny and evaluation. The committees then meet to review and discuss the questions, perhaps as many as fifty or more. A number are rejected as inappropriate. Others are not used but kept in the pool for future consideration. Some are also designated for the pool, but with specific instructions for restructuring. Eventually, the required number of questions is selected, though the committee as a whole rewords many.

These final questions will be reviewed and, if necessary, reworked twice more, by mail and sometimes during another committee meeting. Thus, they will have been examined, dissected, and reconstructed by at least seven people, separately and together, several times before they are finally sent to be printed as part of the examination.

In choosing (and rejecting) questions a number of factors are considered by the development committees. The group of questions finally selected is usually balanced on the basis of chronology, geography, and theme; there are also crossover and comparison questions covering more than one time period, theme, or region. Questions from previous years are examined to maximize coverage of themes and minimize repetition. And the committees avail themselves of the chief reader's report of the previous AP reading (i.e., grading of examinations) to determine how effectively those earlier questions worked. For example, a lesson was learned from an otherwise successful European history question that began with a quotation from Barbara Tuchman: "Every successful revolution puts on in time the robes of the tyrant it has deposed." The question asked students to evaluate the quotation with regard to three specific revolutions. The problem encountered with the quotation, and thus the question, is that it forced students to judge revolutions as deteriorating into tyrannies. Students, therefore, were being made to accept a point of view, a bias if you will, as historical fact. An alternative and satisfying approach would have been to ask students to agree or disagree with the quotation as it related to the specific revolutions. Still another approach would have abandoned the quotation altogether but preserved the question's intent by asking students to balance the achievements of one or more revolution against its (their) shortcomings or failures.

In evaluating and reworking questions development committee members add and subtract words and phrases to arrive at a question that will most effectively elicit the best possible responses. Two examples from the 1981 European history examination will suffice. One question was initially submitted as follows: "Napoleon is sometimes called the last and greatest of the enlightened despots. Evaluate the validity of this claim in terms of his policies and accomplishments." A little editorial work tightened up the wording, and the addition of another sentence enabled knowledgeable students to rise above the ordinary: "Napoleon is sometimes called the greatest enlightened despot. Evaluate this assessment in terms of Napoleon I's policies and accomplishments. Be sure to include a definition of enlightened despotism in your answer." Another question reached the committee as follows: "Compare the respective roles assumed by the state in the direction of the economic systems of France under Colbert and the Soviet Union under Stalin." It was reconstructed to assist students by broadening the question slightly with the inclusion of the names of those economic systems and the time periods in which they functioned: "Compare the economic roles of the state under seventeenth-century mercantilism and twentieth-century communism. Illustrate your answer with reference to the economic system of France during Louis XIV's reign under Colbert and of the Soviet Union under Stalin."

Sometimes the order of a question's wording will be reversed in order to determine whether the new emphasis might be an improvement. For example, this question appeared on one AP examination: "How did the disintegration of the medieval church and the coming of the Reformation contribute to the development of nation-states in western Europe between 1450 and 1648?" Although this was the desired question, a reversal could have provided another, though not necessarily better option: "How did the development of nation-states in Western Europe between 1450 to 1648 contribute to the disintegration of the medieval church and the coming of the Reformation?"

Graders of AP examinations are especially sensitive to the need for carefully worded questions. They—and by extension, AP development committees—are aware that a vague question, one without clear demands or a precise topic, does not offer students the margin of freedom that some would think.

Unfortunately, vague questions force students to use and waste time and energy guessing what the question is really asking. Instead, instantly upon reading a question students should know what is called for so they can begin immediately. They should know precisely what is wanted of them, and they—and graders—should subsequently be able to tell if they have done it.

As the above indicates, there is concern among AP development committees that essay questions be as clear as possible. Although the flawless question may be perpetually elusive, and the perfect examination administered only in Utopia, a concerted effort is made nonetheless. In 1979 I prepared a guide to essay construction (i.e., dealing with goals, language and wording, directions, sequencing of questions, breadth and specificity, questions within questions, compare and contrast questions, quotations in questions, use of dates, right or wrong questions) based upon the collective feedback from AP examination readers and the evaluation of chief readers covering a quarter of a century of experience in both European and United States history. Hindsight played a key role as sometimes the best or poorest questions were not discovered until after examinations were graded. Still, approaching essay construction with a sense of what has or has not "worked" has been able to help avoid past mistakes. What originated as a document for the development committees only was subsequently expanded and published in *Social Education* (March 1981) so as to be disseminated to a larger audience.

If free-response questions are the subject of considerable attention, then document-based-questions are pampered. A typical gestation period is two years. A DBQ begins as an idea in the mind of at least one development committee member. That idea is presented to the rest of the committee whereupon it is determined whether it is worth pursuing further. If the committee agrees that the subject is appropriate and the number and kinds of documents needed are probably available, then the originator of the idea returns home to develop the question, prepare a historical setting statement, and select a variety of possible documents. If necessary, other members of the committee search for documents too. Completed copies of this material are forwarded to all committee members for their evaluation. Then, as with the review of other questions when the committees convene, all material relevant to the DBQ is confronted. The actual question may be reworded and the historical setting statement rewritten. Some documents are eliminated and others are edited. Where additional documents are required these are secured later. The documents are also placed in a specific order. All of this work, plus whatever new documents have been added, are subsequently mailed to committee members for an additional review. A final examination of the DBQ comes at another committee meeting when the completed package is seen just as students will see it at the end of that school year. Incidentally, as with the free-response question, some members of the committees, at various stages in the process, answer the question themselves in an attempt to discover—and suggest possible resolutions to—unseen problems.

Documents are selected on the basis of both the information they convey about the topic and the perspective they offer on other documents used in the question. Thus, documents are significant not only as separate items, but also as a part of the entire series of documents. Questions are designed to be exercises in both analysis and synthesis. In other words, what is expected from students is a coherent essay that integrates the analysis of documents into a treatment of the topic.

Clearly, then, the AP examination that students see in May of each year is the work of both individual and group effort some two years in the making. But there is more to these questions than the work of a benevolent cabal. At the annual reading those secondary and college teachers present (about fifty in European history, one hundred in United States history) are encouraged to offer their criticisms and suggestions. At mini-conferences, meetings, and conventions AP teachers present their views to committee members and ETS consultants. And concerned teacher send letters to the development committees. All of this information and feedback is considered, with much of it either directly or indirectly having an influence on the establishment of policy and the construction of examinations.

What follows now is appended as a postscript. Although the checklist below is not actually used by the development committees, it is in effect considered in the preparation of essay questions. Some teachers, therefore, may find it helpful.

1. Is the question phrased clearly and specifically? Are ambiguous terms eliminated or explained?

2. Is it possible to use an innovative or uniquely stimulating (as opposed to conventional) approach to the housing or phrasing of the question, and thus encourage students to merge remembered or studied information with creativity and imagination?

3. What knowledge is the question intended to elicit? Should students be reasonably expected to be familiar with such knowledge?

4. Does the question ask students to recall information alone, or does it combine recall with reflection, analysis, or application?

5. What writing skills does the question require of students? Should they be prepared to exercise those skills?

6. Does the question clearly specify the mode of development required (e.g., comparison, description, cause-effect)?

7. Can the question be answered fully in the amount of time allotted?

8. Is the subject of the question appropriately related to the material covered in the course?

9. Is the basis for evaluating responses clearly specified?

One final note: question 6 above refers to modes of development, by which it is meant to suggest that good answers to essay questions depend in part upon a clear understanding of the meanings of important directive words. These are the words that indicate the way in which the material is to be presented. Students should be told that while background knowledge of the subject matter is essential, mere evidence of this knowledge is not enough. For example, if they only describe when they are asked to compare, or if they merely list causes when they have been asked to evaluate them, the results will be less than satisfactory. An essay only begins to be correct if it answers directly the question that is asked. What AP examinations cannot provide, but what individual teachers can, is help so that their students are familiar with the meanings of, for example, the following (and know how to proceed when so directed):

Assess: judge the value or character of something; appraise, evaluate. "Assess the relative importance of social factors and economic factors as causes of the Reformation."

Compare: examine for the purpose of noting similarities and differences. "Compare the leadership qualities of Lenin and Stalin."

Contrast: compare in order to show unlikeness or points of difference. "Contrast the rights of serfs in Western and Eastern Europe."

Criticize: make judgments as to merits and faults; criticism may approve or disapprove, or both. "Criticize the Alien and Sedition Acts."

Define: give the meaning of (a word, phrase, concept); determine or fix the boundaries or extent of. "Define the term enlightened despotism."

Describe: give an account of; tell about; give a word picture of. "Describe the events that led to America's entrance into World War II."

Discuss: talk over; write about; consider or examine by argument or from various points of view; debate; present the different sides of. "Discuss the policy of internment of Japanese-Americans during World War II.

Enumerate: mention or list separately; name one after another. "Enumerate the main points of the Bill of Rights."

Evaluate: give the good points and the bad ones; appraise; give an opinion regarding the value of; discuss the advantages and disadvantages. "Evaluate the role played by the United States in the Westernization of Japan."

Explain: make clear or plain; make known in detail; tell the meaning of; make clear the cause or reason of. "Explain how the Medici family were able to rule without holding office."

Illustrate: make clear or intelligible as by examples. "Illustrate the ways in which Europeans exploited Africa and Africans in the nineteenth century."

Interpret: explain the meaning of; make plain; present your thinking about. "Interpret the processes by which medieval civilization declined."

Justify: show good reasons for; present your evidence; offer facts to support your position. "Justify American isolationism in the 1930s."

Prove: establish the truth or genuineness of something by giving factual evidence or logical reasons. "Prove that the Industrial Revolution was or was not a benefit to humankind."

Summarize: state or express in concise form; give the main points briefly. "Summarize the major causes of the Protestant Reformation."

Trace: follow the course of; give a description of the progress of; ascertain by investigation. "Trace the course of nineteenth-century French-German relations.

11. BULL'S-EYE

A Teacher's Guide for Developing Student Skill in Responding to Essay Questions

Are you a hardworking teacher whose students react favorably to what you teach, enjoy time spent in your classroom, and claim to appreciate and learn from your subject matter? Are you also frustrated when students fail to respond on essay exams as you expect? Do their intelligence levels and the quality of their other work suggest that their performance on essay exams does not reflect their abilities? Do your students insist that their essays do not represent their abilities or what they have learned?

If your answer to any of these questions is yes, you are not alone. The problems involved in writing successful essays are not limited to level of teaching or type of student. Graduate students suffer as much as high school students, and gifted students require assistance as well as average students.

Responding effectively to essay questions is not a new problem, but many educators believe it has been aggravated by the erosion of writing and critical thinking skills within our culture as a whole. However serious the problem, I shall contend that it is not irremediable. Persons who seek a solution to the problem may be reminded that a link exists between clear thinking and clear writing, that responding effectively to essay questions is a skill, not an art, and that helping students write essays that reflect their abilities requires extra effort by both teachers and students. It is an effort worth making, because other forms of writing do not replicate skills acquired or perfected by taking essay tests. Essay tests give students practice in writing under pressure and help them learn to create a first draft that communicates clearly, though without the polish of revised and edited prose.

What follows then is a series of suggestions designed to assist teachers and students in developing these skills. Teachers should be aware that what is involved is a process. Just as writing teachers have come to recognize that students improve with instruction in the process of writing (and not merely from more writing, the study of grammar, or the number of the teacher's marks), responses to essay questions can be improved if instruction is understood and presented as a process. Before beginning, however, teachers must prepare the way on their own.

Introspection. The initial step in teaching essay exam writing skills does not involve students. Teachers must take time to reflect upon how their courses are organized and determine what students are expected to learn. Much of the factual material that appears in textbooks and fascinates teachers will, most assuredly, soon be forgotten. In order to do a service to students and our world, we must therefore teach students to think so as to reflect our discipline's contribution to a broad base of wisdom and understanding. As most students will be unable to make this discovery without help, they must be shown how to use facts in essay writing and how critical thinking works within a discipline.

Teachers who routinely demonstrate relationships between parts, explain why something is important, examine a range of interpretations, call attention to prejudices (including their own), and draw comparisons and contrasts exemplify what will help students study, take exams, and move beyond mere note taking and regurgitating recitation. Determining, synthesizing, and linking facts, significance, meaning, analysis, and cause and effect are central to virtually all courses. They are also keys to good citizenship and success in life. They must, therefore, be repeatedly demonstrated in class as part of all assignments so as to impress upon students their value over and above course content. For the process to work and improvement to be evident, students must practice constantly—at first orally in class and then on exams.

Question writing. The second step, like the first, also involves teachers working alone—or preferably in consultation with other teachers who review one another's material—because effective student responses to essay exams depend on well-constructed questions. Questions that are awkwardly phrased, carelessly worded, unclearly related to course goals, or vague in the directions provided make the students' task more difficult. Although these concerns are not the focus of this paper, their importance is illustrated by the following question: "Were the victorious powers in World War I justified in including a 'war guilt clause' in the Treaty of Versailles of 1919 blaming Germany for the war?"

If such a question does not explicitly ask that the answer given be justified, then "yes" or "no" would be a complete answer. Although the writer of the question might expect students to address political, social, intellectual, and economic developments in Germany and elsewhere to support the position taken, that intent is not evident in the question itself. Instead, the question would be clearer and much improved with the addition of the following: "Defend you answer by demonstrating whether conditions in Europe warranted such action."[135]

General directions. Once good questions have been formulated and teachers have demonstrated the thinking of their disci-

---

135. For more specific direction, see my articles, "A Guide to the Skill of Essay Construction in History," *Social Education* 45, no. 3 (March 1981): 178-82; "How Advanced Placement History Questions Are Prepared—and How Yours Can Be Too," *AHA Perspectives* 20, no. 8 (November 1981): 23-25. Of related value are "Designing Effective Writing Assignments," chap. 6 in *Teaching and Assessing Writing*, ed. Edward M. White (San Francisco: Jossey-Bass, 1985) and J.C. Bean et al., "Microtheme Strategies for Developing Cognitive Skills," in *Teaching Writing in All Disciplines*, ed. C.W. Griffin (San Francisco: Jossey-Bass, 1982).

plines, they may provide helpful instructions to assist students to perform their best.

Students should be advised to read the examination directions carefully and then the entire set of questions before them. If they are to choose from several questions, they should be instructed to select questions they are best prepared for. If several questions are required, time will need to be budgeted, including setting aside five-to-ten minutes for proofreading. Teachers should point out that it is better to write something on all required questions and that questions assigned a higher value in points should be answered first. Students should also be instructed to respond directly to the question asked, not to different questions that result from their own reformulations. Key words in the instructions may be underscored to make instructions clearer. For example, if part A or part B of a question is to be answered (but not both), 'or' should be underlined and the words 'but not both' added to prevent both parts from being addressed.

Directive words. Good answers to essay questions also depend upon clear understanding of important directive words. Good answers do not require covering the entire territory by writing down everything known; the so-called "shotgun" approach usually backfires. Essay tests measure students' skill in selecting, organizing, and analyzing material in answering a question. Such words as 'analyze,' 'discuss,' and 'compare,' for example, indicate how material is to be presented.

Although background knowledge is essential, merely to display it is insufficient. If students are asked to compare the constitutions of Britain and the United States, they should receive little credit if they only describe them but fail to indicate similarities or differences. If they are asked to evaluate the causes of the French Revolution, they do not answer the question by listing the causes without ranking them in order of significance and justifying their ranking.

An essay answer is satisfactory if and only if it directly answers the question asked.

Teachers should have their own clear understanding of the directive terms they employ in formulating essay questions, and they should with definitions and examples clearly and adequately communicate to student examinees the meanings of such frequently occurring directive terms as *analyze*, *assess*, *compare*, *contrast*, *criticize*, *define*, *describe*, *discuss*, *enumerate*, *evaluate*, *explain*, *identify*, *illustrate*, *interpret*, *justify*, *list*, *prove*, *summarize*, and *trace*.

Planning and organization. Another important prewriting step involves planning an essay response. Students typically, like race horses reacting to the starter's gun, lunge headlong into their answers, hastily writing down everything of direct or even remote relevance they can think of. Thus they should be made aware of the value organization has for achieving clarity. Teachers may wish to establish a "reading period" of five-to-ten minutes, before students are permitted to begin writing in order for them to plan and organize their answers.

Planning and brainstorming and clustering. After choosing the question to be answered and considering the directions provided, students should be advised about the value of brainstorming—that is, to prepare a list of major points to be covered. They should jot down, on the test sheet itself or on scrap paper, what comes immediately to mind as they react to the question in their heads. This resolves the problem of forgetting points thought of at first but not at that moment written about in the essay proper. Students can assess items on the list and expand upon the most important ones, avoiding repetition, addressing elements in order of importance, and grouping—or clustering—them where connections should be made or relationships are observed. The list of points resulting from brainstorming need not be complete, as additional one can be incorporated later, but it is an effective way of seeing the components of an answer at the outset and in perspective. It is also vital for analyzing the question, i.e., for examining it carefully, word for word, to determine precisely what is (and what is not) being asked; equally, it can be of tremendous help in formulating a thesis.

Introduction and thesis. The reading or planning period should be used for outlining and structuring the essay. A well-organized essay, complete with a thematic introduction, body of supporting evidence, and conclusion, will be more favorably received than one that lacks clear structure. Stressing this, the teacher should explain what an introduction is and its role in the essay. Emphasis should be placed on the role and value of a thesis statement that answers the question directly, shows that thought will likely inform the response, and points out the direction the paper will take. A thesis statement should state a brief answer to the question, as if a sentence or two would suffice (supporting evidence follows); it should not merely describe the scheme of organization. In other words, instruct students, instead of stating what they will discuss, to state the meaning and significance of what they will discuss. Valuable time should not be spent (wasted?) repeating or paraphrasing the question that is already on the exam itself.

Historical setting (background and consequences). History students should be instructed how to establish a historical setting for their responses; what happened before the subject of the question and what resulted afterward should be considered in planning a complete essay, although such background should be concise and directly relevant to the rest of the essay. This will help students to think historically and encourage them to understand the significance of an event in the broader context of what preceded and followed it. Teachers of other disciplines can provide instructions that reflect the characteristics of their fields.

Body and thesis. The body of an essay should not consist only or primarily of factual information. Answers are stronger if historical (literary, scientific, etc.) analysis or argument is provided. Students should be encouraged to express opinions, but such thinking should show use of material to arrive at an understanding of the question. Arguments should be sound and their conclusions based on facts presented; examples should be relevant to the question. Instruct students to use evidence to substantiate all generalizations and to draw generalizations and conclusions from factual material presented. As the body of the essay is developed, the thesis must be kept in mind and even modified if warranted by the evidence adduced. Time is limited, so students must guard against being distracted by tangential issues. Everything contained in the essay, including the conclusion, should support the thesis and be relevant to answering the question.

Conclusion. In addition, the differences between a conclusion and a summary require explanation and examples. Students typically understand a conclusion to be primarily a repetition of the main points (that is, a summary), but they will better demonstrate thinking skills if they determine the significance, meaning, and results of those points—that is, a conclusion—as well.

Proofreading. Several minutes for proofreading should be scheduled in the time allotted for the examination. It is common to misspell even simple words, omit letters or words, or transpose numbers and letters when writing under pressure. Students should be alerted to reread their essays in order to confirm that the words they use convey the meaning they intend. Although unity, organization, and development are most important to communicate clearly in an essay examination, correct spelling and grammar improve the quality of every essay.

In-class practice. All these suggestions will have minimal effect if they are only cited orally or in writing. The most effective way to ensure that students both understand and know how to implement them is to devote class time to practicing what is preached, to going through the essential steps of responding to essay questions.

Teachers should outline on the white- or blackboard an effective answer to sample essay questions, thinking aloud as they proceed step-by-step, showing how to analyze a question, brainstorm, formulate an introduction and thesis, provide supporting evidence, and finally draw a conclusion implied by the evidence that answers the question and incorporates the thesis. Students can then, orally and as a class, practice the same exercise, with as many students as possible contributing while the teacher outlines their collective contributions on the board for all to see. Students can also gain appreciation for effective responses when they create their own essay questions and respond to those of their classmates; evaluating others' answers is a constructive learning experience.

Model and practice essays. Whenever possible, model essays—both well done and poorly done—should be distributed (or otherwise made available) and reviewed by the class, with the teacher highlighting positive and negative characteristics; students could also, collectively or in small groups, critique essays in a like fashion. After students see these differences and internalize the process of essay writing, they should be given practice essay questions to answer.

Teacher comments. When the practice essays are completed, two important steps that remain are (1) teachers writing comments and (2) students rewriting their practice essays. Most teachers, at best, make only a few general comments, like captions to cartoons, to go along with the essay grade— for example, "well done," "good evidence but weak conclusion," "the question is answered only indirectly." Most do not ordinarily allow students to rewrite their answers. General comments, however, are inadequate as constructive direction. To improve students' essay-writing skills, extensive teacher comments and student rewriting are necessary. If students are not shown a better way, they will perpetuate their mistakes rather than learn from them.[136]

In marginal and in general comments on student essays, teachers should explain what students do well or poorly and why. Comments are most effective when they lead students themselves to make the corrections or improvements. For

---

136. See my article, "Writing in the Major: A Novel Approach That Works," *Perspectives* 24, no. 5 (May/June 1986): 10-13; and Barbara E. Fassler Walvoord, *Helping Students Write Well: A Guide for Teachers in All Disciplines* (New York: Modern Library Association, 1982).

example: "Introduction provides general information only and lacks a thesis or point of view relevant to the question; try using enough of that information to whet the reader's appetite and then lead into a thesis based directly on the question"; "How is this material relevant to your answer? You leave it to the reader to make the connection when you should be doing the work, and the thinking"; "This is a summary of earlier points, not a conclusion. A proper conclusion should answer the question by amplifying on the thesis and demonstrating what is important about the subject based on the evidence you have provided." The more specific the comments, the better, and they may be in the form of statements or questions.

Teacher comments should focus on written expression as well as content. Emphasis on content alone does not enable students to appreciate the link between knowledge and expression, between information and communication. (An alternative approach, albeit a less personal one, for those teachers who recognize the value of such comments but find it difficult to allot the time to write as many as are necessary, would be to prepare a checklist of commonly used comments. Such a list, appropriately marked and returned to students along with their essays, could be an effective compromise between individualized notations and doing little or nothing; it could be to teachers what proofreaders' symbols are to editors. Still another time-saving alternative would be to require students to submit a blank cassette tape with each exam. Teachers could then read and react audibly, connecting specific comments and suggestions to particular pages and paragraphs. The would enable teachers to be more thorough with limited time, and it could also be used to help students develop an *ear* for the sound of good writing [e.g., "John, listen to what you wrote!...How does that sound compared to this?... It should sound clearer and more to the point. I want you to try rewriting the following sentences:…].)

Rewriting. With the benefit of teachers' pointed comments, students should be asked to respond again to the same question. Experience has shown that with repetition of the process, students show improvement. Teachers should further consider allowing students to earn a higher grade by revising their graded essay exams (also turning in the first response at the same time so as to make grading the rewrite less time-consuming). Students will thus more likely make an effort to understand and use teacher suggestions. Or, the essay test could serve as a first draft for a brief out-of-class assignment to revise and resubmit the essay. Students would have more time to develop ideas, polish their prose, focus on the shortcomings of their essays, and consider what they might do to improve.

Additional suggestions. A few related suggestions are worth considering: (1) As dedicated teachers are usually overworked, one way to assign sufficient practice essay writing, but without the burden of most of the grading, is to use what I call the "fish skeleton approach"; this is where a standard essay is assigned but students turn in only the following: a paragraph introduction and thesis statement, an outline of the body of the response (i.e., listing, but not developing, what the evidence would be), and then another paragraph by way of a conclusion. The student still must prepare as if writing a full answer, but the teacher has much less to read and yet can still gauge the student's performance and progress.

(2) In written and oral comments, it is constructive if teachers make at least some positive comments so as to encourage even the poorest students. (3) If possible, teachers should arrange to meet individually with students to review their essays and the teacher's comments; it is a way to determine whether instruction is understood. (4) Finally, over-marking should be avoided. Just as students will not learn if teachers fail to say anything useful, they may not learn if teachers write so many comments that they are overwhelmed; instead, consider focusing on two or three major issues and, until rewrites or subsequent papers, ignore the rest.

The above suggestions will consume valuable class time, but developing writing and thinking skills is vital to learning and should not be relegated to English teachers alone. What is sacrificed in subject matter will be offset by what is gained in improved skills and comprehension.

12. ADVANCED PLACEMENT EUROPEAN HISTORY

An Anatomy of the Essay Examination, 1956-2000

The College Board's Advanced Placement European History examination, like the program it reflects, is akin to a living organism. Accordingly, it has evolved over the course of its first half-century of existence in virtually all respects: the types and subject matter of questions asked (and not asked); the nature of the history those questions reflect; the number of questions both offered and to be answered, as well as how they have been and not been grouped; the time allotted to answer those questions; the way questions have been worded in order to elicit thought-induced responses rather than those based on memorization of facts; in terms of sensitivity to issues of class, gender, geography, ethnicity, and matters of faith.[137] This is perhaps the kind of *evolution* we all can agree on: a reflection of the mixture of change and continuity that characterizes both history itself and the evolution of the survey of European history course, a reflection, too, of how we as teachers and scholars evolve during the

---

137. For an overview of the AP Program writ large, see Eric Rothschild, "Four Decades of the Advanced Placement Program," *The History Teacher* 32:2 (February 1999): 175-205. Not incidentally, AP is owned by the College Board which, in turn, has a contract with the Educational Testing Service to develop and score the exams.

course of our careers, all in an effort, one hopes, to do a still better job, to get closer to ever-elusive perfection, to learn from our own history as we would hope our students have learned from the history we teach them.

What follows is an examination of the exam, a window into its soul, an anatomization of forty-five years of essay questions (540 such questions in all, with a high per exam of thirty-one, in 1956, to the current seven, which it has been since 1976) with the idea that they will reveal some useful, if not provocative, characteristics about a program—as well as the discipline of history—in which thousands of secondary school and college/university teachers have invested so heavily.

Now, it is probably fair to say that the essay exam questions we construct as individual teachers tend for the most part to be predictable—at least in terms of their being based on the questions we answered when we were students and on those we have already constructed ourselves—and not especially creative. After all, with that exam we are preparing to administer only a week or two (or even a day or two) away, and with all the other responsibilities—academic and non-academic—competing for our limited time, few of us have the spare hours and energy to do too much more than the ordinary. Surpassing what is generally so routine, however, are the AP essay questions that are meticulously crafted—typically over a period of two-to-three years— by the dedicated teams of secondary school and university historians who have comprised the test development committees in European History.[138] To be sure, there are likely to be shortcomings in the finished product in any given year, and this paper will sometimes call attention to such flaws. After all, with hindsight, and reflecting individual preferences and prejudices, we can often see which questions didn't function according to plan, or how some questions could have been improved, or what subjects and sensibilities were ignored. That said, it is still the

---

138. For further explanation, see Robert Blackey, "How Advanced Placement History Essay Questions Are Prepared—and How Yours Can Be Too," *Perspectives* 20:8 (November 1982): 23-25.

contention here that nothing matches the quality, creativity, and variety of questions written under the umbrella of AP European History (APEH)—and we can all learn from the experience of nearly a half century of essay question writing and careful after-administration analysis.

In the Beginning

The first APEH Examination Committee (as the Test Development Committee was then called) consisted of three college/university professors— Thomas Mendenhall of Yale University, Kenneth Walker of Goucher College, and Henry R. Winkler of Rutgers University[139]—who were assisted by Elizabeth Kimball of the Educational Testing Service and a Ph.D. in history. That first exam in 1956 —taken by fifty-nine students[140] and graded by four Readers, one of whom taught at a secondary school—consisted of thirty-one questions divided into two parts. Part A was itself divided into five time periods (1450-1603, 1603-1715, 1715-1815, 1815-1870, 1870-1939), with each period offering five questions; students were required to answer two questions, both from one period, at a half hour per question. Part B included six questions[141], one of which was to be answered in

---

139. The author acknowledges his gratitude to Henry R. Winkler, professor emeritus and former president of the University of Cincinnati, for his considerate response to an e-mail request for information and insight into the early years of the program. Interested readers should also see Henry R. Winkler, "The Advanced Placement Program and Examination in European History," *Social Education* 25:7 (November 1961): 332-42. This 1961 article also includes the entire APEH exam for 1958, including the multiple-choice questions; the next time a complete exam was published was 1984. Also of note is that the first Examination Committee did not include secondary school teachers.

140. For a year-by-year tally of the number of students taking the exam, from 1956 to 1998, see Rothschild, "Four Decades of the Advanced Placement Program," 206.

141. The wide choice of questions, in Parts A and B, came as a result of not wanting "to prescribe a rigid and arbitrary curriculum" but rather trying

the recommended time of one hour; these were broader, often sweeping questions, dealing with issues that cut across countries and centuries, on such issues as balance of power, revolt versus reform, the characterizations given to historical ages, the conflict between church and state, and international systems set up after wars to preserve the peace.

The Examination Committee held that it was important not "to prescribe a rigid and arbitrary curriculum," and that a wide range of courses and approaches existed that might serve as appropriate preparation for the exam; they "deliberately eschewed unusual or experimental material as likely to be unfair to most of the" students. The hope was to offer questions that were sufficiently broad and varied in order to enable "students to use their own particular strengths most effectively," while demanding "a minimum common denominator of general historical knowledge."[142] Thus the questions that first year (as they mostly were for the first fifteen years) covered traditional subject matter, with the majority classifiable under the rubric of what is now the political/diplomatic theme. For example, "ages" were viewed politically (as the above five chronological periods indicate and when questions were formed around the "Elizabethan era," the "age of Louis XIV," and "between the two world wars") and dates of "turning points" pivoted mostly around wars, revolutions, treaties, and reigns. Where social rank or status were involved, attention was paid to what was accepted as integral to traditional history, such as Renaissance gentlemen, Calvinist theologians, or eighteenth-century philosophes. Religious subjects typically meant aspects of the Reformation; cultural history was often represented by the Renaissance, the Enlightenment, or Romanticism; and economic history usually covered the Price Revolution, mercantilism, or the Industrial

to make it possible for all students, regardless of how the course they took was taught, "to have a fair shot at using their knowledge and reflection in an appropriate way." Winkler's e-mail to author, December 21, 2000.

142. Winkler, "The Advanced Placement Program and Examination in European History," 333.

Revolution.

Following the exam a detailed postmortem was conducted, the results of which were summarized in the annual Chief Reader's Report. Among other things, it was agreed that the exam was "much too difficult for the purposes it is designed to achieve. Its level turned out to be that of perhaps a senior [college] comprehensive.... The scope of the questions was often too broad to be handled both from the point of view of the time allotted and from the standpoint of a reasonable expectation of training for school seniors or college freshmen." But the report also concluded that "the exam unquestionably *carries out the intention of the Advanced Placement Program* in requiring that students of European History go beyond mere accumulation of facts and textbook knowledge and that they exercise critical judgment and show thoughtful interpretation." Thus, what was recommended for subsequent exams were not "fundamental changes in the *nature* of the material, but...that the examination should be posed in sharper, more clearly defined terms, and that the time element be given fuller consideration."[143] Although the nature of the exam has, indeed, changed—just as the way history has been perceived has changed—test development committees from the start have been grappling with the problem of how to be comprehensive in coverage while posing questions sharply and clearly. In other words, a posture of critical self-evaluation has characterized the program from the very beginning.

Structural and Format Changes

The initial structure of the exam did not survive the first year without modification. The Readers themselves recommended consolidating the number of periods (which eventually happened in 1961 and then again in 1970[144]) and reducing the num-

---

143. Winkler, *Chief Reader's Report*, 1956.

144. Between 1961 and 1967 the periods were: 1450-1660, 1660-1789, 1789-1870, 1870-1939. For 1968 and 1969 the four periods were reconfigured

ber of questions offered within each period. Thus, for 1957 each of the five periods in Part A now presented four questions (down from five) while the number of choices in Part B was reduced from six to three (or a total of twenty-three questions).[145] This format effectively remained in place, with modifications—with respect to chronological boundaries, periodization definitions, and numbers of questions to choose from—through the 1972 exam, and there are at least a couple of ways to assess its longevity. First, it recognized and thus reflected the chronological and geographical breadth of the APEH course and the consequent difficulty for teachers to cover all periods effectively and for students to prepare for all equally well. Thus for Part A, students were instructed to choose, according to the directions, "the period of European history in which you consider yourself best prepared." Second, and more cynically, is to see the requirement to choose two questions in Part A from the same period as inadvertently signaling a teaching/test-taking strategy that encouraged a great deal of attention to be focused on one period and less on the others in order to help assure quality work on those two essays. But for students to prepare this way

---

to 1500-1660, 1660-1789, 1789-1870, 1870-1945 (i.e., a later starting date by fifty years and a termination date that incorporated World War II). In 1970 the number of periods was reduced once again: Italian Renaissance to 1715, 1715-1850, 1850-1953 (i.e., a less precise starting date, but understood to include the High Renaissance, or from about 1450, and a termination date that advanced the course to the Cold War). Dividing questions into chronological periods ended with the 1972 exam. The modern termination date would be advanced periodically, to the mid-1960s for the 1973 exam, to 1970 for the 1986 exam, and "to the present" in time for the 1997 exam.

145. From 1961-69 there were four questions in each of the four periods in Part A, three in Part B (a total of nineteen). For 1970 and 1971 there were four questions in each of the three periods in Part A, three in Part B (although in 1971 there were just two questions in Part B, a total of fifteen and fourteen, respectively). In 1972 the three periods in Part A included three questions each, while Part B was returned to three (a total of twelve). When periods and parts were discarded, in 1973, the total number of questions was reduced to ten. Finally, in 1976, the total number of questions was reduced to seven, where it has remained, although in 1994 a new grouping was introduced.

would have been to prepare poorly, as the remaining periods could not be given too short shrift, because Part B typically involved questions requiring students to be familiar with the material from at least two periods, and, of course, the multiple-choice portion of the exam required students to be familiar with all periods.

Almost in anticipation of a more significant change the following year, the 1972 exam invited students, in Part A, to choose their two questions from which ever period or periods they wished; in 1973, the division of essay questions into chronological groups and into two parts was abandoned altogether. The new format presented students with ten questions from which only two had to be answered in the allotted two hours[146]

146. For the first seven years of the program two hours were allotted for the essay portion of the exam. Then, in 1963, ten minutes was removed from the one question chosen from Part B in order to accommodate an expanded multiple-choice section. In 1970 the ten minutes were restored and each of the three questions to be answered was allotted equal weight. When the chronological groupings and the division of the questions into two parts, A and B, were abandoned, in 1973, the total time devoted to answer the two questions chosen (from the ten offered) was one hour and fifty minutes. Next, when the Document-Based Question (DBQ) became a regular feature of the exam, in 1975, students were given sixty minutes to answer it and another sixty for the sole Free-Response Question (FRQ). Then, in 1977, and in order to accommodate additional multiple-choice questions, the FRQ was reduced to forty-five minutes, with the DBQ holding at one hour. The absent fifteen minutes was restored to the FRQ section in 1981. In 1983 some additional juggling was done with the clock: a fifteen-minute reading, planning, and analyzing period was introduced (primarily to accommodate the DBQ) and the suggested time for each question, DBQ and FRQ, was forty-five minutes. Another significant change came in 1994, in tandem with the new requirement of two FRQs: one hour was to be devoted to those two questions (or one-half hour each, as had been the case in the early years of the program), while the fifteen-minute reading period along with the forty-five minutes for the DBQ remained the same. Finally, at least for twentieth-century changes, ten additional minutes were added to the FRQ section in 1996. If you, dear reader, have kept track of all these changes, you may go to the head of your class and you are prepared to face the inevitable changes of the next century. One other point: an additional—but by no means the only—reason for some of these changes in time allotments as well as in

(i.e., up until this time students were always required to respond to a total of three questions). On national history exams, therefore, little is written in stone, as would become obvious in time for the 1975 exam.

Following the lead of AP United States (APUS) History (which launched it in 1973), APEH entered the age of the Document-Based Question (DBQ).[147] It appeared as the only required question among the ten offered, with students having to choose one more from the remaining nine. In 1976, the choice was reduced from nine to six, a distribution—one DBQ and six free-response questions (FRQs)—that has remained in place ever since, with but one modification. In 1994 those six FRQs were divided into two groups, with students now required to answer two, with one from each group, a return to a total of three essays as was the structure from 1956 to 1972, except that the earlier use of grouping questions, it will be recalled, was chronological. This time, however, there was no discernible pattern to the division. That is, in 1994 the groupings were indeed chronological, with Group 1 questions covering the period 1450 through the eighteenth century and Group 2 questions covering the nineteenth and twentieth centuries. But such a division was not the case for the exams in the following years. Other patterns might be discerned within any single exam, but collectively they defy prediction (as does most everything else about the content of AP essay questions). For example, in the 1996 exam all Group 1 questions were introduced with the charge to "compare and contrast," while Group 2 questions dealt with things social (roles,

---

the weighting of essay and multiple-choice questions has to do with ETS's concern for grading consistency and reliability. That is, the more multiple-choice questions and the greater their weight vis-a-vis essay questions—so the thinking goes—the greater the reliability will be the final scores.

147. For more information, see Michael S. Henry, "The Intellectual Origins and Impact of the Document-Based Question," *Perspectives* 24:2 (February 1986): 14-16, and Stephen F. Klein, "The Genesis of Shorter Document-Based Questions in the Advanced Placement American History Examination," *Perspectives* 21:5 (May-June 1983): 22-24.

groups, and consequences); for 1997, Group 1 questions were concerned with the control of some people by others, whereas those in Group 2 seemed to share nothing in common; there was another chronological division in 1998, but then in 1999 all of Group 1 featured questions built around images (paintings and photographs), although they otherwise shared nothing in common; and for the 2000 exam, Group 1 questions focused on political and/or economic themes while those in Group 2 were centered on intellectual and/or social themes. In other words, the only discernible pattern—for those who strain to discover them—is that there is no discernible pattern.

Course Descriptions and Themes

As the founders of APEH constructed the course description, or syllabus (as it was often referred to during the early years of the program), their major consideration was "diversity," by which was meant that introductory college courses in European history were different from one another in a way that did not characterize other disciplines (i.e., there was no commonly accepted core of material). Some, according to Henry Winkler, began in ancient times or in the Middle Ages, while others concentrated on the period since 1815. "Controversy over 'coverage' and 'penetration,' over 'understanding in depth' versus the 'overview' has raged for many years."[148] As a result, the early course descriptions were seen to represent a compromise, with the essay section of the exam confined to Europe after 1450.

The course description, conceived and organized chronologically, also included sample topics (the precursor of what is currently itemized under themes) that might be covered in each of the five (then four, then three) time periods. These topics, as with the terminal dates of each period, were primarily determined according to generally accepted and traditional means

---

148. Winkler, "The Advanced Placement Program and Examination in European History," 332.

of structuring a course in European history. That means that political and politically-oriented events and phenomena were the driving force, although each period usually included mainline aspects of economic, social, cultural, and intellectual history. For example, suggested for the period 1789-1870 were: the French Revolution, Napoleon, and the French imperium; the Concert of Europe; romanticism, liberalism, the conservative reaction; the revolutions of 1848, the impact on liberal nationalism; unification movements; reform movements, English and continental; Socialism, Utopian and Marxian; the industrial transformation of Europe; evolution and mechanism in science and social science. These topics were considered sufficiently broad and varied to accommodate individual courses and to enable students to adapt their strengths to any given exam while demanding from them "a minimum common denominator of general historical knowledge."[149] But that common denominator—part of the compromise that was reached in the development of the course description—is what Winkler recently acknowledged as now being "old-fashioned history—political, economic, cultural and social in largely public context,"[150] which is to say the compromise was over coverage and chronology, not untraditional themes or potentially competing approaches to teaching APEH.[151]

---

149. Ibid., 333.

150. Winkler's e-mail to author, December 21, 2000.

151. For example, for the 1967 exam, the period 1450-1660 included the new learning and art of the Renaissance and economic and social aspects of the Reformation, while the period 1870-1939 included science, literature, and society, the capitalism of the large firm, and the impact of the world-wide depression on the social and economic order. For the 1968 exam, most of the topics remained the same or were similar, although for the period 1870-1945 "science, literature, and society" was reworded to "changing concepts of the universe, man, society, and the arts" and "the capitalism of the large firm" was eliminated. And then for the 1970 through 1972 exams, which was just before the transition from a chronological to a thematic structure, some revised topics were introduced, including the classical Renaissance and the Baroque for the period Italian Renaissance to 1715

And yet, however large the AP program has become, however monolithic ETS and the College Board might appear, test development committees have always sought to be responsive to their constituency. Teachers at the first AP conferences, for example, successfully convinced the European history examination committee to make a change, because "to lengthen the time span of the earlier periods [e.g., from 1450-1603 to 1450-1660] would give them greater flexibility in presenting the material of their courses to their students."[152] Another such conference, in 1972, contributed to more dramatic, even revolutionary, changes. Before turning to them, however, it would be instructive first to dissect the annual exams in order to determine their character.

Between 1956 and 1972, during which time the traditional APEH course description was in place, political/diplomatic questions predominated; where the remaining questions could certainly be classified as being in the domain of intellectual/cultural and social/economic history[153], they were, as Winkler noted, largely in a "public context." Let's be more specific. For the 1956 exam, for example (and always acknowledging that some questions melded two or more themes), of the twenty-five questions in Part A, nineteen were primarily political/diplomatic, while the six involving other themes addressed some of the traditional components of European history courses: conflicting interpretations about the religious side of the Reformation; the degree to which the Renaissance was a

---

and social structures in prerevolutionary Europe and society and culture in the Age of Metternich for the period 1715-1850. But the period 1850-1953 dropped reference to the world-wide depression while essentially retaining "changing concepts of man, society, science, and the arts."

152. Winkler, "The Advanced Placement Program and Examination in European History," 333.

153. Political/diplomatic, intellectual/cultural, and social/economic are the categories of themes that have been in place since 1972-73, and they are being used to describe questions from 1956-72 to lend consistency to the analysis.

rebirth or an acceleration of tempo; mercantilism as a political and economic doctrine; whether persecution was successful in the seventeenth century; reason as an eighteenth-century yardstick for appraising human institutions; and when the Industrial Revolution might best be said to have begun and why.

From 1956 through the 1972 exam, out of a total of 282 questions offered in Part A 182, or 64.5%, were primarily linked to political/diplomatic subjects; the remaining 100, or 35.5%, mostly concentrated on intellectual/cultural (sixty-seven or 23.8%) and social/economic (thirty-three or 11.7%) topics. Questions in Part B followed a similar pattern, but with a difference: they were broader-based, often covering more than one time period or age or region/country (with choices—including choices of themes to emphasize—built into each question); they encouraged students to think more broadly than the way issues are usually treated in textbooks and, perhaps, in class. In that respect, they required students to be creative and to think historically by seeing bigger pictures and more intricate patterns.[154] For example, in 1956 they concentrated on: the idea of worldwide frontiers; turning points; toleration; possession of wealth; balance of power; and the state and society. In 1957 they dealt

---

154. Such questions, however, often presented grading problems insofar as preparing standards and rubrics are concerned, especially when they swept widely and allowed for a great variety of options; according to an e-mail communication to me from Phil Kintner, a former Chief Reader, they also were a challenge to Readers who "were not well enough trained to handle all the quantities involved." [For example, question #21, from 1960: "In which of the following centuries has man's cruelty to man been the most extensive and in which the least extensive? The sixteenth century/ The seventeenth century/The eighteenth century/The nineteenth century/ The twentieth century." Reprinted by permission of the College Entrance Examination Board, the copyright owner.] And such questions have a tendency to encourage students to over-generalize at the expense of specific supporting evidence. Nevertheless, the value of questions that are broader based, at least to a degree (e.g., involving comparisons between events in different countries or from different times periods), was acknowledged by the Test Development Committee when, in 1994, the FRQs were again divided into two groups.

with: Machiavelli's influence on other periods of history; main world problems at the turns of centuries; and the relative value of revolt and reform.

A telling postscript to this domination by traditional questions are a couple from 1957 and 1958 (one on the relative influence of the mob during the French Revolution versus individuals, ideas, or accident, the other on whether the Industrial Revolution substituted the tyranny of the masses for the tyranny of the classes) that can be seen as the first social history questions that fell outside the "public context." But it wasn't until the early 1970s that clearer signs suggested that the times were, indeed, a-changin', at least insofar as themes are concerned and that APEH was reflecting shifts in the larger discipline of history. In fact, the way in which the program was being reformulated coincided with the publication of a new generation of Western civilization textbooks that were giving thorough survey-level coverage, as well as new attention, to social, economic, and cultural history more broadly conceived than in what were then the standard texts, especially *A History of the Modern World* by Palmer and Colton. So, for example, *The Western Experience* by Chambers et al. was first published in 1974 and *A History of Western Society* by McKay, Hill, and Buckler first appeared in 1979.

1970 witnessed the first cultural history question focused entirely on the arts: although it dealt with familiar historical periods (classicism and romanticism), students who chose it had to write about one of three pairs of artists (Mozart/Beethoven, David/Delacroix, Pope/Wordsworth) and how the chosen pair were representative of the two periods. This was a noteworthy detour from traditional APEH questions, and although it was not the selection of many students, future test development committees would periodically include more like it, along with other, less orthodox subject areas. The 1972 exam reflected the existence of additional winds of change and revealed a different kind of shift: although there were still more political/diplomatic-themed questions than either of the other two thematic areas, for the first time the number was only a plurality, not a majority; in fact, that exam was balanced thematically as no previous exam had been.

During the same month the 1972 exam was administered, another AP history conference signaled further changes and challenges. Keynote speaker Charles Keller—historian and first chair of the APUS examination committee—advocated that the history we teach and test should be interdisciplinary and more clearly related to the world around us.[155] The APEH examination committee also considered these issues as it undertook a re-evaluation of goals and methods,[156] with the result that the new course description identified several forthcoming critical changes, the most important of which were that new stress was to be placed on European contacts with other peoples and cultures and that a clear thematic structure was to replace the largely topical/chronological one. And it is this thematic structure— with a few additions and modifications over the years—that has remained as the framework for the APEH course today.[157]

---

155. For a more thorough look at what happened at this conference and at its implications, see Mildred Alpern, "Advanced Placement European History," *The College Board Review* 93 (Fall 1974): 2-6, 26-27.

156. Lawrence Beaber, "Changes in the Advanced Placement in European History Program," *AHA Newsletter* 11:2 (May 1973): 38.

157. Initially there were six themes: (1) Political: Toward Egalitarian National States, including the extension of political democracy and parliamentary governments; the rise of the modern state and the development of its variant forms; the development of political parties, programs, and ideologies; the extension and limitation of individual civil rights and freedoms; forms of political dissent, reform, and revolution; types of political dominance: federalism, colonialism, and imperialism; (2) Intellectual: Changing Concepts of Man, God, and the Universe, including the scientific revolutions: attitudes, concepts, and consequences; the visual and performing arts as statements of cultural values and evidence of historical changes; the developments in philosophical thought and their relationship to traditional religious ideas and institutions; the rise of the social and behavioral sciences and their relation to the development of historical studies; forms and content in fictional literature as reflections of and evidence of historical growth; the development of the mass media

and their influence upon the formation of popular cultural values and egalitarian attitudes; (3) Social and Cultural: The Rise of a Mass Urban Society, including the changing social structures from hereditary classes to egalitarian individualism; the role of the city in the changing of cultural values and social patterns; modes of social mobility and the responses of traditional societies to modernization; conflicts of cultural and social values in emerging and developed mass societies; competitive ideas and theories of the nature of man and societies; the interactions between elites and masses; (4) Economic: The Growth of an Industrial Technology, including the origins and developments of the Industrial Revolution; the growth of competition and interdependence in national and world markets; the relationships between private and state contributions to economic growth; the changing forms and organization of labor supply; transportation, communication, and finance capital in economic modernization; economic theories as a basis for social and political programs; (5) International Relations: The Emergence of World Politics, including the rise and spread of the modern state as a competitive and cooperative form of power relationships; systems of interstate accord and conflict: diplomacy, war, and power blocs; attempts to restrain interstate conflicts from balance of power diplomacy and international law to international organization; reform movements and revolutions as responses to international and intercultural tensions; the rise of major non-European powers and their effect upon the European powers; the consequences of technological advances and egalitarian democracy on the development of international political affairs; (6) Intercultural Responses: Europe and the Wider World, including the impact upon Europe of increasing contact with and involvement in the non-European world; problems of racial and cultural contact and conflict; the missionary aspect of Christianity and its contribution to the spread of European culture; the social and political consequences of economic modernization in the non-European cultures; the rise of Europeanized intellectual and technical elites to leadership in non-European cultures.

Then, for the 1975 exam, some changes were made. The number of themes was reduced from six to five, with the intellectual theme and the social and cultural theme amalgamated and with the descriptions that were part of each theme name dropped. Some of the subjects subsumed under the themes were modified slightly, but most were essentially the same. Only in the newly combined Social and Intellectual theme were the changes more clearly noticeable, but even here it was largely in terms of eliminating some subjects and combining others: the scientific revolutions: attitudes, concepts, and consequences; the visual and performing arts and literature as statements of cultural values and as historical evidence; the developments in social and philosophical thought and their relationship to traditional ideas

The exam in 1973, the first under the new structure, told the story of these changes both in the format and in the types of questions asked. As noted above, the grouping of questions into two parts and several chronological periods was discarded in favor of ten essays (one following the other, and based upon the new themes), two of which had to be selected by students. There

and institutions; the role of the city in changing cultural values and social patterns; the shift in social structures from hierarchical orders to modern social classes and the interaction between elites and masses; the formation of popular cultural values and attitudes in developed and in emerging mass societies.

Finally, with the 1977 exam, additional changes were made to the structure of the themes, and these newly-combined sets of three themes have remained in place ever since: (1) Political and Diplomatic History, including the rise of the modern state in its various forms; the development of political parties and ideologies; the extension and limitation of individual civil liberties; the rise of nationalism; forms of political protest, reform, and revolution; types of colonialism and imperialism; interstate conflict: diplomacy, war, and power blocs; relationship of European and non-European powers, including decolonization; relationship between domestic and foreign policies; efforts to restrain interstate conflict: treaties, balance of power diplomacy, and international organizations; (2) Intellectual and Cultural History, including the secularization of learning and culture; changes in religious thought and organization; the scientific revolution and its consequences; major trends in literature and the arts as statements of cultural values and as historical evidence; developments in social thought (economic and political theory, etc.); the spread of literacy; the diffusion of new intellectual concepts among different social groups; changes in popular culture such as the development of new attitudes toward religion, toward the family, toward work; (3) Social and Economic History, including the role of the city in changing cultural values and social relationships; the shift in social structures from hierarchical orders to modern social classes; changes in the nature of elites and their interaction with the lower classes; the development of commercial practices and their economic and social impact; the origins and development of industrialization; changes in the European demographic structure; changes and continuities in the European family structure and relationships; the growth of competition and interdependence in national and world markets; the relationships between private and state contributions to economic growth.

Subsequently, there would be the occasional modification and addition to the subjects subsumed under each theme, but nothing more.

was also a balance among the ten questions: three representing the political/diplomatic theme (which, for the first time, did not comprise either a majority or even a plurality of the total), three intellectual/cultural, and four social/economic. From the first theme the questions were on the new continental political order between 1815 and 1848; the factors that precipitated the major political revolutions of Europe; and how the defeated states were treated by the victors after 1815 and after 1945. Questions from the second theme dealt with the origins and critics of classical liberalism; Western attitudes toward China and Japan in the nineteenth and twentieth centuries; and the novel as a documentary source for historians. For the third theme, questions focused on how European cities were changed by the Industrial Revolution; incentives to economic development between 1650 and 1800; motives for the European penetration of Africa in different time periods; and the social and cultural roles of hereditary aristocracy in the eighteenth century and of totalitarian elite in the twentieth. Thus, the exam reflected the new thematic approach, but in doing so it also included several traditional-style questions for those students prepared along traditional lines, as well as questions that were a combination of the old and the new.[158]

To conclude this section on course descriptions and themes, let's evaluate how effectively the essay questions from 1973 to 2000 have adhered to the new guidelines. The exams during those twenty-eight years consisted of a total of 205 questions

---

158. Sometimes during these years traditional subject matter was introduced in refreshing new ways, as for example with question #5 from 1991 ("Between 1815 and 1848 the condition of the laboring classes and the problem of political stability were critical issues in England. Describe and analyze the reforms that social critics and politicians of this period proposed to resolve these problems.") and question #3 from 1994, which mixed a traditional political question about women rulers with social history issues, in this case "how issues of gender, such as marriage and reproduction, influenced their ability to obtain and exercise power." Reprinted by permission of the College Entrance Examination Board, the copyright owner.

(including DBQs, which were introduced in 1975), of which eighty-two, or 40%, were political/diplomatic, fifty-seven, or 27.8%, were intellectual/cultural, and sixty-six, or 32.2%, were social/economic. These numbers, then, indicate that a far more equitable balance among the themes was achieved than during the initial seventeen years of the exam. Moreover, during fifteen of those thirty-eight years questions in either intellectual/ cultural or social/economic history equaled or were greater than those offerings in the political/diplomatic realm; and in some years only one or two of the six options among the FRQs were political/diplomatic. But balance did not necessarily signify that all was harmonious among these thematic bedfellows, at least insofar as student responses was concerned.

The new themes and the introduction of the DBQ may have allowed for "more liberal experimentation in course design and teaching strategies" (including a wider use of diverse materials—such as novels, art, and readings from other disciplines— and an emphasis on what is involved in historical thinking and methodology),[159] but actual teaching in the schools across the nation, along with some textbook writing, had not yet caught up universally with the tectonic shifts within the discipline. For years the majority of students continued to opt to write on those subjects that were more traditional. And where they chose questions on subjects such as demography, social structure, the decline of the aristocracy, urbanization, and work behavior and attitudes toward work many did not perform as well. Even when these subjects were eventually covered in most textbooks there was a paucity of the kind of facts, or evidence, or historical signposts around which students usually attempt to build an essay. As often as not essay responses involved vague or sweeping generalizations. But this was probably to be expected, and there never was a move to return to earlier patterns.

Nonetheless, several complementary solutions might help to improve students' abilities to answer questions reflective of the

159. Alpern, "Advanced Placement European History," 2-3; Beaber, "Changes in the Advanced Placement in European History Program," 39.

new history without weakening the presentation of what is so vital about social history: (1) textbook authors could give more thought to how they organize and write about social history, and other non-traditional issues, insofar as what students might be expected to learn and, eventually, incorporate into responses to essays on these subjects; (2) test development committees, and we as teachers who compose our own questions, could try to be more creative in how we write and phrase such questions and in what we ask students to do with what they know about this material;[160] (3) history teachers, in becoming aware of these problems that are faced by students who are learning as well as answering AP questions about social history, could work—individually and with others—to become more creative in how this theme is taught; (4) while in recent years test development committees have usually checked to see that the newer areas being tested are covered effectively in the most widely used textbooks, now and then one escapes their diligence, suggesting

---

160. For example, the following questions, from the 1957 and 1959 exams respectively, were worded in such a way as to engage students' attention without sacrificing the need for evidence or analysis: (1) "As an educated European at any TWO of the following times, what would you conceive to be the main problems of your world? 1500, 1600, 1700, 1800, 1900"; (2) "Imagine that you interviewed any TWO of the men listed below on the subject paired with his name. What explanation of his viewpoint would you have obtained? Bismarck on the revolutions of 1848/Karl Marx on bourgeois society/Pope Pius IX on liberalism/ Alexander II on the Edict of Emancipation." And from the 1985 exam, question #4 was an easier-to-answer example of social history because it also incorporated aspects of political history ("'In seventeenth-century England the aristocracy lost its privileges but retained its power; in seventeenth-century France the aristocracy retained its privileges but lost its power.' Assess the accuracy of this statement with respect to political events and social developments in the two countries in the seventeenth century."), while question #5 is social history in familiar territory that can be tied to actual events, social and political, to enable students to provide substantive answers ("Compare and contrast the roles of the peasantry and of urban workers in the French Revolution of 1789 to those of the peasantry and of urban workers in the Russian Revolution of 1917"). Reprinted by permission of the College Entrance Examination Board, the copyright owner.

that the importance of this task warrants underlining.

So, yes, significant programmatic change is often accompanied by problems—including some that take a long time to resolve—but AP also was, and has been, having a powerful impact upon the way history is taught in the schools. In addition, test development committees have used the essay portion of the exam to introduce new and/or recent material (e.g., architecture as a reflection of monarchy or of religious theologies and practices, the Cold War at its height or its end, the economic revival of Western Europe, social activism after World War II) and to demonstrate that APEH regularly reflects developments at the college level.[161]

Chronological and Geographical Representation

Also during these years there was an increasingly conscious effort on the part of APEH test development committees to see that each year's questions, considered collectively, were balanced chronologically (with at least one question covering each century—although at times the fifteenth and sixteenth centuries were considered together) and geographically (with at least one question focusing on Central and/or Eastern Europe). Chronological coverage was easy enough, but even with maps in hand committees sometimes lost their sense of testing direction—a problem compounded, if not caused, by the western bias of so much of European history teaching.[162]

From 1956 to 1972, when questions were grouped according

---

161. About once every four or five years each AP discipline/subject conducts a college curriculum survey to help guarantee that the program keeps abreast of changing content and instructional approaches; these surveys, in fact, are often catalysts for change in many AP subjects. Before these were begun, in the 1960s, the APEH examination committees periodically examined the most widely used textbooks on European history in order to achieve a comparable purpose with regard to content.

162. Norman Davies' *Europe: A History* (New York: Oxford University Press, 1996) offers readers a better balance between Europe, east and west.

to chronological periods, there could never be any doubt about such coverage, but starting with the 1973 exam committees have had to pay closer attention. Then, from 1973 to 1976, the start of the course was pushed forward to 1650 in an effort to reflect greater interest in more modern European history; as a result, there were no questions covering the fifteenth, sixteenth, and first half of the seventeenth centuries. But this shift in chronological coverage resulted in protests from significant numbers of teachers who recognized the special value of the Renaissance and Reformation periods for an understanding of modern times, and so by the 1977 exam the starting date was returned to 1450, where it has remained.

If providing questions to cover the span of centuries was never an obstacle, devoting appropriate, and annual, attention to the history of Europe east of the Holy Roman Empire or Germany could be more problematic. Russia and the Soviet Union, not surprisingly, have received the most attention among the essay questions, but even this statement comes with the equivalent of an insurance rider. Although APEH has, for the most part, begun in 1450, there has never been an essay focusing on the period before the reign of Peter the Great, and aside from Peter, the only other pre-1800 figure included has been Catherine the Great.[163] Thus, for the most part, and these two rulers and their reigns aside, it has primarily been Russian history of the nineteenth and twentieth centuries that has received the most attention. But then Russia has been the only country in eastern Europe regularly tested.

Sometimes there have been questions where students have had the option of picking any European country in order to answer a question, but traditional teaching provides them with more western ammunition. A question on the 1959 exam, on

---

163. In the forty-five year history of the program, five essay questions have been devoted to or included Peter the Great and seven to Catherine the Great. In contrast, there have been close to fifty questions covering Alexander I, Nicholas I, Nicholas II, nineteenth-century Russia more generally, Lenin, Stalin, Gorbachev, Communism, and the Russian Revolution.

the Austro-Hungarian monarchy, was the first to test students about a central-east European country or empire other than Russia. Austria and Central Europe would be included periodically thereafter (once, in 1964, not insignificantly, with a simple map, the first-ever visual in the exam's history)—although not the Balkans until years later. Another important step toward giving the east its due was a 1961 question on why "Western Europe became industrialized more rapidly than Eastern Europe between 1815 and 1870."[164] But any way the geography of European history is tested, even with the sustained effort to include questions from beyond the pale, the overwhelming majority of questions have been concentrated on Western Europe, and there were years (e.g., 1986, 1988, 1990) when the exam included no such questions, all of which seems to reflect the way modern European history is generally taught.

If Central and Eastern Europe are sometimes lost in the blind spot of the way we study European history, there are a few other countries and areas that are either off the map or marginal to it. In 1968, there was a question offering Gustavus Adolphus as a choice among three participants in the Thirty Years' War, the first and last time any Scandinavian or Scandinavian country was mentioned by name in the essay section of the exam. Turkey and Greece are similarly absent, while the Balkans (in a question in 1998) was saved from testing oblivion by current events (although the region had been incorporated into the 1992 DBQ on nineteenth- and early-twentieth-century Pan Slavism). The first and only time Poland was the subject of an essay question was in 1996. Portuguese history has been ignored, except for the extent to which it has been a part of questions on the age of exploration. Focus on the Netherlands has been limited to the sixteenth and seventeenth centuries. Italian history, naturally,

---

164. Reprinted by permission of the College Entrance Examination Board, the copyright owner. By the way, the Chief Reader's Report of that year makes no mention of whether students had enough information to respond successfully with regard to the Eastern Europe part of the question.

is a major part of the Renaissance, but then is otherwise absent until nineteenth-century unification and the age of Fascism and Mussolini. Spanish history is likewise limited to the fifteenth and sixteenth centuries, while there has been one FRQ (1958) and one DBQ (1990) on the Spanish Civil War. In contrast, virtually the full chronological stretch of the histories of England/Britain (along with Ireland rarely, but never Scotland or Wales), France, and the Holy Roman Empire/Prussia/Germany have comprised the majority of APEH essay questions, which again calls attention to the traditional biases in the way modern European history is taught.

There is a final geographically-related observation to make. As noted above, the dramatic changes that were made to APEH starting in 1972 called for new stress to be placed on European contacts with other peoples and cultures. Prior to that time only two essay questions had addressed that issue.[165] Then, on four of the six exams between 1973 and 1978, there were several such questions.[166] As it developed, however, the responses to these questions were generally not successful: small numbers of students elected to answer most of them and, more importantly, responses were often based on inadequate information. Too much of European history, both among textbooks and

---

165. One, in 1959, dealing with "ways in which the non-European world helped to change the European balance of power between 1715 and 1815"; the other, in 1963, asking students to determine the extent to which "Europe's economy in the eighteenth century [may] be considered a world economy." Reprinted by permission of the College Entrance Examination Board, the copyright owner.

166. Of two questions in 1973, one was on changing Western attitudes toward China and Japan, the other on the European economic penetration of Africa; of two questions in 1974, one was on the reasons for Japan adopting Western science and technology while China did not, the other on the conflicting outlooks for the colonized regions of the world toward Western civilization; of two questions in 1975, the DBQ was on suppressing the slave trade by Britain and the U.S., the one FRQ on the changes in the views of Europeans toward the cultures of China and India; the sole question in 1978 was on the reasons behind Europeans' being able to gain economic and political control over non-European peoples.

teaching, was apparently cloaked in a mantle of Eurocentrism. Thus the APEH examination committee decided to drop the theme dealing with the interaction of Europe and the wider world, because it tended to generate traditional political/diplomatic questions and answers and not address the reverse flow of influences.[167] As such, since that time it has only been the more traditional subjects of European explorations and imperialism that have brought the rest of the globe in the orbit of APEH essay testing.

Document-Based Questions

The DBQ is now more than a quarter-century old. Indirectly, its origins are rooted in the very beginnings of the program, as noted by Henry Winkler when he wrote that the exam had been "drawn up in the belief that students should be exposed as early as possible...to some of the primary materials which give the feel of history-in-the-making."[168] But he was referring to the inclusion of documentary materials in textbooks and classroom discourse. Then, as noted above, the great leap toward an integration of primary source materials into the annual exam itself came with the 1975 DBQ, on the heels of the trailblazing effort of APUS two years earlier. The DBQ itself provides students with the ingredients for constructing a narrative based on analysis and deduction: maps, photographs, cartoons, graphs, and excerpts from memoirs, government documents, newspaper accounts, and speeches. The exercise is designed to test a student's ability to acquire knowledge from the raw materials of history; in fact, with their fifteen minutes of required reading time, students "must demonstrate historical craftsmanship n the spot (something historians are not usually required to do.)"[169]

---

167. James McAree, Chief Reader's Report, 1976.

168. Winkler, "The Advanced Placement Program and Examination in European History," 333.

169. Alpern, "Advanced Placement European History," 4.

The DBQ, however, proved to be a controversial exercise for a number of years.[170] Much of the criticism was leveled at the way aptitude and reading skills seemed to take precedence over thinking historically, especially as outside historical knowledge was not expected to be brought to the task and training students both to "assess the reliability of the documents as historical sources" and to write a narrative in response to the question often proved difficult. But teaching students to respond in proper fashion to DBQs is certainly an appropriate activity for the history classroom, while the DBQ format has proved to be an effective way to introduce non-mainstream, often-esoteric-or-even-exotic subjects[171], as well as social history questions that were themselves more difficult for students to answer as FRQs.[172] In addition, and over time, increasing numbers of teachers have come to see the wisdom in an exercise—however imperfect—that simulates the way in which historians write

---

170. For a list of each year's DBQ, from 1975 to 2000, see Appendix II.

171. The best example is probably the DBQ of 1983. There are any number of subject areas that might surprise students and teachers of APEH, but the Flemings and Walloons in Belgium struck many as a stretch with regard to where the subject matter of the exam should go. In response, however, such a seemingly off-the-wall topic (or one, for example, on hunting in Lapland, or on migration patterns of gypsies in Eastern Europe, or on the rituals of Hasidic Jews in Poland) calls attention to the DBQ as a self-contained exercise where students are not expected, much less required, to bring in outside knowledge. Even when DBQs roam in more familiar territory, such as the French Revolution's Reign of Terror or the role of the S.A. in Hitler's Germany, rarely did students make reference to anything not in the documents provided. To be sure, these latter subjects are ones which students "expect" or ordinarily think of as history, and thus they are not "surprised." But clearly there is more to history than what is familiar, and the AP course description and exam are intended to reflect college-level courses, which in turn should reflect an ever-changing discipline and, at times, the introduction of "new" materials or perspectives.

172. See, for example, the 1981 DBQ, a comparison of middle-class and working-class attitudes toward work and its effect on workers in nineteenth-century Western Europe and whether those attitudes crossed social class lines.

history.

Also over the years, test development committees have wrestled with DBQ directions in an effort, among other things, to encourage students to "NOT simply summarize or repeat the contents of the documents" (added in 1979); and both to "use the documents in a historical context and draw conclusions from them" and to "construct a coherent essay that integrates the analysis of documents into a treatment of the topic" (added in 1980). But then, in the 1983 directions, references to assessing the reliability of the documents, to avoiding summarizing or paraphrasing the documents, and to using the documents in a historical context and drawing conclusions from them were dropped. For the 1984 exam, however, students were now advised, as they analyzed each document, to "take into account its source and the point of view of the author." The importance of this addition was underlined, literally, in the 1987 directions. The wisdom of discouraging students from summarizing, repeating, or paraphrasing documents was restored, in 1989, with the caution, "in no case should documents simply be cited and explained in a 'laundry list' fashion" and, in 1998, with the further admonition not to "simply summarize the documents individually" (a sentence that was placed in bold letters the next year). Not incidentally, this summary of the directions and direction changes calls attention to the main problems students have had in responding to DBQs. Finally, a new grading method— called core scoring—was introduced in 2000, which has modified the way in which the directions are presented (starting in 2001) so as to indicate precisely what must be included in order for essays to earn higher scores: a relevant thesis that is also supported with evidence from the documents; use of a majority of the documents; an analysis of the documents by grouping them in appropriate ways (along with a reiteration of the earlier admonition, still in bold type, not simply to summarize the documents individually); a consideration of the sources of the documents and the authors' point of view.

There have been other, essentially minor, adjustments made

to the presentation of DBQs (especially in terms of lengthening the documents while reducing their number), but as always the fundamental purpose of the exercise is to give students explicit directions and appropriately useful documents with which they can write a short history in response to the question and to enable them in the process to give evidence of their ability to think critically and historically.

Naming Names, Testing Topics

In historiography, "history as biography" was long a standard approach. "There is properly no History," wrote Emerson, "only Biography." And to Carlyle, "The history of the world is but the biography of great men." Such sentiments might seem to have been a governing principle of APEH exams for their first seventeen years. There were always several questions per year that revolved around monarchs, statesmen, religious leaders, philosophers, scientists, and/or artists. Beginning with the 1973 exam, however, a shift seems to have taken place, for in that year—and not for the last time—no question included the name of an individual European; in the years thereafter, individuals, vis-a-vis events, concepts, and forces, have occupied a less important place in the pantheon of questions. (For a list of those individuals named in essay questions, and their frequency, see Appendix III.)

This is not to suggest a teaching strategy that sacrifices the role of individuals in history, because historical figures continue to be part of some questions. In fact, the 1999 exam included two questions in which seven figures were mentioned by name, and the 2000 exam included three questions with five names. There are, however, some observations that can be made about the use of historical figures and the frequency of their being incorporated into questions.

There have been eighty-five such figures, with more than two-thirds (or fifty-seven) incorporated into the first ten years of questions, from 1956 through 1965. Forty-two of the people are part of questions dealing with political/diplomatic history, while all the rest—i.e., effectively, the other half, including religious leaders—falling under the intellectual/cultural theme; Colbert is the only person who can be placed as part of the social/economic theme. The last new political figure introduced was Mikhail Gorbachev, in the 2000 exam, but before that the last new political figure had been Robespierre, in 1970. Between the years for these two men, 1970 and 2000, the only new figures were artists, musicians, and writers.

It all began when the 1956 exam referred to the following, all of whom were heads of state: Holy Roman Emperor Charles V, Charles I of England, Louis XIV, Cromwell, the Great Elector (Frederick William), and William III of England. Louis XIV would be part of eleven years of questions during the first thirty years of the program, but then only once in the last twenty years. On a lesser scale, Charles V would be in questions five times during the first dozen years, and then not again until twenty-three years later. William III's debut was also his only appearance. The 1957 exam included the following, none of whom were heads of state: Marx, John Stuart Mill, Freud, Darwin, Einstein, Nietzsche, and Machiavelli. Marx has been part of more questions—nineteen—than any other historical figure, but only once during the 1990s. Darwin was cited eight times, from 1957 to 1971, but then after a twenty-eight year hibernation returned in 1999 and 2000. Nietzsche—as good as dead—did not return. The 1958 exam included both political and intellectual figures, and by the 1959 exam some individuals began to return for roles in additional questions.

Subsequently, Luther and Calvin would be the two most used religious figures, at eight and seven times respectively, although a Reformation-related question was asked on twenty-four exams. Louis XIV, at twelve times, tops the list for monarchs, followed by Napoleon at nine, and Joseph II of Austria and Elizabeth I tied at eight. Elizabeth is also the most frequently asked woman, followed by Catherine the Great (seven times);

the only other women to be tested by name on any exam is Maria Theresa of Austria. Among twentieth-century dictators, Hitler leads with nine, followed by Stalin at eight, although Hitler has not been mentioned by name in a question since 1972 (whereas Stalin was most recently in 1995 and 2000). Marx, as noted in the previous paragraph, has been the most frequently used philosopher, followed by Locke at eight and Machiavelli at seven. Among scientists, there has been Darwin at ten, Newton at six, and Einstein at four. Freud is the only individual from his field represented, at eight times, which can be interpreted in any number of ways. Figures from the arts have mostly made single appearances (Shakespeare, Mozart, Beethoven, Jacques-Louis David, Delacroix, Wordsworth, Rembrandt, Giacometti, Goya, and Picasso), although three (da Vinci, Michelangelo, and Alexander Pope) have appeared on two exams each; however, prior to the 1970 exam Shakespeare and da Vinci were the only figures from the arts to be subjects of questions.

While no essay question has ever been asked more than once, the author has also identified more than thirty of the most frequently tested topics (see Appendix IV), including the Enlightenment at twenty-five times, the Reformation at twenty-four, the Renaissance at twenty-three, the French revolutionary period at twenty-two, seventeenth-century England at eighteen, the Industrial Revolution at fifteen (but only three times since 1983), the arts (exclusive of Italian Renaissance questions) at fourteen (with eight such questions since 1981), followed by sixteenth-century Spain, imperialism, and Fascism/Nazism tied at thirteen. Mercantilism was a fairly popular subject with six questions between 1956 and 1972, but then only twice since then. Similarly, there were eight questions on the Thirty Years' War between 1957 and 1968, but only two subsequently; there were six questions on the Revolutions of 1848 between 1956 and 1970 and eight on nineteenth-century Russia between 1957 and 1971, but only one on each afterwards. There hasn't been a specific question on communism since the 1981 exam, on conservatism since 1969, on socialism since 1982, on romanticism since 1979, and on enlightened despotism as such since 1980 (although these subjects are at times subsumed within other questions, such as when aspects of communism might be considered as part of a question on the Cold War).

On the flip side of frequently-tested topics are topics that have been virtually ignored or only marginally included on the essay portion of the exam: the Spanish Inquisition, the Military Revolution, the witch craze (except for the 1980 DBQ), the Holocaust (especially as the exam was extended, in 1968, to include events to 1945), anti-Semitism, racism and the interaction between Europeans and other races of peoples within Europe, xenophobia, sexuality, assassinations and executions, economic crashes and crises (although the Great Depression was once the subject of a question), popular culture (except for the 2000 DBQ), peasant revolts and urban riots, organized labor and trade unionism, food, nutrition (except for the 1988 DBQ), and medical practices, and the migration and displacement of peoples (from the Morenos and Moriscos in the fifteenth century, to the Huguenots in the seventeenth century, to Armenians, Jews, and those whose lives were disrupted irretrievably by the Nazis and during the crises in the Balkans in the middle and late twentieth century). Children have only been the subject in a couple of DBQs. There have been questions on Darwin, but none relating to human origins. Most questions on religion have been on the Reformation and a few other early modern topics, but only one centered on the nineteenth century and none for the twentieth century.

To be sure, for some of these topics there have been no FRQs due to a relative paucity of coverage in the textbooks; for others there has been a concern for the sensitivities of some religious groups. But clearly there are areas where APEH has room to expand, even if it must do so with a delicate touch.

The Arts and the Visual

There was a time, a mere few decades ago, when the arts were more peripheral than integral to the teaching of European history. To be sure, one couldn't do justice to the Renaissance without some attention to art, architecture, and perhaps a little poetry and music. There were also the occasional works of art and literature that would be used because they revealed something or other about events, but not too much more. And so it was with APEH. Between 1956 and 1969 there was but one essay question (out of the 294 available to be selected) on the subject, although curiously in its focus it anticipated the regular appearance of such questions starting in the 1970s: "How were social and economic problems reflected in the literature of any TWO of the following nations in the period 1815-1870? England/France/Russia/Germany."[173]

It was, however, the arts-oriented questions of the '70s that established a precedent and that were often pioneering and representative of creative and innovative ways of testing. Over the following three decades fourteen such questions appeared, or an average of nearly one every two years. Those questions have dealt with the arts in all centuries covered by APEH, and most have linked the arts to the non-cultural themes of history. For example, question #6, from 1973, asks students to demonstrate how three eighteenth-century novels might be used as documentary sources for studying the age in which they were written. Question #6, from 1977, requests that students choose two twentieth-century works in either the visual or literary arts that offer images of man that reflect the age. Question #2, from

---

173. Reprinted by permission of the College Entrance Examination Board, the copyright owner. Actually, there were three additional questions that could have involved students in discussing the arts, such as one from 1959 that asked students to discuss aspects of the Renaissance suggested by three of five men, two of whom were Shakespeare and da Vinci. But in each case the question also made it possible for the arts to be avoided.

1984, reproduces paintings by Goya and Picasso in order for students to compare the way in which they express both the artistic styles and political issues of their times, while #2, from 1996, asks for a comparison of the patronage of the arts by Italian Renaissance rulers and dictators of the 1930s. Question #7, from 1987, also reproduces two paintings, but this time in order to prompt an elaboration on the technological and urban transformations that were characteristic of the second half of the nineteenth century.

Questions from 1988 and 1992 introduced architecture, one as a reflection of the conception and practice of monarchy, the other of differing theologies and religious practices. A question from 1990 used two paintings for what they might reveal about social life and leisure in two centuries. Then, for only the second time in the history of APEH (the first being in 1970), a question (#6, from 1997) gave students the option of choosing musicians, as well as artists and writers, to describe the Romantic response to political and socioeconomic conditions, 1800-50. Finally, although lines of poetry have been incorporated into a rare question here and there (e.g., as a source in a DBQ and in the form of a Pope couplet in a 1978 FRQ), question # 6, on the 2000 exam, asked students to determine the accuracy of four lines from a poem with regard to nineteenth-century gender roles. So, with paintings, literary excerpts, and poetry being occasional features of the APEH exam, who knows, given the rapidity of technological change, there may come a time when actual music selections and clips from history-oriented films will be integrated into the questions as well.

As is obvious, many of these questions on the arts have involved significant visual components, either as the sole focus or as launching points for an analysis of larger issues. Where such images had been a part of the multiple-choice section of the exam, the first-ever visual prompt accompanying an essay came in 1964: a simple black-and-white outline map of Europe with broken lines used to identify "East Central Europe," but without the identifying names of countries. A dozen years elapsed before visuals returned, and they did so on the back of the slave-trade DBQ in the form of three tables and an expense account. It remained for the DBQ on the role of the S.A. in Hitler's rise to power, in 1977, to include the first photograph, newspaper headline, and political cartoon as documentary evidence. These and other kinds of illustrations would thereafter become fairly regular components of the documentary make-up of DBQs.

For FRQs, the turning point for the use of visuals came with the 1979 exam: photographs of two chalices, one Catholic, the other Lutheran, with the question asking students to explain how the latter reflected the theology and ideals of the Reformation. Not incidentally, this was probably as perfect a question as any, chosen by a large percentage of those taking the exam and understood to the extent that what the chalices represented was used with varying degrees of effectiveness, thus contributing to a balanced distribution of scores. In addition, Readers at the time not only applauded the use of pictures and encouraged their use on future FRQs, but they also recognized "the leadership role of the AP exam in American education."[174]

And so the visual images kept coming, in the form of sculpture,[175] paintings, architecture (both exteriors and interiors[176]), and photographs. The banner year for such questions

174. Robert Blackey, Chief Reader's Report, 1979.

175. The 1981 exam presented Michelangelo's *David* and Giacometti's *Man Pointing* for students to compare as expressions of "the artistic, philosophical, and cultural values of their times." Although Giacometti's work bears his distinctive style and is reproduced in some textbooks, it is less familiar than the almost-universally recognized *David*; this presented some students with difficulties in answering the question. Nevertheless, both are the kind of art from which students are able to build answers, which is most important. After all, the chalices from 1979 were not familiar to most students who chose and otherwise did well on that question.

176. Question #3, from 1988, showed paintings of two palaces, Philip II's Escorial and Louis XIV's Versailles, and asked students to use them as a starting point for analyzing "the similarities and differences in the conception and practice of monarchy of these two kings." The major problem was that students tended not to know as much about how Philip's palace

was 1999, with three questions, each centered on paintings or photographs from which to build responses; these formed part of a group, one of which students were required to answer.

Other Matters that Matter

Before concluding this anatomy lesson, there are a couple of other matters that require our brief, but still undivided attention. One concerns an effort on the part of the Educational Testing Service (ETS) to avoid, or at least to be sensitive to, subjects that might be offensive to some among the many and diverse constituencies involved in AP or that might adversely affect student performance on the exam.[177] This was brought to my

---

reflected his conception of monarchy as they did about Louis' relation to his much-copied and photographed château. Comparable problems faced those who chose question #2, in 1992, which presented the interiors of a Protestant church and a Roman Catholic church from the seventeenth century, with the task to "explain how these interiors reflect the differing theologies and religious practices of Protestantism and Catholicism at that time." Reprinted by permission of the College Entrance Examination Board, the copyright owner. Another potential problem with the use of visual images is the clarity of their reproduction; such clarity is vital if students are to extract the kind of detail that is usually necessary for an effective response.

177. In its "Fairness Review" process ETS employs a sensitivity review procedure that evaluates its test questions, as well as its other products, "for their awareness of the contributions of various groups to United States society" and in order to avoid language, symbols, and examples "that are sexist, racist, or otherwise potentially offensive, inappropriate, or negative toward any group." At the same time, ETS recognizes that it should also be clear to test takers that its "materials are being used to assess knowledge and do not represent the view of the test developer. For example, it would be acceptable to include material about slavery or the Holocaust in history tests even though these topics would be considered inflammatory in other types of tests, such as reading skills tests." Officials at ETS would also like those of us who evaluate their tests to understand that there is a difference between materials that might be appropriate for use in a monograph, where the reader can choose to put it aside or skip over it, and those included as part of an exam where readers have no choice but to read, interpret, and write about what has been chosen for them.

attention in the years after the 1980 DBQ on the persecution of witches in the early modern period. This DBQ notwithstanding, there has never been another essay question on the subject, and yet when one considers that witchcraft concerns and persecutions spanned more than three centuries, affected most European countries, and victimized in excess of 100,000 people, it can hardly be dismissed as a minor or insignificant topic to test. Textbooks in the 1950s and '60s, and even beyond, might have failed to describe or analyze the witch craze (and thus reason not to ask an FRQ), but for more than a decade now it has been a featured, and fascinating, textbook episode. I recall being told by an ETS official, some years after the 1980 DBQ, that witchcraft is too sensitive a subject, that it might, for example, offend the sensibilities of some parochial school officials, that some parents might not want their children exposed to subjects dealing with the devil and supernatural beliefs, and that a DBQ like the one from 1980 would no longer be approved. Similarly, this may also be why questions having to do with evolution/ creationism or sexuality (e.g., heterosexuality, homosexuality, prostitution, pornography) have been absent from the exam, even as they are considered worthy of historical investigation and are usually integrated, to some extent or other, into college surveys of European history and Western civilization. It may, as well, be why textbooks that treat these subjects are excluded from serious consideration for adoption by some secondary schools and teachers.

A final, and always significant, issue concerning essay exam questions is the way in which they are worded. Taken as a whole, the phrasing of nearly a half century of such APEH questions has reflected the intent of all those university and secondary school historians who have served on the test development committees: to encourage students not only to recall the history they have studied but to write in a way that reflects their ability to think historically. Or as Henry Winkler wrote in 1961: "Clearly, the mastery of specific facts is not the be-all and end-all of teaching European history. Understanding history is the ultimate aim, and the Program tries to foster understanding."[178] Accordingly, students were asked from the first year of the program to develop and justify interpretations, to account for changes or degree of difference, to appraise or compare or explain or clarify.

A number of questions, however, especially during the earlier years of the program, consisted simply of a quotation and then the charge "discuss," but without any further direction, say, toward analysis. (Curiously, the word "evaluate" was first used in an essay question on the 1958 exam and then was used regularly thereafter, but both "assess" and "analyze," so ubiquitous over the last couple of decades, did not join the testing vocabulary until the 1960s, perhaps reflecting existing patterns of questioning, although the intent was that students do those things.) Some quotations were followed by the question, "Do you agree?" but without the request for an accompanying justification that other similar quotation-questions required. There were still other questions, now and then, for which a single word or name would technically suffice as a response (e.g., from 1960, question #11: "In your opinion, which was the more absolute ruler, Catherine the Great or Napoleon?"[179]). Similarly, there were a few questions that merely asked for a listing of items. As Winkler realized, "Over the years many of the essay questions have been of a type to elicit the 'why' and the 'what about it,' although admittedly there is inevitably some of the purely 'what' to be found among them."[180]

Two important steps marked the growing awareness of the role played by the careful wording of questions. The first was the publication, in 1981, of an article that provided an analysis of essay test construction that was, in turn, based on twenty-five years of the annual reports written by chief readers, in both

178. Winkler, "The Advanced Placement Program and Examination in European History," 333.

179. Reprinted by permission of the College Entrance Examination Board, the copyright owner.

180. Winkler, "The Advanced Placement Program and Examination in European History," 334.

APEH and APUS.[181] The second was the initial appearance, in the *Advanced Placement Course Description: History*, in the late 1980s, of a list of the key terms (e.g., analyze, compare, explain) that commonly accompany essay questions; included in the list were definitions of the terms along with sample questions. The introductory paragraph included the following useful advice: "Effective answers to essay questions depend in part upon a clear understanding (and execution) of the meaning of important directive words.... An essay can only begin to be correct if it answers directly the question that is asked. Individual teachers can provide what AP examinations cannot: help with the meanings and applications of...[these] key terms."[182]

Conclusion

The decade of the 1970s was pivotal for the development and maturation of the APEH essay exam section, akin perhaps to one of those turning points historians sometimes still like to identify. While the course and exam have always been designed to reflect their college-level equivalents, as well as the profession's evolving focuses, the shifts that took place in the 70s were more numerous and dramatic than in previous

---

181. Robert Blackey, "A Guide to the Skill of Essay Construction in History," *Social Education* 45:3 (March 1981): 178-82. Reprinted in Blackey, ed., *History Anew: Innovations in the Teaching of History Today* (Long Beach: The University Press, California State University, Long Beach, 1993).

182. *Advanced Placement Course Description: History* (College Entrance Examination Board, 1987), 60-61. A word of caution, however, and with respect to George Santayana's caution to those who do not know history: those who have forgotten or ignored what has been learned about test construction in history will surely repeat past mistakes. Witness the 2000 exam, where one question simply called upon students to discuss certain developments (what Winkler labeled the "purely 'what'" kind of question) and another asked "how accurately" some lines of poetry reflected gender roles, a charge that could be answered either "very accurately" or "not accurately."

or subsequent decades. Among other things, a new delineation of themes was articulated which have remained in effect ever since, with only minor modifications; a more conscious and successful effort was launched to provide something of an equitable balance among those themes, with political/diplomatic questions no longer dominating as before; the innovative document-based question joined the exam format in 1975, thus adding a new dimension to essay testing; where there had been only one question (in 1968) centered on the arts and history, as a theme it began making regular appearances in a variety of questions starting in 1972; visual stimuli (e.g., paintings, photos, cartoons, maps), hitherto confined to the multiple-choice portion of the exam, became part of essay questions, first in a DBQ, in 1977, then as part of FRQs, in 1979; where the names of specific Europeans figured in many of the questions through 1972, afterwards APEH became less "biography" focused, and in some years the questions were nameless; issues, as well as exam questions, relating to women's history became an increasingly integral part of the panorama of European history; along with questions on women, other social history subjects became the focus of questions for the first time (e.g., demography, social structure, decline of the aristocracy, urbanization); and, lastly, with one of the commonly-recognized themes of modern world history—the rise of the West—coinciding with much of the chronology of APEH, the 70s launched an effort to make the study of European history less provincial, to include questions reflective of greater global awareness, to direct us to think of Europe as part of the world beyond what is housed within the walls formed by the Atlantic, the Mediterranean, the North and Baltic Seas, and the Ural Mountains.

AP essay exams, if not quite as rigorous as the civil service examinations of imperial China, have often been as sophisticated and demanding as those offered to undergraduate history majors and even to graduate students (although to be sure they are graded with adjustments as to what can reasonably be expected from secondary school students and their AP classes). Former

Chief Reader Phil Kintner called the essays "the real 'guts' of the APEH endeavor."[183] Founder Henry Winkler declared that "it is very largely the essay section of the examination which appears clearly able to test—and which in fact does test—for a sense of continuity and development. Indeed, it is fairly apparent that whatever may be the results of 'scientific' studies, there is very little of such a sense which can be adequately assessed in any objective test, no matter how carefully devised."[184] These prophetic words anticipated what has from the start been such a vital and successful part of a successful and vital program.

Finally, it should be noted that any patterns which may have been detected during the course of this analysis are products of chance and are random. There is no master plan that dictates the subject matter or types of questions that appear from year to year (except the effort to achieve balance among themes, time periods, and regions, and a conscious effort not to repeat a subject from one year to the next, or at least not in the same form). What further helps to insure freshness and surprise is that members of test development committees, both secondary and university people, serve an average of three years, which means "new blood" is regularly introduced, and all members work conscientiously to keep the program guidelines, and the exam, reflective of current research and of how the subject is taught at the university level. In this sense, the APEH essay exams have been a glorious and effective barometer of the modern study of European history, just as the program itself—warts and all—has helped to lead the way in which history is taught in the schools.

---

183. Kintner's e-mail to author, January 10, 2001.

184. Winkler, "The Advanced Placement Program and Examination in European History," 333.

Appendix I
Themes of the APEH

<u>**1972-1974:**</u> There were six themes:

Political: Toward Egalitarian National States, including the extension of political democracy and parliamentary governments; the rise of the modern state and the development of its variant forms; the development of political parties, programs, and ideologies; the extension and limitation of individual civil rights and freedoms; forms of political dissent, reform, and revolution; types of political dominance: federalism, colonialism, and imperialism.

Intellectual: Changing Concepts of Man, God, and the Universe, including the scientific revolutions: attitudes, concepts, and consequences; the visual and performing arts as statements of cultural values and evidence of historical changes; the developments in philosophical thought and their relationship to traditional religious ideas and institutions; the rise of the social and behavioral sciences and their relation to the development of historical studies; forms and content in fictional literature as reflections of and evidence of historical growth; the development of the mass media and their influence upon the formation of popular cultural values and egalitarian attitudes.

Social and Cultural: The Rise of a Mass Urban Society, including the changing social structures from hereditary classes to egalitarian individualism; the role of the city in the changing of cultural values and social patterns; modes of social mobility and the responses of traditional societies to modernization; conflicts of cultural and social values in emerging and developed mass societies; competitive ideas and theories of the nature of man and societies; the interactions between elites and masses.

Economic: The Growth of an Industrial Technology, including the origins and developments of the Industrial

Revolution; the growth of competition and interdependence in national and world markets; the relationships between private and state contributions to economic growth; the changing forms and organization of labor supply; transportation, communication, and finance capital in economic modernization; economic theories as a basis for social and political programs.

International Relations: The Emergence of World Politics, including the rise and spread of the modern state as a competitive and cooperative form of power relationships; systems of interstate accord and conflict: diplomacy, war, and power blocs; attempts to restrain interstate conflicts from balance of power diplomacy and international law to international organization; reform movements and revolutions as responses to international and intercultural tensions; the rise of major non-European powers and their effect upon the European powers; the consequences of technological advances and egalitarian democracy on the development of international political affairs.

Intercultural Responses: Europe and the Wider World, including the impact upon Europe of increasing contact with and involvement in the non-European world; problems of racial and cultural contact and conflict; the missionary aspect of Christianity and its contribution to the spread of European culture; the social and political consequences of economic modernization in the non-European cultures; the rise of Europeanized intellectual and technical elites to leadership in non-European cultures.

<u>1975-1976</u>: There were five themes. The above themes generally remained in place with the following exception:

Intellectual and *Social and Cultural* themes, as above, were amalgamated. The changes in this new category were clearly noticeable, largely in terms of eliminating some subjects and combining others: the scientific revolutions: attitudes, concepts, and consequences; the visual and performing arts and literature as statements of cultural values and as historical evidence; the developments in social and philosophical thought and their relationship to traditional ideas and institutions; the role of the city in changing cultural values and social patterns; the shift in social structures from hierarchical orders to modern social classes and the interaction between elites and masses; the formation of popular cultural values and attitudes in developed and in emerging mass societies.

1977- present: Three themes combined many of the previous themes:

Political and Diplomatic History, including the rise of the modern state in its various forms; the development of political parties and ideologies; the extension and limitation of individual civil liberties; the rise of nationalism; forms of political protest, reform, and revolution; types of colonialism and imperialism; interstate conflict: diplomacy, war, and power blocs; relationship of European and non-European powers, including decolonization; relationship between domestic and foreign policies; efforts to restrain interstate conflict: treaties, balance of power diplomacy, and international organizations.

Intellectual and Cultural History, including the secularization of learning and culture; changes in religious thought and organization; the scientific revolution and its consequences; major trends in literature and the arts as statements of cultural values and as historical evidence; developments in social thought (economic and political theory, etc.); the spread of literacy; the diffusion of new intellectual concepts among different social groups; changes in popular culture such as the development of new attitudes toward religion, toward the family, toward work.

Social and Economic History, including the role of the city in changing cultural values and social relationships; the shift in social structures from hierarchical orders to modern social classes; changes in the nature of elites and their interaction with the lower classes; the development of commercial practices and their economic and social impact; the origins and development of industrialization; changes in the European demographic structure; changes and continuities in the European family structure and relationships; the growth of competition and interdependence in national and world markets; the relationships between private and state contributions to economic growth.

Subsequently, there would be the occasional modification and addition to the subjects subsumed under each theme, but nothing more.

Appendix II
Subjects of DBQs, 1975-2001

1975	Suppressing the slave trade
1976	Population trends in France & Germany, 19th & 20th centuries
1977	Role of German paramilitary groups in Hitler's rise to power
1978	Encouraging education for women, Renaissance to 18th century
1979	Advantages & disadvantages of the Terror during the French Revolution
1980	Persecution of individuals as witches, 15th through 17th centuries
1981	Working- & middle-class attitudes toward work in 19th-century W. Europe
1982	Child-rearing among English upper classes, 16th through 18th centuries
1983	Differences between Flemings & Walloons in Belgium, 19th-20th centuries
1984	Role of the army in the German aircraft industry, 1908-1918

1985	Views on juvenile crime & its effects on the legal treatment of juvenile offenders in 19th-century Britain
1986	Pressures on Britain's Liberal government during the Sudan crisis, 1884-85
1987	Variations in the levels of literacy in Old Regime France
1988	Arguments for & against restrictions on the sale of gin in 18th-century England & their influence on the Gin Act of 1751
1989	Points of view concerning women's suffrage & its potential affects on the political & social order
1990	The ways in which the defenders of the Spanish Republic represented their aims & attitudes
1991	The views of those addressing the issue of slavery during the Enlightenment & the French Revolution
1992	The political & cultural issues in the debate over Pan-Slavism
1993	The values & purposes of Renaissance education & how they changed over time
1994	The controversies over the relationship between the English & Irish, 1800-1916
1995	Responses to the outbreaks of plague, 15th to 18th centuries
1996	The challenges to the security, unity, & prosperity of the Dutch Republic, 1650-1713
1997	Attitudes & reactions toward the participation of women in the sciences, 17th & 18th centuries
1998	The views of those concerned about the problems of political, economic, & social order in the German states before the revolutions of 1848

1999   Perceptions of Russians to the condition of the Russian peasantry, 1861-1914, & the proposals to change that condition

2000   The purposes served by rituals & festivals in traditional European life

2001   Character & condition of Greeks in the Ottoman Empire during the Greek movement for independence, 18th & early 19th centuries

Appendix III:
Individuals named in FRQs

Adolphus, Gustavus	1968
Alexander I	1964
Alexander II	1958, '59, '63, '65, '70
Beethoven	1970
Bentham, Jeremy	1966
Bismarck	1958, '59, '61, '65, '66, '68, '88
Burke, Edmund	1963, '64
Calvin	1959, '61, '62, '64, '66, ' 69, '95
Catherine II	1959, '60, '63, '66, '71, '95, '99
Cavour	1958, '67, '68
Charles I	1956, '60, '63, '66, '68
Charles II	1960, '65, '66, '68
Charles V	1956, '60, '63, '64, '67, '90
Colbert	1961, '81
Copernicus	1959, '64, '84
Cromwell, Oliver	1956, '59, '67
Darwin	1957, '59, '62, '64, '66, '68, '70-71, '99-00
David, J.-L.	1970
da Vinci, Leonardo	1959, '64

Delacroix	1970
Descartes	1966, '69
Disraeli	1963, '68, '69
Einstein	1957, '60. '68, '74
Elizabeth I	1961, '62, '63, '65, '67, '68, '69, '99
Erasmus	1959, '64, '66, '67, '69, '71
Frederick II	1959, '62, '63, '66, '70, '99
Freud	1957, '60, '66, '68, '70, '74, '85, 2000
Giacometti	1981
Gladstone	1961
Gorbachev	2000
Goya	1984
Great Elector	1956, '68, '69, 70
Henry IV of France	1963, '65, '99
Henry VIII	1961, '70
Hitler	1961, '62, '65, '66, '68, '69, '70, '71, '72
Hobbes	1958, '64, '68
James I	1960, '62, '63, '67, '69, '93
James II	1960, '65, '66
Joseph II	1959, '61, '62, '65, '66, '67, '68, '71
Lenin	1961, '64, '65, '66, '67, '68, '83
Locke	1958, '65, '67, '69, '70, '72, '74, '83
Louis XIII	1966
Louis XIV	1956, '59, '61, '64, ;65, '67, '68, '69, '72, '75, '78
Louis XV	1964
Louis XVI	1966, '68
Loyola	1964
Luther	1959, '64, '66, '69, '70, '83, '85, '95
Machiavelli	1957, '62, '64, '67, '68, '84, '99
Malthus	1966

Maria Theresa	1963
Marx	1957, '59, '60, '61, '62, '63, '65, '66, '68, '69, '70. '71, '72, '75, '83, '85, '87, '88, '99
Medici, Lorenzo de	1959
Metternich	1958, '64, '69
Michelangelo	1972, '81
Mill, John Stuart	1957, '64
Montesquieu	1963, '65
More, Thomas	1967
Mozart	1970
Mussolini	1959, '61, '65, '66, '68, '70
Napoleon I	1959, '60, '61, '63, '64, '68, '69, '71, '81
Napoleon III	1960, '64, '65, '66, '68, '70
Newton	1966, '68, '74, '78, '83, '84
Nicholas I	1969
Nicholas II	1968, '82
Nietzsche	1957
Owen, Robert	1966
Peter the Great	1965, '68, '69, '70, '89
Philip II	1959, '65, '67, '68, '88, '92, 2000
Picasso	1984
Pope, Alexander	1970, '78
Pope Leo XIII	1963
Pope Pius IX	1959
Rembrandt	1972
Richelieu	1968
Robespierre	1970, '89
Rousseau	1962, '64, '65, '67, '75, '84
Savonarola	1964, '67
Shakespeare	1959

Smith, Adam	1961, '70
Stalin	1967, '68, '70, '75, '81, '82, '95, 2000
Voltaire	1962, '71
William II, Kaiser	1968
William III	1956
Wordsworth	1970

Appendix IV
Frequently Tested Topics

Age of Exploration	1958, '63, '64, '67, '69, '71, '78, '80, '82, 89, '92, '97
Arts, The	1962, '70, '72, '73, '77, '78, '81, '84, '87, '89, '90, '92, '97, '99
Communism	1952, '58, '60, '61, '63, '65, '66, '74, '81
Congress of Vienna	1956, '64, '76, '93, '99
Conservatism	1957, '58, '69
Darwinism	1956, '59, '64, '68, '71, '99
1848 revolutions	1956, '59, '60, '64, '66, '70, '90
England, 17th century	1956, '57, '59, '60, '62, '63, '64, '65, '66, '67, '68, '69, '73, '78, '82, '87, '93
Enlightened Despotism	1959, '62, '63, '65, '71, '76, '80
Enlightenment	1956, '57, '61, '62, '63, '64, '65, '66, '68, '69, '72, '76, '77, '80, '82, '83, '84, '86, '88, '90, '92, '93, '94, '98, 2000
French Revolution	1957, '58, '59, '60, '61, '62, '63, '64, '65, '66, '67, '68, '69, '70, '71, '72, '78, '84, '85, '86, '89, '96
Imperialism	1960, '61, '64, '65, '66, '67, '69, '73, '74, '76, '82, '90, '97

Industrial Revolution	1956, '58, '59, '61, '68, '69, '71, '72, '73, '75, '77, '78, '83, '89, 2000
Liberalism	1956, '58, '61, '62, '68, '69, '73, '77, '82, '95
Marxism	1957, '63, '65, '69, '75, '83, '87, '88, '91, '99
Mercantilism	1956, '58, '59, '62, '70, '72, '81, '95
Nationalism	1957, '61, '62, '63, '67, '89, '95, '98
Nazism/Fascism	1956, '58, '60, '61, '63, '64, '65, '66, '68, '71, '72, '74, '83
19th-Century Russia	1957, '58, '59, '60, '65, '69, '70, '71, '84
Price Rise	1957, '62, '67, '89
Reformation	1957, '58, '59, '61, '62, '63, '64, '65, '66, '68, '69, '70, '71, '77, '79, '83, '85, '86, '87, '88, '91, '95, '96, '98
Renaissance	1956, '58, '59, '60, '61, '62, '63, '64, '65, '66, '67, '69, '71, '72, '77, '82, '84, '85, '86, '88, '94, '96, '98
Reign of Louis XIV	1959, '64, '65, '67, '68, '72, '75, '88
Romanticism	1958, '60, '70, '79
Russian Revolution	1964, '67, '71, '72, '78, '80, '85, '87, '94
Scientific Revolution, 17th-Century Intellectual	1957, '58, '68, '69, '76, '78, '84, '90, '91, 2000
Socialism	1959, '67, '82
Spain, 16th-Century	1957, '59, '61, '64, '65, '66, '67, '68, '69, '70, '93, '97, 2000
Thirty Years' War	1957, '58, '60, '61, '63, '64, '65, '68, '80, '99
Treaty of Versailles	1956, '58, '60, '64, '67, '76, '99
Women	1978, '88, '89, '90, '93, '94, '95, '96, '97, '98, '99, 2000

World War I   1959, '62, '63, '65, '98

13. SO MANY CHOICES, SO LITTLE TIME

Strategies for Understanding and Taking Multiple-Choice Exams in History

"Don't worry, Howard," says a wife to her husband in a *New Yorker* cartoon (by Victoria Roberts) from a few years ago, "The big questions are multiple choice." And so they may be if the ubiquity of standardized and regular classroom testing is any indication. Taking these often high-pressure, high-stakes tests presents, if not overwhelms, students with numerous questions and four-to-five times as many choices accompanied by time constraints. When the correct answer is not immediately identified, many students guess randomly or choose blindly. To guess or choose this way, however, is also to increase the chances for poor grades. There are, instead, more effective ways to resolve the virtually inevitable indecision when taking such exams.

Whether students will be taking the SAT, ACT, AP history exams, multiple-choice exams in college courses, the GRE, or any other standardized examinations that include multiple-choice questions in history, including required statewide 6-12 grade-level exams, learning as much as possible about what to expect and how best to select among response choices will enable them to improve their scores so as to reflect more fully their knowledge and abilities. With this in mind, many students enroll in test preparation courses while others search web sites or purchase test prep books, some of which do, indeed, provide useful information and suggestions along with sample questions—although many of these sample questions are available online or have been published by state teaching commissions or boards and testing organizations such as The College Board. What follows is a thorough collection of strategies and insights that are useful, if not critical, for maximizing performance, especially in the areas of history and social studies (although most can also be adapted to other academic areas). By way of a caveat, however, it should be stressed that these strategies will work optimally only when coupled with the development of skills to think historically[185] as well as with significant understanding and studying of course or subject matter material.

For his own preparation to write this essay, the author has compiled more than thirty years' experience writing and reviewing multiple-choice questions for Advanced Placement and other College Board and Educational Testing Service programs; he has served on several test development committees at the state and national level; he has read and, in some cases, adapted suggestions from published test preparation books[186];

---

185. See Thomas C. Holt, *Thinking Historically: Narrative, Imagination, and Understanding* (New York: The College Board, 1990); Robert Blackey, ed., "Thinking Historically in the Classroom," *Perspectives* 33:7 (October 1995): 1, 4, 23-35, 37; Robert Blackey, ed., *Perspectives on Teaching Innovations: Teaching to Think Historically* (Washington, D.C.: American Historical Association, 1999); Samuel Wineburg, *Historical Thinking and Other Unnatural Acts* (Philadelphia: Temple University Press, 2001); Thomas Andrews & Flannery Burke, "What Does It Mean To Think Historically?" *Perspectives* 45:1 (January 2007): 32-35. In addition, the following web sites offer videos wherein historical thinking is demonstrated: http://teachinghistory.org and http://historicalthinkingmatters.org/why/.

186. Grace Roegner Freedman, *Cracking the SAT U.S. and World History Subject Tests* (New York: The Princeton Review/Random House, 2007); Kenneth Pearl, *Cracking the AP European History Exam* (New York: The Princeton Review/Random House, 2006); *DAC Study Guide for AP European History* (DAC Educational Publications, 2001); Nathan Barber, *AP European History* (Stamford, CT: Arco/Thomson Learning, 2001); Martha Moore, *AP European History* (New York: Kaplan Publishing,

he has examined published multiple-choice questions from the California Standards Tests (CST)—administered to secondary school students—and from the California Subject Examinations for Teachers (CSET)—taken by prospective secondary school teachers; he has reviewed banks of multiple-choice questions that are available to teachers and typically accompany textbooks for United States, Western, and world history survey courses; he has surveyed recently published multiple-choice questions from United States, European, and world history AP exams; and he has written, and revised, many multiple-choice questions for his own courses.[187]

To begin, let's become aware of a few commonly used *terms*.[188] Multiple-choice questions typically direct students to pick the correct answer from among four or five choices or **options**. Ordinarily, all the options will be approximately the same length (or no fewer than two of them will be a comparable length but different from the others that are of approximately equal length), so that no single option, and certainly not the correct one, stands out by virtue of its length or brevity. The **stem** is the part of the question that precedes the options. The wrong answers among the options are called **distractors**, whereas the correct answer option is the **key**.

2008); Michael Romano, *CliffsAP European History* (Hoboken, NJ: Wiley Publishing, 2003); Chris Freiler, *AP Achiever Advanced Placement European History Exam Preparation Guide* (New York: McGraw-Hill, 2008); Louise Forsyth and Lenore Schneider, *Fast Track to a 5: Preparing for the AP European History Examination* (Boston: Houghton Mifflin, 2008).

187. For advice on constructing multiple-choice questions, see Ann McCormick Scott, "Life Is a Multiple-Choice Question" and Ray W. Karras, "A Multidimensional Multiple-Choice Testing System," both in Robert Blackey, ed., *History Anew: Innovations in the Teaching of History Today* (Long Beach: The University Press, California State University, Long Beach, 1993).

188. These are the terms used by The College Board and the Educational Testing Service, among others.

So as to minimize students being surprised, and thus caught unawares when actually taking multiple-choice exams, teachers should familiarize themselves with the exam to be taken in order to prepare their students to expect some among the following *types of questions*, although not all multiple-choice exams include all types:

(1) questions in the form of questions, for which the correct—or sometimes the most correct—answer to the question is to be chosen.

(2) complete the stem questions, in which the stem is the first part of an incomplete sentence whereupon a decision has to be made about which of the possible options (answers) most accurately completes the sentence.

In terms of the structure of multiple-choice exams, these first two types of questions are typically the most common, even as they may incorporate some of the following additional variations on these types:

(3) analysis questions, which ask that a conclusion be drawn or a judgment rendered about a specific topic, or that an assessment be made about the impact of a movement, or that a judgment be rendered about the most important cause of some event, or that a characterization be made about a policy, a person, or an event, or how something has changed over time. Analysis questions require familiarity with historical context and greater understanding than simple factual recall or mere recognition.

(4) missing word, words, or phrase, in which the stem is almost complete, except that one or more words are missing, with the correct word or words being among the available options.

(5) questions that include visuals, such as graphs, tables, maps, prints, posters, paintings, sculptures, political cartoons, photos, and engravings; these images should neither frighten students nor should they be over-analyzed or over-interpreted, as

the questions themselves are typically straightforward; instead, questions with visuals test students' ability to understand and interpret them, especially within historical context and with an awareness of possible distortions or bias.

(6) questions based on quotations or short passages from a book or other source, which might ask for the author to be identified or for the name of the concept or episode the quotation or passage refers to; presumably, the authors of the quotations and the sources from which the passages are taken should be familiar to the well-prepared student.

(7) a complete statement of a problem to be solved, which as often as not is the form taken by questions based on quotations or short reading passages.

(8) cross-chronological and cross-geographical questions, which call attention to the importance of understanding the roles played by chronology and geography in making sense of cause-and-effect, historical interpretations, degree of change over time, or seeing how some themes and subjects (e.g., the African slave trade, the Industrial Revolution, Imperialism) connect chronologically and geographically.

Ordinarily, but especially on both college-level exams and on standardized exams such as the SAT and those within the AP program, only a small number of questions will involve simple recall of factual material, whereas most will instead require *understanding the material* (as opposed to merely memorizing it), although such questions will surely cover a range of degrees of difficulty. In most cases, students will *not* be able to choose the correct option just by recognizing it. And, as already noted, many questions will blend more than one of the above types of questions.

In addition, *dates* are often included in question stems on standardized tests (in the form of specific dates or years for events, or as centuries for movements or broader trends)— because questions are not typically, if ever, based solely on the memorization of dates (which is an approach to history teaching that results in students associating the subject with the word "boring"). What is more vital than memorizing dates in developing an understanding of history is to improve one's sense of chronology, to be aware of the order of key events and people and of their relationship to one another, including, say, in terms of cause and effect.

Students should also be prepared for the stems of some questions to include the following phrasing:

(1) "all of the following EXCEPT," "which of the following was NOT," or "all but which one of the following."

(2) "the BEST answer," "the MOST important," "the MAIN point," or "the LEAST important." [As an aside, note that AP, SAT, and other standardized multiple-choice questions rarely, if at all, include the following options: "all of the above" and "none of the above."]

Questions that include these or similar words or phrases tend to be more difficult for some students. As such, students should be clear about what is being asked. For questions that include one of the three directive groupings in (1) earlier in this paragraph, students might try rewording the negative phrasing in the stem to positive phrasing (i.e., instead of having to decide which answer to exclude because it is the exception, such rewording leads students to identify which ones among the options actually apply, whereupon the one that does not will be the correct answer to the question). By way of example, the following question appeared on the 2006 United States History AP exam:

All of the following contributed to the decline of open-range cattle ranching at the end of the nineteenth century EXCEPT
(A) excessively cold winters
(B) federal recognition of American Indian land claims
(C) a drop in cattle prices

(D) over grazing
(E) production of crops for distant markets[189]

If reworded in the positive, the question reads: "Which four among the following options contributed to the decline of open-range cattle ranching at the end of the nineteenth century?" In this way, the option that is the least correct or is incorrect (B) becomes more readily apparent and is thus the correct choice.

For questions that include one of the four phrases in (2) at the beginning of the previous paragraph, students should be prepared to make a judgment or to discriminate between or among more than one option that might appear to be correct and thus to *understand* the material being tested at a more sophisticated level. In questions of both these types, students should be certain to weigh all the options carefully, and to look for nuances and subtleties, before deciding which one is the best possible answer. Consider the following example from the 2002 World History AP exam in which, upon consideration, at least two of the options might be safely eliminated because they are out of the time period covered in the stem, and two others can also be rejected with a little understanding of what the states represented and where their trading energies were focused:

Which of the following are the states that dominated the Mediterranean trade during the sixteenth century?
(A) Italian city-states and the Ottoman Empire
(B) The Byzantine Empire and the Ottoman Empire
(C) Spain and Portugal
(D) The Habsburg Empire and France
(E) The Crusader states[190]

---

189. Copyright © 2008 The College Board. Reproduced with permission.
http://apcentral.collegeboard.com

190. Copyright © 2008 The College Board. Reproduced with permission.
http://apcentral.collegeboard.com

Option B can be eliminated because the Byzantine Empire effectively ended with the fall of Constantinople, in 1453. Option E can be dropped from consideration because the Crusader states (i.e., twelfth- and thirteenth-century feudal states created by western European crusaders in Greece, Asia Minor, and the Holy Land) did not survive very long after the Crusades. The trade of Spain and Portugal was focused on the Atlantic and Indian Oceans, not the Mediterranean, whereas that of the Habsburg Empire and France never dominated in the Mediterranean. Thus by a process of elimination and some understanding of the roles of states involved in trade the correct answer can be deduced as option A.

In answering the questions themselves, it is important to impress upon students the value of always *reading all answer options* for each question, because more than one choice might appear to be right—which they often have a nagging habit of sounding—whereas the first one to appear to be correct might not be the best—and thus the correct—answer. Before deciding which choice *is* correct, students should be directed to try to *identify which among the options might be safely eliminated* because, for example, it:

(1) is out of the time period covered in the stem (or main part) of the question (e.g., see the sample question above from World History, option B);

(2) involves absolute phrases (e.g., "never," "always," "all," "every," "complete") that cannot be qualified; options that include such words effectively indicate that the phrase or statement is universally true—which is seldom the case.

(3) might be true in another context but otherwise has little to do with the subject covered in the stem (e.g., see the incorrect options in the last sample question, from United States history, below).

(4) includes two distractors that are opposites (i.e., that contradict each other), which could mean that one of them

might be the correct option (e.g., see the sample question above from World History, options A & B), but care should be taken nonetheless to read all options just to make sure.

As students read each question they should, if permitted, *underline the critical words in the stem*; this will help them to focus precisely on what is being asked and thus to reduce the chance of making careless mistakes with regard to the intent of the question. And as they read the stem—but before they actually read the options—a useful strategy to employ is one where students have been trained to *anticipate* what the correct answer might be, after which they can compare their anticipated answer to each of the options before deciding which best answers the question; this approach has the advantage of encouraging students to think about the subject before they choose or guess, which in turn should help to minimize any potential confusion that might result when more than one option appears to be correct. The following example from the 1994 European History AP exam can be used to illustrate how this can be made to work:

Which of the following best expresses Voltaire's views concerning religion?

(A) Catholics should obediently follow the dictates of the pope.

(B) Protestants should be excluded from French government service.

(C) Religious unity is fundamental to enlightened monarchies.

(D) Organized religion perpetuates superstition and ignorance.

(E) Criticism of religious doctrines and authorities should be condemned.[191]

---

191. Copyright © 2008 The College Board. Reproduced with permission. http://apcentral.collegeboard.com

By reading the stem first, as well as underlining the most important words (i.e., *best expresses Voltaire's views concerning religion*), students should think about what Voltaire's views on religion were: as most textbooks emphasize, he relentlessly criticized the Catholic Church and he was associated with the phrase *Écrasez l'infame* ["Crush the infamous thing"], which referred to the superstition and ignorance by which he was convinced the Church manipulated believers. Armed with that information, not only does the correct answer, option D, readily reveal itself but the four distractors also become clearly wrong.

To differentiate among given options, especially with questions that appear to be more difficult or complicated, another helpful strategy encourages students to *translate or summarize each option* either into more familiar words and/or fewer words; that is, students could rewrite the answer choices in their own words so that each option possibility makes more sense to them. Doing this also promotes understanding much the same way that re-reading or re-typing one's class notes does; it is also a variation on what teachers often do when they explain and rephrase sophisticated or difficult ideas and concepts to their students. This practice can be illustrated with the following question from the 2006 United State History AP exam:

In 1950 a major factor in President Harry Truman's commitment of American troops to combat North Korean aggression was a desire to

(A) force Congress to appropriate more money for the armed services

(B) preserve South Korea's markets for United States exports

(C) overcome the stigma that the Democratic party had "lost" China to communism

(D) convince Americans that containment was an insufficient way to deal with communist expansion

(E) direct the focus of American postwar foreign policy away

from Europe[192]

Following pre-exam practice with this technique, students might be able to simplify the stem and the options to a more manageable, easier to understand question and thus be clearer about concluding that C is the correct option:

A major reason Truman sent troops to fight in North Korea was to
  (A) get Congress to vote more money for the army
  (B) help U.S. trade interests in South Korea
  (C) show the Democrats to be tough enough to stop communism
  (D) show that containment didn't stop the spread of communism
  (E) prove that we had vital interests away from Europe

Yet another helpful technique is to train students to read the stem along with each of the options, one at a time, as if the combination of stem and each option were either a *true or false statement or answer*. If doing so makes the statement or answer false, that option should be rejected; if it seems to be true, it should be considered as a possible correct answer, but students should be reminded of the importance—as with other suggestions made above—to use this approach with all options before one is finally chosen as the best possible choice. This approach to answering multiple-choice questions can be demonstrated with the following question from the 1994 European History AP exam (note: after each option, in brackets, is my thinking behind determining whether it is true or false; this bracketed material is not part of the original question):

---

192. Copyright © 2008 The College Board. Reproduced with permission. http://apcentral.collegeboard.com

Which of the following was a major demographic change in Western Europe between 1850 and 1914?

(A) A dramatic shift of population to urban areas
[Urbanization and growing urban populations were characteristics of the time period, so this option appears to be true, but before marking A as the correct answer I want to test the accuracy of each of the other options in a similar manner.]

(B) A rapidly increasing birth rate
[This is false, as advancing industrialization saw birth rates decline, even in the face of overall population increase.]

(C) A rapidly increasing death rate
[This is false, as urbanization and health improvements saw the death rate decrease.]

(D) A pronounced trend toward larger families
[This is false, as greater longevity and enlightened attitudes toward child labor contributed to a diminishing need for large families.]

(E) A marked decline in emigration[193]
[This is false, because figures show no abatement in emigration. Thus option A is, indeed, the correct answer.]

Because there is a quarter-point penalty in many standardized exams for a wrong answer (as opposed to not choosing any answer at all, i.e., leaving the box to be filled in blank), the decision to leave any question unanswered should be based on whether students can eliminate one or more of the options. Statistically, it is actually advantageous to guess when at least one option can be eliminated, but *guessing intelligently* increases the odds of guessing correctly. In addition to the suggestions described above for doing so, another way to guess intelligently is to teach students to divide the history they have been taught and are studying into the periods or eras they should already be familiar with as the exam date nears—thinking of each of

---

193. Copyright © 2008 The College Board. Reproduced with permission.
http://apcentral.collegeboard.com

them as "boxed" time periods or labeled groups or perhaps even as rooms in a house. Organizing the subject matter of history into these familiar periods (or boxes or groupings or rooms) should help students to recall the material more readily during the exam, especially if they are encouraged to visualize in their mind's eye what is in each period (or group, or box, or room). This ancient technique to improve memory is a form of *association* that can help students to make connections and prompt them to think about what comes to mind in reference to periods, such as the Age of Exploration, or the Mughal Empire, or the Reformation, or the Industrial Revolution, or any other periods being tested. [This, not incidentally, is akin to the technique of *brainstorming*, which is often recommended for use in preparation to respond to essay exam questions.] Remembering key themes, names, and events from each period should help students to eliminate clearly wrong options and thus guess more intelligently. When students do not readily know the correct answer, they should start by deciding which period (or group, or box, or room) the question refers to (or is situated in). Then they should read all the options—all of which, once again, should always be read—to determine which ones clearly do not relate to the period in question. Of the remaining options, the one that best relates to the era being tested is the one to chose. This makes for intelligent guessing. Let's see how this plays out with the following example from the 2002 World History AP exam (note: once again, my thinking—what my mind's eye visualizes—is reflected in what is written within the brackets):

Which of the following is true of both Russia and Japan by 1914?
[I quickly call to mind the period from the second half of the nineteenth century to the eve of World War I and what I know belongs in both my "Russia box" and my "Japan box" that will help me to evaluate each of the options.]
(A) Both were characterized by a high degree of ethnic homogeneity.

[I remember that Japan, a culturalist state, was ethnically homogeneous, but Russia, a pluralist state, especially as it expanded to the Pacific Ocean, was ethnically diverse. Thus I eliminate this option.]

(B) Both had effective democratic institutions that restrained the power of their monarchs.

[Although both countries had government institutions below their autocratic rulers, they could hardly be described as democratic, much less as effective in restraining the power of their monarchs. I reject this option.]

(C) Both had low literacy rates.

[This may have been true for Japan, but I'm pretty certain it's not true for Russia. So, unless both of the remaining options are clearly false, I will eliminate this option.]

(D) Marxism had become a strong influence among urban workers in both countries.

[This was probably true for Russia but not so for Japan, although Japan would later develop a communist party that was perceived by many as a threat to the emperor in the waning days of World War II. So this option is rejected.]

(E) Rapid, state-sponsored industrialization had occurred in both countries.[194]

[Yes, this was true of both countries starting in the second half of the nineteenth century; this was covered in the required readings on industrialization as well as on the world on the eve of World War I. E, therefore, is the correct option.]

Teachers should advise students that a distractor being true in and of itself does not make it the key (or correct option) if it is not correct in connection with the stem or if it is only partially correct in relation to the stem. Questions including distractors of this variety are likely to be fairly common in standardized and other challenging multiple-choice exams; preparing for them

---

194. Copyright © 2008 The College Board. Reproduced with permission. http://apcentral.collegeboard.com

accordingly makes for effective test preparation. A variation on this type of distractor is where the distractor is plausible but otherwise is incorrect with regard to the stem. All this is to say that *understanding the material is critical to answering questions accurately*. The following question from the 2006 United States History AP exam should help to explain the importance of mastering this strategy (note: remember, the material within the brackets represents my thinking and is not part of the actual question):

Parliament enacted the Stamp Act (1765) primarily to...
(A) regulate trade between the colonies and European nations
[This is plausible in that the British government wanted to regulate trade with the colonies, which didn't preclude trade with other nations, but it's not the case with the Stamp Act.]
(B) strengthen the communication network within the colonies
[This is plausible insofar as Britain wanting the colonies to cooperate, but that has nothing to do with the Stamp Act.]
(C) raise revenue to pay for British troops in the colonies
[This is true in that the Stamp Act was meant to raise revenue rather than to regulate trade, which would have been an aim more difficult for the colonists to oppose. Thus, this is true both as a British intention and as it relates to the Stamp Act; C is the correct option.]
(D) regulate commercial activity within colonies
[Here again is a plausible characterization of British policy, but not as it applied to the Stamp Act.]
(E) control population movement to the colonial back-country[195]
[If the stem had focused on the Quebec Act (1774), this option would have been correct; but it is irrelevant to the Stamp Act.]

---

195. Copyright © 2008 The College Board. Reproduced with permission.
http://apcentral.collegeboard.com

A frequently asked question is: Should students *second-guess themselves* and change an answer previously entered? Ordinarily, they should not, unless it is subsequently determined that the student has misread the question or some of the options. It is natural to be of two-minds about some questions, perhaps even about many questions: to be fairly certain one has chosen correctly and, simultaneously, to fear one may have chosen wrongly. As long as students have prepared well, they should trust that they have chosen correctly the first time. They should also be cautioned against assuming that their choice must be wrong because they found the question and answer too easy. Questions are generally meant to be straightforward, not purposely complicated or confusing, and most multiple-choice exams include a variety of questions that run the gamut from fairly easy to especially challenging. So, yes, there will be some truly difficult questions, but their difficulty will likely be the result of the subject being tested, not the trickiness of the choices or the caliber of the words employed to express them.

For AP exams as well as for exams based on comparably structured programs, students will need to *be familiar with the following major components*:

(1) themes and trends;
(2) changes occurring over time and across geographical regions;
(3) events and movements;
(4) documents;
(5) historical figures from all theme areas;
(6) writings by key figures;
(7) concepts and terms (including some in their original language that are also typically included in current textbooks).

Some logistical advice to pass along to students is that when taking the exam itself, they would be wise to check periodically to make sure the number of the question on the test page they are reading corresponds to the number of the answer on the bubble sheet they are filling in; this is the equivalent of the carpenter's rule of measuring twice so as to cut once. This *check for consistency* is worth the second or so it takes, with the consequence for making a mistake along these lines being self-evident, as well as potentially disastrous. At the same time, students should, prior to actually taking an exam, know the maximum time allowed to complete the multiple-choice section as well as how many questions comprise the exam, so as not to miss any accidentally, as some students invariably do. Armed with this information, they might want to divide the allotted time into quarters or halves so as to determine which number question should be reached when, for example, a quarter of or half the time has elapsed. Doing so will help students to *pace* themselves and to increase their chances of responding to all or at least most of the questions. Because each multiple-choice question is worth the same number of points as every other one, students should always skip those that cannot be answered quickly rather than dwell on or worry over them. These more difficult questions can always be returned to, time permitting, after all others have been answered.

Popular impressions and conventional wisdom notwith-standing—and even if the term appears in newspaper and magazine articles—for AP exams there is no such thing *as a passing score* (typically identified as a three on a scale of one to five). Instead, each college and university (and sometimes each academic department) determines what number scores they will accept (or whether to accept any score at all, as it is their choice) and how they will apply those scores (e.g., for advanced standing; in lieu of lower-division courses but without units earned); secondary schools also utilize reported scores as they wish in terms of the courses that have prepared students to take the exam (e.g., counts toward the course grade; is indepen-dent of the course grade). That said, if a student's scores on the Multiple-Choice Section, the Document-Based Question, and the Free Response Question(s)[196] are at comparable levels, then in order to earn a reported score of three on the entire exam the student should leave no more than twenty unanswered multiple-choice questions; and of the sixty questions that are answered (out of a total of eighty, at least for United States and European History AP; in World History AP there are seventy multiple-choice questions), if only nine are wrong (and factoring in the deduction of one-quarter point for wrong guesses), that should support a reported score of three. In other words, a score equivalent to a 64% on the multiple-choice section works to secure a reported score of three as long as the DBQ and FRQ scores are at comparable levels. To be sure, on teacher-generated multiple-choice exams in their classes such a percentage would be unacceptably low to most students and teachers—perhaps equivalent to a letter grade of D—but in this pivotal way AP scoring is decidedly different. Realizing this is an important psychological component for taking AP exams, and being aware of it should help to relieve student anxiety as the exam is being taken, especially for those students who might otherwise find their confidence waning as they read questions they are unable to answer. In addition, the organizations that sponsor or generate standardized exams, including The College Board for AP exams, usually compile and make available the statistics on the percentage of students who receive the range of reported scores.[197]

Although the authors and editors of test preparation study

196. For more on writing free response questions as well as for preparing students to respond to essay questions, see Robert Blackey, "A Guide to the Skill of Essay Construction in History," *Social Education* 45:3 (March 1981): 178-82; Robert Blackey, "Bull's-Eye: A Teacher's Guide for Developing Student Skill in Responding to Essay Questions," *Social Education* 52:6 (October 1988): 464-66.

197. For example, on the 2006 AP history exams, in European History 69.1% of students taking the exam earned a grade of 3 or higher; for U.S. History it was 53.1%; for World History it was 51%. On the 2007 exams, for European History it was 65.9%; for U.S. History it was 53.2; for World History it was 54.2%.

guides no doubt do their best to characterize the exams generated by The College Board accurately, this does not mean that those guides are free of *misinformation*. For example, with regard to the AP European History exam, some assert that the multiple-choice questions on the exam are organized in rough chronological order. Any careful review of actual published AP exams, however, will demonstrate the inaccuracy of such an assertion, although there often are more pre-1789-to-1815 questions in the first half of the test and more post-1789-to-1815 questions in the second half. Other test prep guides state, with regard to AP tests in general, that the first twenty-to-twenty-five questions are usually the easiest, with the most difficult questions coming at the end of the test. This, too, is not borne out—at least not universally—by reviewing published exams, although the assertion is perhaps based upon the usually good test construction practice of avoiding confronting students with more difficult questions at the outset. Still other guides suggest that questions tend to be organized in groups of four-to-seven questions, with each group focused on a chronological period and with the difficulty of the questions increasing within each group, with the first question in that group being the easiest. Once again, a study of published AP history exams reveals otherwise. Actually, the degree of difficulty of AP and other standardized exam questions is not something that can be determined readily by so-called test-prep experts, as the work involved in determining questions' degree of difficulty and how many of which level will be used and with what distribution is undertaken, for example, following an analysis of the statistics compiled on pre-tested questions (i.e., pre-tested in college classrooms across the country) by the statisticians at the Educational Testing Service, the results of which are not made public. For example, questions answered incorrectly by students whose total scores are otherwise high indicate a difficult question, whereas questions answered correctly by those who score poorly on the entire exam are considered easy. Another piece of advice proffered by study guides is that students should look for hints or bits of information from previously answered questions that might serve them in figuring out a question they are having difficulty with. Although some teachers might not peruse their own multiple-choice exams for such unintended hints and information, standardized exams are usually carefully scrutinized to root out any such overlapping of question information and to avoid giving clues to a question within the correct option.

So it would seem that there is much to learn about multiple-choice questions and the variety of strategies that can be employed when taking such exams. It follows, therefore, that for both students and their teachers, knowing what to expect before multiple-choice exams are taken, along with developing good study habits and historical thinking skills, may be almost as important as what students have actually studied and learned. All are vital to being thoroughly prepared, including in the sometimes underrated area of mental preparation and building confidence.

14. THE LITTLE ID

A Guide for Answering
Identification Questions Effectively

Identifications test both factual knowledge and an understanding of the significance of people, events, and concepts in the context of their times—unlike essay questions which rely on an ability to interpret historical events, use judgment, and include factual knowledge in appropriate ways to support a thesis and to draw conclusions based on evidence and that thesis.

Unfortunately, typical written responses by students to identification questions on exams include enough information to show they are vaguely familiar with the person, event, or concept, but little or nothing that reveals an understanding as to why the item is important. Thus, in a curious way the word *identification* is a misnomer; it can easily be—and often is—defined narrowly to mean nothing more than the ability to merely recognize or identify the item. In many a student's mind, the charge *to identify* does not involve analyzing significance. What follows are suggestions to guide students both in knowing how to study for exams and for improving ways to use what they have read so as to respond effectively with their answers to identification questions.

Following these suggestions (offered here in two variations) should not be especially taxing, but it does take an understanding of what to look for when one studies and then practicing enough so as to incorporate the thinking behind these suggestions into one's own routine exam preparation. After sufficient practice, this broader way of studying and thinking should become easier, if not second nature, and it will likely also result in improved grades.

One approach, or variation, follows the journalistic principles of *what, who, where, when,* and *why.*[198] These five principles are easy enough to remember, as they guide students toward covering the areas necessary to write a thorough identification response that will reveal a thinking mind at work. By way of example, let's use the Spanish Armada of 1588.

What is the term (i.e., name, person, event, or concept)? Say who it was if it's a person or what it was if it's an event or concept. In the case of our example, the Spanish Armada was a naval flotilla sent against England by Philip II of Spain with the aim of picking up seasoned Spanish troops in the Netherlands, invading England, and ultimately overthrowing Elizabeth and returning England to the Catholic faith.

Who or what was involved, under what circumstances, and with regard to what relevant background? This should be specific but concise: Philip II, Habsburg King of Spain, and Elizabeth I, Tudor Queen of England; the Duke of Medina Sidonia, who was a last-minute replacement as admiral of the Spanish fleet, and Sir Francis Drake, one of the commanders of the English navy. The intended attack by the Armada was part of the war between Spain and England that was itself the result of years of increasingly intense rivalry and conflict—religious, military, economic—between the two countries. Including a couple of brief examples of this larger conflict would demonstrate a student's fuller understanding of the key issues involved.

Where and how did it happen? Provide just enough information to demonstrate familiarity with events: The Armada sailed from Spain toward the English Channel and then east for a planned rendezvous with the Duke of Parma, whose troops

---

198. I liberally adapted this description of the use of these journalistic principles from Dr. Carol Pixton, my wife and a history teacher at the Polytechnic School (Pasadena, CA).

the Armada was to ferry across the Channel to England where the actual invasion and assault would begin. But the Spanish were attacked successfully in the Channel, then at Calais, and then again at Gravelines where the English used *hellburners*, or fireships, to damage the fleet further. After this Spanish defeat, the remaining ships of the Armada, in retreat, sailed north and then around the British Isles, suffering further losses, including the grounding of ships on the Irish coast—especially due to weather and rough seas—before finally hobbling back to Spain.

When did the event happen, or when did the person live, or when was the concept formulated or introduced? Some terms or names elicit an exact date, others an era: in this case it's a specific year, 1588. If the exact year or specific date(s) are not remembered, students should try to place the date as close as possible to the date(s) in question; sometimes the use of the part of the relevant century will be sufficient (e.g., late-16th century in the case of the Armada). Many teachers, however, in an effort to render history more about understanding and meaning than about the memorizing of dates, will provide the necessary dates on the exam page.

What is its significance? *Why* is the event, person, or concept important, both in and of itself and in a broader historical sense? For example: What led up to or caused the event, or helped set the stage for the concept, or made it possible for the person to achieve what makes him or her significant in history? What were the short- *and* long-term influences and consequences? Who or what was affected, and in what ways? Think in terms of *cause and effect, impact upon, connections, links or relationships* as the significance is being analyzed: The Armada was launched as the culmination of the growing conflict between Queen Elizabeth and King Philip II, especially over the fate of Catholic Mary, Queen of Scots (cousin of Elizabeth and her possible successor) and the religion of England. The Spanish defeat was a blow to Spain's prestige and finances, whereas it helped to crystallize English feelings of pride and nationalism. In this regard, the defeat of the Armada signaled the beginning of the decline in the fortunes of Spain (i.e., the end of Spain's Golden Age), even as Spain continued to be the dominant European power into the first quarter of the seventeenth century. In contrast, England's rise could be marked by the event, although the unsuccessful attack by the Armada also added to negative perceptions—perceptions that would linger for centuries—that English Protestants had of English Catholics. Including examples or specifics would further strengthen the impression of the student's understanding. This section, with its emphasis on significance, is the critical part of responding to identifications, and it should be the longest, most detailed, and best supported; it should reflect the student's thinking and feel for history.

In responding to identifications by using the *what, who, where, when,* and *why* approach, all this information and analysis should be combined together into one or more smooth-flowing, essay-like paragraphs; that is, students should not answer each of the parts separately or one at a time in a Question-&-Answer format. In addition, any references to books read or from class lectures/discussions that might support the analysis would be a welcome bonus.

An alternative approach to the above journalistic principles is one that can be remembered easily via the acronym I-BAD, with the letters representing *identify, before, after,* and *during* with regard to identifying and analyzing the significance of a person, event, or concept. Thus if we use *mercantilism* as our sample ID, we could *identify* it as the economic concept (i.e., a set of ideas or policies or even a doctrine, really, rather than a formal theory) that argues in favor of placing the economy in the service of the state in order to add to its power and wealth by regulating as much of the national economy as possible; the doctrine also accepts as fact the erroneous belief that the amount of wealth in the world is finite and that a nation must attempt to secure as much of it as possible in order to sustain and increase its power, yet that could only be made to happen at the expense of other nations.

The background—the *before*—is that mercantilism developed in western Europe from the latter part of the sixteenth century and prevailed during the early modern period, as some states, such as France and England, began to become more centralized and unified in an effort to build up their military and industrial strength as they competed with other states for dominance in Europe; in fact, it was also believed that war could help to advance the economy and strengthen the state simultaneously.

The *during* segment of this I-BAD approach—mercantilism as practiced—should call attention to the ways mercantilism was implemented: by accumulating as much gold, silver, and other precious metals as possible (as these, like trade, were also mistakenly considered finite and thus limited in quantity; this aspect of mercantilism is known as bullionism); by exporting more than importing in order to improve the balance of trade; by building a strong navy; by encouraging the growth of domestic industry so as to increase the potential tax base; by implementing domestic reforms, such as improving roads, revising the tax structure, and establishing standards for weights and measures; and by acquiring colonies to provide raw materials and, eventually, protected markets for goods produced by the parent country. Providing examples of these means—say by referring to Colbert's measures in France under the reign of Louis XIV, England's navigation acts, and the creation in several countries of East and West India companies—would demonstrate a student's understanding of the concept as a living, functioning phenomenon.

The *after* segment—the consequences and significance of mercantilism—should call attention to how mercantilism led some governments to regulate commerce during the seventeenth and eighteenth centuries as well as to engage in economically motivated wars. Along with specific examples, the shortcomings of mercantilism (e.g., how the cost of the wars also contributed to some mercantilist goals not being fulfilled, as was the case with Colbert), the reasons behind the unevenness of success among mercantilist countries, as well as its critics (e.g., the *Physiocrats* and others advocating an economic system characterized by *laissez-faire*) should comprise what is addressed as part of an analysis of significance.

Just as the advice when employing the journalistic principles is to write one or more coherent paragraphs—in short essay fashion—incorporating the specifics that these principles call to mind, so it should be with the I-BAD approach, with each of the four parts flowing from one another and with references made to materials read and to what was heard and discussed in class.

One goal of these approaches is to help students demonstrate their ability to think historically. It is also to help them see people, events, and concepts not as isolated from the world around them—something to be memorized but little understood and soon forgotten—but integral to their surroundings, their pasts, and their connections to the future. Thus it would not be farfetched to say that learning how to respond effectively to identifications, along with essays and constructive discussions, contributes to creating better students and, ideally, better and more active citizens. To paraphrase the French philosopher Pierre Teilhard de Chardin, nothing is understandable except through history. Learning how to think historically as well as critically contributes to an informed and thinking citizenry.

ACKNOWLEDGMENTS

THESE ESSAYS WERE previously published as follows, and are reprinted (with some editing, updating, and textual modifications) by permission of the author:

"Early Bird Specials: Some Thoughts on Use of Class Time Before Class Begins," was first published in *Teaching History: A Journal of Methods*, 35:1 (Spring, 2010): 3-11. Copyright © 2010, 2011 by Robert Blackey.

"So Many Choices, So Little Time: Strategies for Understanding and Taking Multiple-Choice Exams in History," was first published in *The History Teacher*, 43:1 (November, 2009): 54-66. Copyright © 2009, 2011 by Robert Blackey.

"To Illuminate History: Making Teaching Picture-Perfect," was first published in *Teaching History: A Journal of Methods*, 30:2 (Fall, 2005): 59-71. Copyright © 2005, 2011 by Robert Blackey.

"Advanced Placement European History: An Anatomy of the Essay Examination, 1956-2000," was first published in *The History Teacher*, 35:3 (May, 2002): 311-42. Copyright © 2002, 2011 by Robert Blackey.

"New Wine in Old Bottles: Revitalizing the Tradition History Lecture," was first published in *Teaching History: A Journal of Methods*, 22:1 (Spring, 1997): 3-25. Copyright © 1997, 2011 by Robert Blackey.

"Words to the Whys: Crafting Critical Book Reviews," was first published in *The History Teacher*, 27:2 (February, 1994): 159-66. Copyright © 1994, 2011 by Robert Blackey.

ABOUT THE AUTHOR

ROBERT BLACKEY is a professor of history at California State University, San Bernardino, where, after receiving his Ph.D. from New York University, he began teaching in 1968. By training he is a specialist in the history of Britain and early modern Europe, but once at Cal State he expanded his expertise to include the causes of revolutions across the globe and what they had in common. He not only teaches courses in these areas, but also in world history and expository writing. A major tranistion in his professional life developed after he became a Reader of examinations for the Advanced Placement Program in European History (1970). He advanced quickly to the position of Chief Reader, and later still, became a member of that program's Test Development Committee—and in 1986, its chair. This led to his being asked to write an article on the grading of AP history exams for the American Historical Association, and then to serve for fifteen years as editor of the teaching column in the AHA's monthly magazine, *Perspectives*. In 1991 he was elected Vice President of the AHA, with primary responsibilities overseeing the Teaching Division.

He is the author and editor of five books—four having to do with revolutions, one with history teaching and learning—and editor of two booklets for the AHA (on teaching world history, and on teaching to think historically). He has also written some twenty articles covering a variety of fields, including on robots and travel abroad. His many noteworthy activities include memberships on the AHA's World History Task Force to Review the National History Standards Project (1992), the College Board's National Academic Assembly Council (2001-04), and the Steering Committee that established the College Board's National Task Force on the Arts in Education (2008-10). In addition, he has conducted scores of workshops for secondary school teachers all across the U.S. and abroad, and every year he gives presentations to hundreds of pre-college students.

Included among his many awards and honors are the following: Cal State San Bernardino's Outstanding Professor Award (1983-84) and Distinguished Service Award (1995); Distinguished Service Award, The College Board (Western Region, 1999); Eugene Asher Distinguished Teaching Award, American Historial Association (2001); Wang Family Excellence Award of the California State University twenty-three-campus system (2003).

He is married to Dr. Carol Pixton, a historian at the Polytechnic School (Pasadena, CA). He has two sons, Richard and Jeffrey (both of whom work in business), as well as four grandchildren, Sarah, Breanna, Nicholas, and Hunter. For a boy who grew up in the multi-ethnic, multi-racial, and religiously-diverse working-class neighborhood of Manhattan's Lower East Side, he considers himself to be most fortunate.